A Guide to

NATURAL AREAS
of SOUTHERN INDIANA

INDIANA NATURAL SCIENCE

Gillian Harris, *editor*

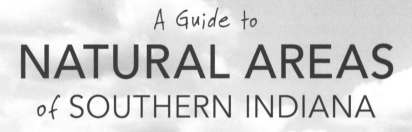

A Guide to
NATURAL AREAS
of SOUTHERN INDIANA

119 Unique Places to Explore

Text and Photography by
STEVEN HIGGS

Foreword by James Alexander Thom

INDIANA UNIVERSITY PRESS
Bloomington & Indianapolis

This book is a publication of

Indiana University Press
Office of Scholarly Publishing
Herman B Wells Library 350
1320 East 10th Street
Bloomington, Indiana 47405 USA

www.iupress.indiana.edu

The paper used in this publication meets the minimum requirements
of the American National Standard for Information Sciences—
Permanence of Paper for Printed Library Materials, ANSI Z39.48-1992.

Manufactured in China

Cataloging information is available from the Library of Congress.

ISBN 978-0-253-02090-1 (paperback)
ISBN 978-0-253-02098-7 (ebook)

1 2 3 4 5 21 20 19 18 17 16

This book is dedicated to Raina and Amara, who endured heat, hills, bugs, and miles to share this epic journey with me—and to Vale, whose time to share is drawing near.

I never saw a discontented tree. They grip the ground as though they liked it, and though fast rooted they travel about as far as we do. They go wandering forth in all directions with every wind, going and coming like ourselves, traveling with us around the sun two million miles a day, and through space heaven knows how fast and far!

—JOHN MUIR

Southern Indiana Highways

* This section of Interstate 69 was under construction in 2016.

Natural Regions of Southern Indiana

SOUTHWESTERN LOWLANDS NATURAL REGION	SOUTHERN BOTTOMLANDS NATURAL REGION	HIGHLAND RIM NATURAL REGION	BLUEGRASS NATURAL REGION
Glaciated Section		*Mitchell Karst Plain Section*	*Scottsburg Lowland Section*
Plainville Sand Section	**SHAWNEE HILLS NATURAL REGION**	*Brown County Hills Section*	*Muscatatuck Flats and Canyons Section*
	Crawford Upland Section		
Driftless Section	*Escarpment Section*	*Knobstone Escarpment Section*	*Switzerland Hills Section*

Contents

Foreword

Fourscore and two years ago, I decided that I wanted to be born in the most interesting part of Indiana, and so it happened, in a very small town called Gosport, which stood on a bluff above a bend of White River's West Fork.

Conveniently for me, the parents I'd selected had their doctors' office in that picturesque little town of seven hundred souls, and I was born in a bedroom upstairs from their office, which had a real human skeleton in it. Birth and death!

I take credit for my excellent choices of place and parents, but I must admit my timing wasn't that great. It was deep in the Great Depression, and even in the best of times, Owen County wasn't very prosperous. In their first year of practice, the Doctors Thom made $25.

But as a newborn Hoosier, I was even less interested in money than I am as an old man. What tickled me then and has ever since was that I was in the Indiana hill country instead of that vast, flat part of the Midwest that I think of as Ohiowa.

So I grew up with steep, wooded hills and stony creek bluffs to climb, limestone quarries to risk my neck in, and caves to crawl through. I was so much a ridge-runner that I never played Indiana's sacred sport, basketball, because I couldn't find anyplace level enough to dribble on. (That makes a better-sounding excuse than my inherent slowness and ineptitude.)

It was due to my childhood in these hills that, when I got to college, I elected for a science course titled Geomorphology, a course so boring to most college kids that everyone else had dropped out within weeks, and the professor had to keep teaching it the rest of the semester just for me. I was fascinated by the formation of uplands.

My college was Butler University in Indianapolis, a city so flat that I felt "steep deprived." So I began shaping my career in ways that would take me into hills and mountains for research and eventually bring me back to Owen County, where I built myself a log house on a ridge overlooking the ranked ridges of what is called the Crawford Upland Section of the Shawnee Hills Natural Region. I live with, appropriately enough, a Shawnee wife from the Ohio hill country who can't stand flatlands any better than I can. Up here we intend to stay until we wake up and smell the coffin in this most interesting part of Indiana where I chose to be born.

* * *

But I didn't come here to talk about me. I came to talk about Steven Higgs and this book. This guidebook is the latest of many reasons why I would designate Steve an honorary gnome.

Gnomes, if you remember your folklore, have the sacred duty of protecting the Treasures in the Earth. Gnomes live close to the earth, far from the skyscrapers of financiers and profiteers.

Steve has spent much of his life working to protect our native Indiana from those who don't care what they do to it as long as there's money to be made from its resources. I'm proud to be in his company. We've come a long way as fellow gnomes, but he's been better at it than I.

He first inspired me with a book he wrote many years ago titled *Eternal Vigilance: Nine Tales of Environmental Heroism in Indiana*. It was about Hoosiers who had risked all in their efforts to stop enterprises that would destroy the natural assets or harm the environmental health of our state. It was, let's say, a book about Great Gnomes he had Gnown and their courage and ingenuity. It was one of the most heartening Indiana books I ever read.

Steve and I have trodden much of the same ground—literally, as the Indiana soil underfoot, and figuratively, in our careers. Both of us have written environmental news for the same Bloomington newspaper. We've both taught in the Indiana University School of Journalism. We've both written nonfiction books and magazine articles about the special nature of Southern Indiana and its earthiest inhabitants, man and beast. We've canoed and hiked many of the same streams and sanctuaries.

We're both tall guys who don't go to the barbershop.

Steve had the courage and enterprise to publish a good, truthful, print and online newspaper for many years, the *Bloomington Alternative*. In it he published many of my articles and commentaries, some on politics and other forms of comedy, some on environmental matters. Usually I wrote under my own name, but I used for nature articles the name "Gnome de Plume." A gnome de plume is, of course, like Steve and me, a gnome who writes.

In my mug shot for those columns, I wore one of those tall red dunce caps that the stereotypical garden gnome wears, and with these white whiskers, I looked like one of them. How many editors would allow a contributor to engage in that kind of fun?

But we gnomes don't joke around about the importance of the Creator's works and the proper use of the blessings we have received. All that is sacred, because the Creator made it, and it is real.

Money was created by man, so it is artificial. If God believed in making money, he would sell us this day our daily bread. Money isn't sacred, except to those who choose to worship it.

Those who worship it are dangerous to the natural world, because they will wrest from the earth every resource the Creator put there and won't stop until it's all gone, as long as it's profitable to them.

I've spent about half my life writing about Indiana and the Wabash and Ohio watersheds as they were in historical and prehistorical times, when they were still occupied by the Natives, whom we call "Indians." This area was given the name meaning "Land of the Indians" just when it was being taken away from them. Grim irony. The Indians didn't use money, didn't sell resources for profit, which may explain how they lived for ten or twenty thousand years on this continent without destroying it or using it up.

They wouldn't recognize it after a mere two centuries of Paleface domination: exhausted resources, deforested landscapes, exterminated species, disrupted climate, poisoned soil, air, and water.

For one little thing, imagine a Miami or Delaware or Shawnee of those old days looking up and seeing something that's so common to us we hardly notice it: a blue sky crisscrossed with white jet contrails. It would terrify him. And what would he make of a billboard, say, of a gigantic blonde with cleavage, brandishing a can of beer?

What little there is left that such an Indian would recognize is in this book. Here are the places that have been saved, or restored, and protected by those few visionaries among us who held the earth sacred. Call them gnomes, or land stewards, or conservationists. Somehow they realized that a true measure of civilization is what it leaves unspoiled. Writers like Thoreau and Muir may have sparked the notion in them.

Politicians like Theodore Roosevelt lent them clout. Hoosier citizens such as Richard Lieber pressed for a state parks system and developed government bureaus to oversee the protection of woods, game, and streams. The first state park Colonel Lieber got established was McCormick's Creek, an easy three-mile walk from my boyhood home in Spencer, and I practically grew up in it. My ambition was to become a park ranger.

A great land-stewarding program in the Great Depression was the Civilian Conservation Corps. Being an Army Reserve doctor, my father spent much time, between serving in both World Wars, as a CCC camp physician, keeping those tough, disciplined CCC boys hale and healthy so they could work in reforestation, erosion control, and state park development, whose results we still enjoy.

The Indians who lived here so long believed that Manitou, the Great Good Spirit, gave them everything they needed to live, and he told them that they, and their children and children's children, would always have enough if they took only what they needed and gave their bodies back to nourish the earth. Manitou didn't teach them anything about money or the profit motive, so they were able to live by that simple principle of eternal renewal, the Sacred Circle always turning and in balance. Everything was round.

Then came the Europeans, or "the boat people," as my Shawnee wife, Dark Rain, calls them, who saw the process not as a circle but as a straight line from Point A to Point B, with progress measured in earnings and the notion that the Creator's work should be improved upon, with more and more wealth always being made. That meant getting the old Indian land stewards, with their archaic Sacred Circle idea of leaving something unexploited, out of the way. That was done, cleverly and ruthlessly, and the earth skinning was soon almost total.

But one thing that can't be destroyed is a good idea, and renewal is the best idea ever. Even greed can't quite wipe it out. So now we are conceiving ways to protect and conserve what's left.

Part 1 of this guidebook to Southern Indiana's natural treasures is titled "The Land Stewards." It is the best compilation I've ever seen of the institutions and people dedicated to sustaining the life of our corner of this earth. They aren't perfect. They're up against the juggernaut of what we call "progress." But they're managing and learning the old wisdom that the Native people already had here. As long as the natural world can be seen and enjoyed, people will care about it, cherish it, and start thinking like gnomes: *This is a treasure. It must endure.*

In this guidebook, Steven Higgs has compiled and written a hundred times more good, useful information about my native state's natural treasures than I ever learned in eighty years of crawling, hiking, riding, swimming, and paddling all over them.

I believe he deserves an honorary red gnome hat.

James Alexander Thom
Owen County, Indiana, springtime, 2015

Pioneer Mothers Memorial Forest, Hoosier National Forest, Orange County.

Preface

While this book's overarching purpose is utilitarian, it also represents the latest phase of a personal life journey that's entering its fifth decade. When IU Press sponsoring editor Linda Oblack asked in January 2014 about turning my Natural Bloomington Ecotours & More project into a guidebook, I declined her invitation to "think it over." I've been photographing and writing about the Southern Indiana environment since the mid-1970s, when I began my adult life on a ridgetop overlooking Monroe Lake and discovered Edward Weston's photography. My final master's project at the IU School of Journalism in 1985 was titled "Clearcutting the Hoosier National Forest: Professional Forestry or Panacea?"

The opportunity Linda offered me to share with other nature lovers the places I've explored and photographed since my Weston days appeared as a clearly marked turn on a long and twisting wilderness path. I wrote her right back and said yes. By the time we met six months later at the Soma Café & Juice Bar in downtown Bloomington to negotiate the contract, I had already written forty thousand words.

The eighteen months I spent researching and writing this book were indeed a logical next step. Throughout my thirty-five-year career as an environmental journalist, I've researched and written millions of words about the Indiana environment as a graduate student, newspaper reporter, author, Indiana Department of Environmental Management senior environmental writer/editor, magazine freelancer, and online publisher/blogger. I have spent an inestimable number of hours physically immersed in that environment, the majority with a Nikon around my neck. I've walked among the oldest trees in the state and stood inside a combined sewer overflow.

But that was all prelude to this guidebook. From January 2014 to May 2015, I logged 4,500 miles on the road, hiked at least partway through more than one hundred natural areas, and uploaded roughly 3,500 digital photographs to the Natural Bloomington and related websites. I plotted a couple hundred routes with Google Earth and my 2001 Honda Accord odometer (learning that they're almost always close but seldom match). I got us lost, some, and relearned a literary truism: asking directions is an integral part of the travel writer's journey.

Usually with traveling companions, sometimes alone, I perspired, panted, slipped, and itched my way through the Southern Indiana wilds, following trails, roads, roadbeds, stairways, train tracks, blufftops, creek- and riverbeds, bridges, and, more often than not, steep hills, wherever they led. I always turned around too soon. I once ended up disoriented, dehydrated, and, I learned a couple days later, seriously bug bitten. I was damned lucky more times than I will ever admit to.

I gathered and perused information from hundreds of websites, relying heavily upon those of the property owners' opinions on what is noteworthy. I spoke with botanists, ornithologists, geologists, archaeologists, professors, property managers, public affairs officers, and fellow travelers we encountered along the roads and trails. (One bought us dinner at the Overlook Restaurant in Leavenworth for returning his iPhone, which we found on the trail in the Mouth of the Blue River Nature Preserve.)

I read books, some I've had on my bookshelf for decades, others that I had never seen before. Most notably, I turned to *The Natural Heritage of Indiana* by Marion T. Jackson. For species identification, I relied on John Whitaker, Jr.'s *Habitats and Ecological Communities of Indiana: Presettlement to Present* and multiple field guides from IU Press, the Audubon Society, and others.

The result is the first compilation of information about all of these Southern Indiana natural areas ever collected in one volume, designed for use on the road. (See the introduction for the definition of *natural area*.)

I didn't get to explore all of the sites included here. Due to time and logistics, I missed Nine Penny Branch Nature Preserve and Splinter Ridge Fish & Wildlife Area. There are several individual areas on larger properties, like the Hoosier National Forest and Patoka National Wildlife Refuge, that I included but didn't visit.

Every time I pulled away from one of these areas, I swore I would return. I've already begun.

Acknowledgments

I've told anyone who cared to listen about my journey through the Southern Indiana wilds the past year and a half that I feel more editor than author of this volume. That's because, aside from my observations from the roads, trails, overlooks, bluffs, valleys, creekbeds, lakeshores, and so on, this book is a compilation of others' work, which I rewrote, reorganized, and embellished with additional research and my own experiences.

So, before acknowledging any of the individuals who assisted me directly in this guidebook's preparation, I want to thank the communications folks at the organizations that own and manage the natural areas I included. There were some places where I simply couldn't say things better than they did and merely tweaked their prose. Informed by four years in the late 1990s as a senior environmental writer/editor at the Indiana Department of Environmental Management, I can say from experience that they all did it well.

That said, I want to start with Michael A. Homoya (state botanist and plant ecologist for the past thirty years) from the Indiana Department of Natural Resources Division of Nature Preserves and naturalist Cathy Meyer from Monroe County Parks & Recreation. Both read and commented on the entire manuscript, and they were always available to answer questions. Their insights and expertise more than compensated for my weaknesses. The same is true for John C. Steinmetz, state geologist and director of the Indiana Geological Survey, who fact checked the natural history section.

For proofing their properties' individual sections, appreciation goes to U.S. Fish & Wildlife's Daniel Wood, Joe Robb, Heath Hamilton, and Alejandro Galvan; the U.S. Forest Service's Teena Ligman and Nancy Myers; Monroe Lake naturalist Jill Vance; Sycamore Land Trust assistant director John Lawrence and communications director Katrina Folsom; The Nature Conservancy marketing manager Chip Sutton; Wesselman Nature Society director John Foster; and Oxbow Inc. president Jon Seymour.

Without former IU Press sponsoring editor Linda Oblack, this project would have never existed. It was her idea. I'm proud to be involved in one of the last projects she shepherded through the conception and approval phases at IU Press. Interim sponsoring editor Sarah Jacobi carried on Linda's support and enthusiasm for the project.

I want to express my sincerest gratitude to my old friend and historical novelist James Alexander Thom for writing the foreword and allowing me to share a book jacket with him—also to our mutual friend Jaime Sweany for shooting my author photo.

Finally, I want to mention the hundreds of friends and followers who have liked, shared, read, and commented on this project through the Natural Bloomington website and social media. Their support and encouragement left no doubt that I was engaged in a worthy pursuit.

It's been an honor working with and learning from them all. This book is much more than it would have been without them. That's for sure.

A Guide to

NATURAL AREAS
of SOUTHERN INDIANA

Stillwater Marsh, Monroe Lake, Monroe County.

Introduction

This book is designed as a tool for travelers who enjoy, desire, or require nature for their recreation and inspiration. Its pages provide details on, anecdotes about, and directions to 119 natural areas in Southern Indiana, identified ecologically by natural regions and socially by transportation corridors.

The Indiana Division of Nature Preserves defines a natural area as land and/or water that has retained or reestablished its natural character, has unusual plants and animals, or has "biotic, geological, scenic, or paleontological features of scientific or educational value." While state nature preserves, and most of the individual sites included in this guidebook, are protected against extractive uses, the state and national forests allow logging. Hunting and fishing are allowed on most. A few properties are periodically burned or otherwise managed to restore native plant species. Others offer developed recreation, lodging, and other amenities.

Some, like Greene-Sullivan State Forest and Blue Grass Fish & Wildlife Area, are former strip mines that are anything but natural. Minnehaha Fish & Wildlife Area west of Dugger in Sullivan County is leased from a coal company and has shrunk in size as the company has taken back land for mining. Yet the Audubon Society has designated ten thousand acres of Minnehaha and a nearby portion of Greene-Sullivan State Forest as an Important Bird Area.

All of the sites—many of which are rare remnants of the Indiana landscape that existed before the Europeans arrived—lie on or south of Interstate 70. They range from some of the state's highest elevations in the Switzerland Hills northeast of Brookville to its lowest, some eight hundred feet below in the Southwestern Bottomlands south and west of Mt. Vernon.

The book is organized from west to east, around Southern Indiana's six Natural Regions and six major highways: I-70, State Road 67, I-69, State Road 37, I-65, and I-74. It's divided into three parts.

Part 1 tells the story of those who have fought for and now steward the six hundred thousand acres of land highlighted here. They include the U.S. Forest Service, U.S. Fish & Wildlife Service, various divisions of the Indiana Department of Natural Resources, local governments, and nonprofit groups like The Nature Conservancy, Sycamore Land Trust, and Friends of the Oxbow.

Part 2 provides brief overviews of the Southern Indiana landscape's ever-evolving natural history and features.

The natural history section traces billions of years of geologic evolution to the land's present state, where every drop of precipitation that reaches its surface flows southwest toward the swamplands near the confluence of the Ohio and Wabash Rivers. Not too many million years ago, the water flowed north to a west-flowing river.

The natural features section discusses Southern Indiana's six Natural Regions and eleven Sections, each of which is categorized by a distinctive assemblage of natural characteristics, including plants, animals, climate, soils, glacial history, topography, bedrock, and physiography.

Part 3 lists the individual natural areas and provides details about them, including ecological characteristics and natural and human histories, as well as anecdotes, activities, and specific directions from the nearest highways, with GPS coordinates.

Natural Area Etiquette

BEHAVE LIKE AN ECOTOURIST

By the time I started writing this book in early 2014, I was fairly well schooled in the field of ecotourism. Since launching Natural Bloomington Ecotours & More in the spring of 2013, I had read up on the subject, led a few ecotours, and become a regular guest speaker at ecotourism and sustainable tourism classes in the IU School of Public Health. I'm no expert, but I have invested some time in the subject.

One thing I had learned is that ecotourism, defined by the International Ecotourism Society as "responsible travel to natural areas that conserves the environment and improves the well-being of local people," has been advancing for decades. Its roots are directly traced to the dawn of the environmental movement in the 1960s and 1970s. My favorite theory dates its birth to Alexis de Tocqueville, whose early nineteenth-century American guests on the Michigan frontier were stunned when the French writer and historian said he wanted to explore the surrounding wilderness for the sake of curiosity.

The United Nations designated 2002 the International Year of Ecotourism to generate greater awareness about ecotourism's capacity to help conserve natural and rural areas while helping improve local standards of living. In December 2012 the UN General Assembly declared the effort a success in a landmark resolution that cited ecotourism "as key in the fight against poverty, the protection of the environment and the promotion of sustainable development."

Domestically, however, I didn't find much of a story line. Internet searches returned scant results; one in Oregon seemed to match my vision, kind of. Most of what I found was self-guided ecotourism, where, for example, local tourism groups provide information about natural places to explore and environmentally sensitive ways to behave. To this day in May 2015, my daily online alert for ecotourism features, almost exclusively, links to posts from places like Myanmar and Colombia, not Maine and Colorado.

So, as a proud, lifelong, environmental radical blazing what appeared to be some new ground, I knew that if I were going to lead or encourage any form of nature-based tourism—through ecotours or guidebooks—I would subscribe to the field's highest ethical standards. Despite my journalistic aversion to clichés, my Natural Bloomington brochures prominently feature the old ecological saw, "Take only photographs. Leave only footprints."

The best way to protect what's left of our wild places, of course, is to practice environmental abstinence—to stay out altogether. I worry about "loving-it-to-death syndrome." But natural noncontact is neither practical nor, perhaps, even desirable. A basic ecotourism tenet is the notion that human beings have innate attractions to other life forms and need to interact with natural living systems. The emphasis on awareness raising reflects the belief that humans must physically experience nature to fully appreciate its grandeur. Preservation is dependent upon sensory interaction. To truly love nature, the theory goes, we must touch, smell, hear, feel, and see it up close.

To accomplish these goals, the International Ecotourism Society identifies a set of principles for ecotourism that, relevant and adapted to Southern Indiana, include the following: minimize physical, social, behavioral, and psychological impacts; build environmental and cultural awareness and respect; provide positive experiences for both visitors and hosts; provide direct financial benefits for conservation; generate financial benefits for local people; and deliver memorable interpretative experiences to visitors that help raise sensitivity to host communities' political, environmental, and social climates.

According to David Fennell, founding editor in chief of the *Journal of Ecotourism* and professor of tourism and environment at Brock University, St. Catharines, Ontario: "Ecotourism is a sustainable, non-invasive form of nature-based tourism that focuses primarily on learning about nature first-hand and which is ethically managed to be low-impact, non-consumptive, and locally oriented (control, benefits and scale). It typically occurs in natural areas, and should contribute to the conservation of such areas" (Fennel 2008).

In short, ecotourists know the natural areas and local cultures they visit, leave no adverse trace of their incursions therein, support those who steward the land, and contribute to the local economies in which the lands are preserved.

AN ECOTOURIST TIP LIST

Plan your adventure

Most of the natural areas included in this guide are not developed. Some are vast and remote—by midwestern standards, anyway—and can be forbidding, even if their most secluded tracts are seldom more than a mile or two from a road. You're not going to get lost for days in the Southern Indiana backcountry. But you can end up disoriented, befuddled, bug bitten, and frustrated. So know your weaknesses and learn everything you can about your destination before you go. Study maps and learn the terrain. Familiarize yourself with timing, trails, and weather.

Nearly all the natural areas in this guide have rules and special concerns that you should likewise research before your exploration. Don't count on information kiosks indicated on property maps. They are often empty, or they no longer exist.

Wear seasonal- and locational-appropriate clothing. Well-fitting hiking boots are a must. Except during hunting season, wear earth tones—browns, blues, and greens—so you are less visible. Reds, oranges, and yellows visually intrude into the spaces and solitude that are part and parcel of the outdoor experience.

Be prepared for nature's challenges, extreme weather, and emergencies. Always carry more than enough water, maps, first-aid kit, compass, and cell phone (service is available in some of the most far-flung places). Make sure someone knows where you are.

Southern Indiana wild places teem with insects between frosts, and a strategy to combat them is essential, starting with repellent. To DEET or not to DEET is the question. DEET stands for the active chemical ingredient N,N-diethyl-meta-toluamide in the more powerful products. I find non-DEET sprays effective, but I've been surprised by others' choices. Tucking pant legs into socks and shirttails into pants helps block the path to your skin.

Tread lightly, on the trail and in camp

The footprints you leave behind should follow only those who preceded you—on established trails and in campsites. That means stick to the trail. Don't take shortcuts or cut switchbacks. Groups should walk single file in the middle of the path, even when it is wet and/or muddy.

If you must stray from the trail, tread with extreme caution. Photographers are particularly bad about leaving the path in search of light, color, and form. If you must bushwhack to find the optimum camera angle, watch where you plant your feet. And remember, the more plants you come in contact with, the more bugs come in contact with you.

If you backpack into wilderness or backcountry areas, use existing campsites when possible. It is seldom necessary to alter an area for camping. If you must establish a new site, keep it small and in areas without vegetation. And use a portable backpacking stove rather than a campfire for cooking. Stoves prevent fire-blackened rocks in areas where people camp.

Whether you are staying at a developed campsite or along a backcountry trail, exercise caution with campfires. Check the fire danger in the area—a simple Internet search for "Indiana fire danger" produces multiple resources. Some properties put restrictions on fires during dry periods. To avoid spreading pests, like the emerald ash borer, do not bring in firewood from other locales. Use only dead and downed wood from the area you camp in.

Campfires in backcountry areas should be in pits twelve inches or less in diameter, with an area three feet in diameter cleared around the fire. Before breaking camp, mix ashes with the soil, fill the pit, and cover the cleared area with the humus layer you originally removed.

GARBAGE IN, GARBAGE OUT

No respectable nature lover would ever litter on a city street, let alone along a wooded trail or creek bank deep in the wild. But many nature lovers do, sometimes knowingly—trash left behind at campsites, for example—and sometimes unknowingly—upstream trash that washes ashore on downstream riverbanks. (The Ohio River preserves are the worst.) Sycamore Land Trust had to close the parking lot at Eagle Slough Natural Area by Evansville due to illegal dumping.

Whether you are hiking or camping, carry trash bags in so you can carry the trash you generate or find back out. Campers should pack out all trash, spilled or leftover foods, toilet paper, and hygiene products.

HANDS OFF THE NATURAL GOODS

To preserve the past and conserve the future, you should never touch cultural or historic structures and artifacts, and you should leave rocks, plants, and other natural objects where they are. State law prohibits disturbing or removing anything from dedicated state nature preserves without a special permit. Do not build structures or furniture, and do not dig trenches.

LET THE CRITTERS BE

Wildlife should be observed from a distance and then left alone. Animals should never be fed. It can hurt their health, alter their natural behaviors, and expose them to predators and other dangers. Leave them alone when they are mating, nesting, raising young, or wintering.

Pets should be controlled at all times or, better yet, left at home. Keep all pet waste well away from the trail, and don't allow your dog to bark at or chase other trail users or wildlife. Bring food and water for your dog.

RESPECT YOUR FELLOW TRAVELERS AND NEIGHBORS

You can rest assured that anyone you encounter in any of the natural areas in this guide is a nature lover almost by definition. You don't sweat, swat, and stumble your way through the Southern Indiana wilds for long if you're not committed. Be courteous, and respect the quality of their experiences. When you encounter horse riders, step to the downhill side of the trail.

To eliminate waste on the trail and in areas where restrooms are not provided, stay a couple hundred feet from any water supply and camping area. Dig a hole approximately eight inches deep and then cover it with loose soil and leaf litter to promote decomposition and sanitary conditions.

Most of the natural areas included here are adjacent to or surround private properties. Do not trespass.

Stop talking and listen. Let nature's sounds prevail.

Part 1

THE LAND STEWARDS

Waldrip Ridge, Hoosier National Forest, Monroe County.

The Land Stewards

The natural area destinations in this book are owned and managed by a variety of public and private entities, including federal and state governments and private, nonprofit conservation organizations. Some are owned jointly, mostly between Indiana Division of Nature Preserves and nonprofits. Others are contiguous to one another with separate owners and are managed under cooperative agreements.

While the six hundred thousand acres of land highlighted here are stewarded by their owners, some are neither *protected* nor *preserved* in the sense that they are off limits to human intervention. Timber harvesting, always a controversial subject in public lands management, is practiced on most state and national forest acreage in Indiana. Since 2005 the Division of Forestry has logged portions of Back Country Areas, which, according to a 1981 news release from Republican governor Robert D. Orr, were established "to be enjoyed by the wilderness seeker as a place of solitude and repose."

Fish and wildlife areas managed by the state may include crop plantings that are intended to feed game species.

U.S. Forest Service

The U.S. Forest Service, an agency in the U.S. Department of Agriculture, owns and manages the Hoosier National Forest, which is one of 155 the agency oversees in the National Forest System (NFS). Along with twenty grasslands, the system totals 193 million acres in forty-four states, Puerto Rico, and the Virgin Islands. That's roughly 9 percent of the entire U.S. land mass.

The Forest Service's mission is to "sustain the health, diversity, and productivity of the nation's forests and grasslands to meet the needs of present and future generations." The NFS is divided into nine regions. The 202,000-acre Hoosier is part of Region 9, also known as the Eastern Region, which is headquartered in Milwaukee.

The Forest Service dates its origins to 1876, when Congress created the Office of Special Agent in the Department of Agriculture whose mission was to assess the quality and conditions of the nation's forestlands at a time when they were at great risk. Settlement patterns and technological changes in the 1800s had resulted in scarred and damaged landscapes in Southern Indiana and across the nation, ultimately leading to concerns of a nationwide *timber famine*. Five years later, in 1881, the Office of Special Agent became the Division of Forestry.

Congress passed the Forest Reserve Act of 1891, which gave then President Benjamin Harrison authority to designate public lands in the West as *forest reserves*. Harrison, the only president from Indiana, had pushed the legislation. The reserves became national forests in 1905, when President Theodore Roosevelt transferred them to his newly created U.S. Forest Service. The agency's first head was Gifford Pinchot, whose vision was to manage the forests "to provide the greatest amount of good for the greatest amount of people in the long run."

While the National Forest System, like the National Park System, has land preservation as a function, its managerial priorities differ from parks. National forests are open to logging, livestock, oil and gas drilling, and other commercial activities, as well as recreation and amenities-based activities like hiking, nature study, photography, and wildlife watching.

Each national forest is assigned a forest supervisor and one or more district rangers who oversee land management. The Hoosier National Forest supervisor's office is in Bedford, with a district office in Tell City.

U.S. Fish & Wildlife Service

The U.S. Fish & Wildlife Service, a division of the U.S. Department of the Interior, owns and manages the Muscatatuck, Patoka, and Big Oaks National Wildlife Refuges, all of which are located in Southern Indiana. Their combined 65,731 acres in 2015 are part of the 93-million-acre National Wildlife Refuge System, which is composed of more than 520 National Wildlife Refuges and thousands of small wetlands and special management areas nationwide. The agency's National Fish Hatcheries Program operates sixty-six National Fish Hatcheries, sixty-four fishery resource offices, and seventy-eight ecological services field offices, including one in Bloomington that serves Central and Southern Indiana.

Fish & Wildlife's mission is "working with others to conserve, protect, and enhance fish, wildlife, and plants and their habitats for the continuing benefit of the American people." The service is headquartered in Washington, D.C., and has seven regional offices and nearly seven hundred field units. Indiana is part of the Midwest Region, which also includes Illinois, Michigan, Minnesota, Missouri, Ohio, and Wisconsin.

Key agency functions include enforcing federal wildlife laws; protecting endangered species; managing migratory birds; restoring nationally significant fisheries; conserving and restoring wildlife habitat, such as wetlands; and helping foreign governments with international conservation efforts.

Fish & Wildlife traces its origins to the U.S. Fish Commission, created by Congress in 1871, whose mission was to study the nation's declining food fishes and recommend ways to reverse the trend. In 1885 Congress created the Office of Economic Ornithology in the U.S. Department of Agriculture to study the food habits and migratory patterns of birds. After several name changes, it became the Bureau of Biological Survey in 1905.

The survey studied birds and mammals, managed the nation's first wildlife refuges, controlled predators, enforced wildlife laws, and conserved dwindling populations of migratory birds. The Bureau of Fisheries and the Biological Survey transferred to the Department of the Interior in 1939 and combined the next year into the Fish & Wildlife Service.

In addition to the ecological services field office in Bloomington, the U.S. Fish & Wildlife Service has field offices for each of the refuges that are located in Seymour for Muscatatuck, Oakland City for Patoka, and Madison for Big Oaks.

Indiana Department of Natural Resources

The Indiana Department of Natural Resources (DNR) is the state government agency entrusted with protecting, enhancing, and preserving the state's natural, cultural, and recreational resources for the public's benefit. These include state nature preserves, parks, forests, and fish and wildlife areas in Southern Indiana.

The agency is divided into two teams. The Land Management Team oversees the state's natural areas and manages them for preservation, recreation, and extractive activities like timber harvesting. Its divisions include Nature Preserves, State Parks & Reservoirs, Fish & Wildlife, Outdoor Recreation, and Forestry. The Regulatory Team has authority over entomology and plant pathology, historic preservation, oil and gas, reclamation, and water.

DNR is overseen by the autonomous, twelve-member Indiana Natural Resources Commission (NRC), which is composed of seven citizens chosen on a bipartisan basis, three ex-officio members from state agencies, and a member of the Indiana Academy of Science.

DIVISION OF NATURE PRESERVES

The DNR Division of Nature Preserves identifies, protects, and manages more than 250 nature preserves totaling more than 46,000 acres in all twelve of the state's natural regions. Its mission is to maintain natural areas in sufficient numbers and sizes to maintain viable examples of all of the state's natural communities and to provide living museums of natural Indiana as it was when the European settlers arrived. The first state nature preserve—Pine Hills Nature Preserve at Shades State Park—was dedicated in 1969.

Established by an act of the Indiana General Assembly in

1967, the Division of Nature Preserves provides permanent protection for natural areas, defined as land and/or water that has "retained or re-established its natural character, or has unusual flora or fauna, or has biotic, geological, scenic, or paleontological features of scientific or educational value." The Division also manages and maintains viable populations of endangered, threatened, and rare plant and animal species.

Inclusion as a dedicated state nature preserve requires agreement of a site's landowner, the DNR, and the NRC. Once dedicated, a preserve is protected in perpetuity from development that would harm its natural character.

Dedicated state nature preserves are owned by DNR Nature Preserves, Parks & Reservoirs, Fish & Wildlife, and Forestry, as well as city and county park and recreation boards, universities and colleges, and private conservation organizations, including The Nature Conservancy, Central Indiana Land Trust, Whitewater Valley Land Trust, Ouabache Land Trust, Sycamore Land Trust, Indiana Karst Conservancy, and Oak Heritage Conservancy.

As part of its management protocol, the Division of Nature Preserves uses prescribed burning, removes nonnative plants, and maintains preserve boundaries and trails. It also inventories the state for previously unknown natural areas, maintains a registry of natural areas, and dedicates new preserves.

The Indiana Natural Heritage Data Center, a program administered by Nature Preserves, locates and tracks the state's rarest plants, animals, and natural communities. It maintains a database of this natural diversity to help set priorities for protection.

Dedicated state nature preserves, regardless of ownership, are managed to maintain and/or restore their natural ecological conditions. With a few exceptions, they are open to the public for hiking, nature study, photography, wildlife watching, and, with advance permission, scientific research. Visitors are asked to stay on trails to reduce erosion and damage to the fragile plant communities that thrive on the preserves' floors.

Some preserves do not have parking lots or hiking trails.

The Division of Nature Preserves and the organizations that own the individual sites can answer questions about access and visitation.

As the Division of Nature Preserves says on its website, nature, not recreation, is priority no. 1: "More than any other reason, nature preserves are set aside to protect the plants, animals, and natural communities which are found on them. Visitation is allowed to the extent that the features can tolerate it without deterioration."

State law prohibits disturbing or removing anything from dedicated state nature preserves without a special permit.

DIVISION OF STATE PARKS & RESERVOIRS

The Division of State Parks & Reservoirs, DNR's largest division, manages thirty-five parks, lakes, and recreation areas across the state, sixteen in Southern Indiana. The properties range in size from the 165-acre Falls of the Ohio State Park to almost 16,000 acres at Brown County State Park. They include eight U.S. Army Corps of Engineers reservoirs and the state-built Hardy Lake.

The division's mission is to "manage and interpret our properties' unique natural, wildlife, and cultural resources using the principles of multiple use and preservation, while sustaining the integrity of these resources for current and future generations." Multiple use means properties are managed for a variety of public uses, from, in the case of state parks and reservoirs, scenic drives to fishing, camping, hiking, horse riding, biking, and nature study. State and national forests allow logging and other resource-extractive uses under the multiple-use umbrella.

Some Parks & Reservoirs properties, like Monroe Lake and Patoka Lake, have multiple recreation areas under their supervision. Many, like Shakamak, O'Bannon Woods, and Whitewater Memorial State Parks, have dedicated state nature preserves within their boundaries. Others, including Brown County State Park and Brookville Lake, abut other state, federal, and land trust properties to create more expansive natural areas than each provides on its own.

Hornbeam Nature Preserve, Whitewater State Park, Union County.

As of 2016 the Parks & Reservoirs division managed more than 2,000 buildings, nearly 8,400 campsites, 700 miles of trails, 631 hotel and lodge rooms, 75 marinas, 200-plus shelters, 160 or so playgrounds, 149 cabins, 16 swimming pools, and 15 beaches.

HISTORY OF INDIANA STATE PARKS

Indiana State Parks history dates to 1916, when Col. Richard Lieber, an Indianapolis businessman who came to be known as the "father of Indiana state parks," recommended creation of a state park system to coincide with the state's centennial celebration. Lieber became a national leader in the state parks movement and served as the Indiana Department of Conservation's first director for more than a decade.

Under Lieber's direction, the state purchased 350-plus acres in Owen County for $5,250 at auction and established McCormick's Creek as Indiana's first state park on May 25, 1916. In almost a century, the number has grown to twenty-two, with parks stretching from ever-changing sand dunes on Lake

Michigan to four-hundred-million-year-old fossil beds at the Falls of the Ohio River.

As with national and state forests, parks, and other public properties, Indiana's state park history is inextricably linked to President Franklin D. Roosevelt's New Deal–era Civilian Conservation Corps (CCC). A division of the Works Progress Administration, the CCC hired unemployed workers during the Great Depression to reclaim Hoosier landscapes devastated by overlogging, ill-fated agricultural operations, and other poorly planned development projects by planting trees. They implemented erosion-control measures where needed. They also built lakes, roads, shelters, restrooms, gatehouses, trails, bridges, and other structures, many of which are still in use at state parks and other state and federal properties today.

Versailles State Park features a life-size commemorative statue celebrating the CCC workers' contribution to the country's natural heritage. It is one of fifty-nine such sculptures in thirty-eight states nationwide.

A stated goal of the division's parks side is to "give Hoosiers the ability to experience what the Indiana landscape was like prior to settlement . . . mature forests, wetlands and prairies. Additionally, we interpret the historical and archeological context of our state. All of this involves what is known today as resource management."

The reservoir side traces its roots to Cagles Mill Lake just north of McCormick's Creek in Putnam County, which was built in 1952 as the first U.S. Army Corps of Engineers reservoir in Indiana. While recreation and wildlife management opportunities were among the goals for all Corps dam projects, the primary reason for the state reservoir system was flood control—impounding water in some areas to slow downstream flooding in others. The Corps owns the reservoirs and leases the water and surrounding landforms to the DNR for management.

DIVISION OF FISH & WILDLIFE

The Indiana Division of Fish & Wildlife manages Indiana's fish and wildlife populations on more than 150,000 acres of land on twenty-six properties statewide through research, regulation, and restoration. Eleven are located in Southern Indiana. The emphasis is on game species for hunting, fishing, and trapping, along with rare and endangered species.

The division's mission is to "professionally manage Indiana's fish and wildlife for present and future generations, balancing ecological, recreational, and economic benefits." Under state law, it shall "provide for the protection, reproduction, care, management, survival, and regulation of wild animal populations, regardless of whether the wild animals are present on public or private property."

Among the division's stated values are the following: fish and wildlife resources belong to all the people of Indiana; regulated hunting, fishing, and trapping are important wildlife management tools; fish and wildlife resources enrich the quality of human life; public participation is essential for effective resource management; and regulated hunting, fishing, and trapping are legitimate pursuits when conducted in fair chase.

"Fish and wildlife resources are renewable, and when wisely managed will indefinitely provide numerous public benefits such as hunting, fishing, trapping, and wildlife viewing," the division says on its website.

The Fish & Wildlife division also raises and stocks fish in public waters, provides access to public lakes and rivers, and offers advice and incentives to landowners who wish to develop wildlife habitat.

The Nongame & Endangered Wildlife section focuses on the conservation and management of 750 species of nongame, endangered, and threatened wildlife throughout the state. Nongame is any species that is not pursued through hunting and fishing—more than 90 percent of the state's mammals, birds, fish, mussels, reptiles, and amphibians.

The nongame program receives no tax support and is funded through citizen donations to the Nongame Fund. Donations can be made on state tax forms or online through the agency's website. Nongame programs also receive reimbursements through the State Wildlife Grants program from the U.S. Fish & Wildlife

Service. Grant funds must be used on species of greatest conservation need.

Many Fish & Wildlife areas have been designated as Important Bird Areas by the National Audubon Society. Goose Pond Fish & Wildlife Area, for example, is considered a Global Important Bird Area.

DIVISION OF FORESTRY

The Indiana Division of Forestry manages more than 150,000 acres of woodlands on twelve state forests and two state recreation areas, all but one in Southern Indiana. The forests range in size from 355 acres at Selmier State Forest in Jennings County to roughly 24,000 acres each at Morgan-Monroe, Clark, and Harrison-Crawford State Forests. Several feature dedicated nature preserves within or contiguous to their boundaries.

State forests are managed for multiple uses that include timber harvesting, recreation, and watershed protection. Timber harvesting on state forests, however, has been one of Indiana's more controversial environmental policy issues since the 1990s. Conflicts over state forest logging have led to protests and, in some cases, arrests.

The state forest system is open to the public; includes remote backcountry areas, campgrounds, trails, fire towers, lakes, shelters, and other amenities; and is actively managed for fish and wildlife populations. "Recreational development will not take precedence over natural resource conservation and protection and will continue to be structured on the natural rather than the 'built' environment," according to the division's website.

District foresters assist private landowners with inspections and forest management stewardship objectives. The forestry division also operates nurseries that provide stock for landscaping, windbreaks, fire control, and other uses.

INDIANA HERITAGE TRUST

The DNR's Indiana Heritage Trust does not own any natural areas, but it funds acquisition of lands for other DNR agencies to manage that represent outstanding natural resources and habitats or have recreational, historical, or archaeological significance.

Created in 1993, the Heritage Trust program is funded through Indiana environmental license plate sales. In the twelve years between its creation in 1992 and 2014, more than fifty-six thousand acres across the state were purchased.

Among the higher-profile projects the trust has underwritten in Southern Indiana are the Goose Pond Fish & Wildlife Area in Greene County, Beanblossom Bottoms Nature Preserve in Monroe County, and Saunders Woods Nature Preserve in Gibson County.

Indiana Heritage Trust buys land from willing sellers. In addition to environmental license plates, funds for natural area purchase are drawn from General Assembly appropriations and public donations.

The Nature Conservancy

The Nature Conservancy's (TNC) Indiana Chapter has protected more than eighty thousand acres of forests, wetlands, prairies, lakes, and streams on nearly five dozen properties in all twelve of the state's natural regions. Twenty-three of them are located in the state's southern six Natural Regions.

Founded in 1951, TNC pursues a mission that is both prodigious and succinct, expressed in a mere ten words: "Conserve the lands and waters on which all life depends."

To accomplish that charge, the nonprofit conservation organization protects and preserves ecologically important lands and waters in all fifty states and thirty-five countries. TNC has more than one million members worldwide and has protected more than 119 million acres of land and thousands of miles of rivers worldwide. The organization also operates more than one hundred marine conservation projects around the globe.

On its website, The Nature Conservancy traces its history to the formation in 1915 of the Ecological Society of America, which included disagreement about its mission from the get-go: "Should it exist only to support ecologists and publish research

Pennywort Cliffs Nature Preserve, Jefferson County.

or should it also pursue an agenda to preserve natural areas?"

In 1917 the society's activist wing formed the Committee for the Preservation of Natural Conditions, which in 1926 published *The Naturalist's Guide to the Americas,* which attempted to catalog all the known patches of wilderness left in North and Central America.

The Nature Conservancy dates its direct roots to 1946, when "a small group of scientists formed the Ecologists Union, resolving to take 'direct action' to save threatened natural areas." In 1950 the Ecologists Union changed its name to The Nature Conservancy, which incorporated as a nonprofit on October 22, 1951.

Land acquisition has been the organization's primary conservation tool since 1955, when TNC purchased a sixty-acre tract along the Mianus River Gorge on the New York–Connecticut border.

In 1970 TNC created a biological inventory of the United States, providing the impetus for the Natural Heritage Network.

"Its sophisticated databases provide the most complete information about the existence and location of species and natural communities in the United States," the organization says on its website. "The methodology becomes the national standard and is adopted by numerous partner organizations and federal and state governments and universities."

INDIANA CHAPTER OF TNC

The Indiana Chapter formed at a time when conservation was only beginning to take root in Indiana. "The Indiana Chapter of the Nature Conservancy formed in 1959 and struggled for a decade to justify its existence," former Indiana University professor emeritus Lynton Keith Caldwell wrote in the foreword to Marion T. Jackson's *The Natural Heritage of Indiana*. "Then with unforeseeable rapidity and external funding the Indiana Chapter grew to become one of the most active in the nation."

Sycamore Land Trust

Sycamore Land Trust (Sycamore) is a regional, nonprofit conservation organization founded in 1990 with the mission to "preserve the disappearing natural and agricultural landscape of southern Indiana." Sycamore is headquartered in Bloomington and serves twenty-six counties, roughly from Morgan County down to the Ohio River. By early 2015—the organization's twenty-fifth anniversary—Sycamore owned and managed more than eight thousand acres across ninety properties.

The organization protects and conserves land with unique, natural characteristics by purchasing it outright or managing private land through conservation easements that limit harmful uses. Sycamore also runs an environmental education program that connects people of all ages to nature through guided hikes, field trips, and other outdoor experiences. Sycamore protects a variety of different types of land, from forests and family farms to prairies and wetlands, applying the following criteria to each site. Priority areas include those that are adjacent or close to other protected land; in a relatively natural, undisturbed condition, preferably with valuable wildlife habitat; home to threatened or endangered species; and/or protecting a significant stream, river, or wetland.

Private donors are Sycamore's primary funding source. Others include foundation grants and matching funds for land acquisition from government agencies. Sycamore Land Trust preserves are maintained in part by volunteers.

Central Indiana Land Trust

The Indianapolis-based Central Indiana Land Trust, Inc. (CILT), protects more than a thousand acres of land on seventeen nature preserves and forests in Central and Southern Indiana. Five are closed to the public, and several others have limited access. Another three thousand acres on dozens of sites are protected through conservation easements and management agreements with landowners.

Through land protection, stewardship, education, vigilance, and manual labor, the organization's mission is to preserve unique natural areas and help improve air and water quality while enhancing community life for present and future generations.

CILT is an active steward, monitoring the conservation values of its nature preserves and conservation easements and working with landowners, volunteers, and other conservation organizations to protect them.

Each preserve has a science-based management plan that is focused on the land and region's best interests and monitored for rare and endangered species and invasive and exotic species.

Central Indiana Land Trust accepts lands for protection based on three criteria, according to the organization's website:

> **Core conservation areas**—Rich with biodiversity and special ecological attributes, these lands represent the best examples of Central Indiana landscapes.
>
> **Greening the Crossroads**—A plan that identifies a green infrastructure network for Central Indiana, Greening the Crossroads helps to guide restoration and

protection of lands that provide ecological benefits and opportunities for Hoosiers to connect with nature.

Lands of community significance—These lands play integral roles in communities and include family farms and forestlands that serve as legacies for future generations.

CILT's mission is to protect intact natural ecosystems, as well as preserves, parks, and working landscapes that add to a sense of place. The organization seeks to provide places for plants and animals to thrive and for humans to escape the stresses of everyday life and find solace in nature.

"We envision a future where the Central Indiana Land Trust fosters sustainable communities that maintain a healthy environment, a vibrant economy, and a better quality of life," the mission statement says.

Oak Heritage Conservancy

The Oak Heritage Conservancy is a nonprofit land trust that protects nearly seven hundred acres of land on eleven preserves in Southeastern Indiana. Its mission is "to preserve, protect, and conserve land and water resources that have special natural, agricultural, scenic, or cultural significance." Another purpose is to educate the public about the importance of honoring land, water, and local culture.

Oak Heritage focuses on ten counties from Washington to Decatur and Dearborn to Clark. It purchases land outright and accepts donations, bequests, and conservation easements, under which landowners retain ownership of their properties but give up their development rights to ensure the land's long-term protection. Natural resource inventories are developed to understand each property's needs. Land management techniques include invasive plant control and trash removal.

Oak Heritage Conservancy, established in 2002, grew out of the Historic Hoosier Hills Resource Conservation and Development Council. Its operating principle is that the acquisition and protection of natural land and green space are important to the region's quality of life.

Oxbow, Dearborn County.

"We see ourselves as an organization to which landowners may turn to in order to see long term preservation of ancestral lands, or lands that they have become so attached to that they do not wish to see developed or drastically changed," the organization's website says.

Oxbow Inc.

Oxbow Inc. is a nonprofit conservation organization that protects a little more than eleven hundred acres of floodplain at the confluence of the Ohio and Great Miami Rivers at Lawrenceburg. The organization is named after an oxbow lake that formed when the river changed course, and its primary purpose is to manage the property's lakes, ponds, and marshes as stopover, resting, and roosting areas for migrating birds, especially waterfowl and shorebirds.

Active land management practices include agriculture, trash removal, limited burns, and control of noxious plants and destructive wildlife.

Oxbow Inc. organized in reaction to plans announced in the summer of 1985 by political and business leaders to create a new port authority and build a seven-hundred-acre commercial barge-shipping center on the site. A coalition of sportsmen, environmental, and other conservation groups argued the Oxbow was a key area of vital importance to native wildlife. Ultimately, the General Assembly dropped plans for legislation that would have created the port authority.

Within two years, the organization boasted seven hundred members, raised more than $50,000 in private sector donations, and purchased a 27.5-acre block of farmland in the heart of the area. Since then, Oxbow Inc. has purchased more than 850 acres of wetlands and entered into conservation easements to manage another 260 acres of private land.

In addition to protecting the Oxbow's unique natural characteristics, the nonprofit emphasizes public education. "The Oxbow is a classroom for teaching all generations about ecology and the close interaction between wildlife and their habitats. Educational activities for children and adults will bring knowledge to new generations that they may also be encouraged to preserve the natural world," its website says.

National Audubon Society— Important Bird Area Program

Neither the National Audubon Society nor any of its state or regional affiliates in Indiana owns any publicly accessible natural areas in Southern Indiana. But Indiana's local Audubon Society chapters have conducted extensive research that helped identify Important Bird Areas (IBA) across the state.

The IBA program was initiated in Europe in the 1980s and now identifies bird species of concern in more than 8,000 areas in 178 countries. "Hundreds of these sites and millions of acres have received better protection as a result of the Important Bird Areas Program," National Audubon, the program's U.S. administrator, says on its IBA website.

The Audubon Society is a multilayered conservation organization whose mission is "to conserve and restore natural ecosystems, focusing on birds, other wildlife, and their habitats for the benefit of humanity and the earth's biological diversity." Named after nineteenth-century artist and ornithologist John James Audubon, who lived in Kentucky and painted in Indiana in the early 1800s, the society has more than five hundred state and local affiliates around the nation. Four local chapters—Wabash Valley in Terre Haute, Sassafras in Bloomington, Knob and Valley in New Albany, and Evansville—are active in Southern Indiana.

National Audubon launched its IBA initiative in 1995, establishing programs in each state. IBAs are designated as either global, continental, or state and, by definition, are sites that support species of conservation concern (e.g., threatened and endangered species); range-restricted species (species vulnerable because they are not widely distributed); species that are vulnerable because their populations are concentrated in one general habitat type or biome; and/or species or groups of similar species (such as waterfowl or shorebirds) that are vulnerable because they occur at high densities due to their congregatory behavior.

Initially relying on a volunteer coordinator and technical committee, the Indiana Important Bird Areas Program was initiated in 1998. With funding help from the Amos Butler Audubon Chapter in Indianapolis, a full-time coordinator was hired in January 2005. The state's first IBAs were identified that September.

Forty-one Indiana sites, totaling more than 750,000 acres, have been designated as IBAs.

Part 2

THE SOUTHERN
INDIANA LANDSCAPE

The Southern Indiana Landscape

Sculpted by Rock, Ice, and Water

BILLION-YEAR-OLD BEDROCK

From the majestic hills of Dearborn County to the surreal swamps of Posey County, Southern Indiana's physical landscape, formed over billions of years, is a tilted physiographic plane that, while many of its landforms are treacherously precipitous, is in the geologic sense a rather soft, gentle descent.

Like the rest of Indiana, the state's southern landscape is underlain with layers of sedimentary bedrock, formed through the ages by the compression of various materials into limestone, dolomite, siltstone, sandstone, and shale. Depending on the location, from east to west, the rock at or near the surface is between 505 million and 266 million years old and was formed during one of five geologic periods, identified in Marion T. Jackson's *The Natural Heritage of Indiana* as Ordovician (505–438 million years ago), Silurian (438–408 million years ago), Devonian (408–360 million years ago), Mississippian (360–320 million years ago), and Pennsylvanian (320–266 million years ago).

Beneath those layers are two more rock layers from geologic periods that are older still and never approach the surface in Indiana: Cambrian (570–505 million years ago) and Precambrian (4.6 billion–570 million years ago). The oldest earth rocks are estimated at four billion years old. Indiana's geologic record dates back a billion years. That's eight hundred million years *before* the dinosaurs.

While the earliest fossils discovered on earth are three and a half billion years old, physical evidence of Precambrian life

Bluffs of Beaver Bend Nature Preserve, Martin County.

anywhere is exceedingly rare. Fossils show that most of the major animal life forms appeared during the Cambrian period, when invertebrates were common. This period has been called the Cambrian Explosion.

The oldest surface bedrock formed in Indiana during the Ordovician period, when fish first appear in fossil records and invertebrates began diversifying. A narrow slice of Ordovician rock runs north and south along the Ohio border from Wayne County just south of Richmond to Dearborn County, where the Ohio River marks the state line with Kentucky. Fossils embedded in the limestone along Laughery Creek in Versailles State Park are 475 million years old.

From that Ordovician strip, the bedrock tilts to the southwest beneath younger rock layers deposited during the progressively younger Silurian, Devonian, Mississippian, and Pennsylvanian periods. This southwestern tilt, from Brookville to Hovey Lake, on average, follows only a half-degree slope. Over the two hundred or so miles a great blue heron would fly from the highest point in the Dearborn Upland to the Ohio River locks by Mount Vernon, elevations drop eight hundred feet. Along the riverbank, nearly four hundred twisting miles from Lawrenceburg past Evansville, they drop a little less than a hundred feet.

Southern Indiana's landforms, of course, run the gamut—a dizzying array of highlands and lowlands forged through the eons by epic forces that include tectonic plate shifts; continental-size glaciers; the eternal, erosive impacts of oceans, rivers, and streams; and climatic shifts.

Three hundred and fifty million years ago, much of the landmass that is now Southern Indiana occupied the bottom of a shallow inland sea—near the equator. The world-famous limestone quarried in Monroe and Lawrence Counties formed through the eons as sea-dwelling creature shells solidified after they died.

Three hundred million years ago, coal swamps covered the southwestern part of the state with vegetation that transformed from peat and, through compression and heat over millions of years, formed the coal that is still mined there today.

Over the past couple million years, advancing and retreating glaciers and flowing waterways from the melting ice sheets have carved cliffs, bluffs, gorges, and canyons through the bedrock. The elevation at Clifty Falls State Park on the Ohio River at Madison drops three hundred feet from the north gate to the south gate.

PROFOUND ICE AGE EFFECTS

Southern Indiana's physiography began its last and most relevant transformation roughly seven hundred thousand years ago during the Pleistocene Epoch, also known as the Ice Age, when an ice sheet blocked and redirected drainage patterns in the region and began forming the Ohio River Valley. Prior to that glacial advance, rainwater and snowmelt in the Midwest drained to the north to a preglacial river called the Teays, which stretched from its North Carolina headwaters through Northern Indiana to the Mississippi River in Western Illinois.

As explained on the Indiana Geological Survey website: "No other event since the extinction of the dinosaurs sixty-five million years ago can compare to the Ice Age in terms of the profound effect it had on our landscape and the natural environment in which we live today. In fact, virtually all of societal affairs are in one way or another affected by some facet of the Ice Age."

The Pleistocene began two million years ago, presumably lasted until roughly ten thousand years ago (we may be in between ice events), and is divided into four periods, each named after the states in which their impacts are most evident: Nebraskan Glacial (2 million–770,000 years ago), Kansan Glacial (700,000–220,000 years ago), Illinoian Glacial (220,000–70,000 years ago), and Wisconsin Glacial (70,000–10,000 years ago).

During this time, snowfall on large portions of the Hudson Bay and Labrador sections in Northern and Eastern Canada accumulated and formed massive ice sheets. Under the pressure of their own weights and influenced by temperature fluctuations to the south, these glaciers eventually advanced and retreated to and from the south. Believed to be as much as a half-mile to a mile thick, they ground the Earth's surface into new configurations of hills, valleys, flats, lakes, and rivers and carried sediment from north to south. Glacial deposits left when the glaciers retreated in Northern Indiana are several hundred feet thick.

Geologists estimate there may have been between twelve and eighteen different glacial events that caused continental-sized ice sheets to develop, but it's unclear how many of them impacted Indiana. Geologists believe there may have been eleven.

The first ice sheet known to reach Southern Indiana arrived seven hundred thousand years ago during the Kansan Glacial and came down from Michigan. Both the Kansan and Illinoian Glacial events reached the Ohio Valley through a small portion of Southwestern Indiana and a larger expanse in Southeastern Indiana. The Illinoian events occurred between 220,000 and

70,000 years ago and are evident in slightly smaller parts of those same areas.

The last and most influential of the ice sheets in Indiana advanced and retreated during the Wisconsin Glacial, which began in the state about 50,000 years ago and retreated some 13,600 years ago. It was largely responsible for the flat landscape in the northern two-thirds of the state. The Wisconsin ice sheets stopped north of Martinsville, along an uneven line from Brookville to Terre Haute.

None of the Kansan or Illinoian events covered what is called Indiana's unglaciated or driftless region, whose boundary forms an upside-down U from New Albany to Martinsville to the White River on the Martin-Dubois county line before jutting southwest to the Wabash just north of the Ohio.

But that's not to say the unglaciated region was untouched by Pleistocene ice. The 360-degree view from just about any fire tower in any state or national forest in the Norman and Crawford Uplands reveals not the ups and downs typical of hill country. Rather, the horizon appears as a flat plane that, through the ages, glacial meltwater eroded and carved into the eclectic mix of hills, valleys, canyons, flatlands, cave lands, and lowlands it is today.

And even though the glaciers themselves were absent for many tens of thousands of years between the advances—known as *interglacial* periods—their formative work continued unabated. As the Indiana Geological Survey further explains: "Rivers cut great valleys, sediments weathered to form thick soils, and forests and prairies dominated by temperate vegetation pushed the tundra and spruce forests northward. Evidence for these ancient landscapes can still be observed at a few places in Southern Indiana, where the older glacial deposits are at the modern land surface."

The drainage conduits and landforms that these Ice Age rivers created in Southern Indiana follow that gentle bedrock tilt from the northeast to the southwest. Every drop of water that is not captured by a lake or a pond or absorbed by the ground ultimately flows to the Ohio, through its confluence with the Wabash River, on the way to the Mississippi and the Gulf of Mexico. Indeed, those two waterways drain the vast majority of the state, save for three small watersheds in the far north that feed the Maumee River, Lake Michigan, and Illinois River.

THE WATER FLOWS SOUTH AND WEST

The Ohio River and Wabash River watersheds together drain the entire Southern Indiana landscape, steadily flowing southwest from some of the state's highest elevations in southwestern Wayne County to its lowest, where the Ohio and Wabash meet southwest of the Posey County swamplands. Every ounce of water that reaches the state's far southwestern boundary ultimately flows through one of its two mightiest rivers.

The Ohio River

The 981-mile Ohio River—named after the Seneca word *ohiyo,* for "great river"—now bears little resemblance to the serpentine waterway seventeenth-century French explorers dubbed *la belle rivière,* "the beautiful river." It's more like a series of lakes controlled by the U.S. Army Corps of Engineers through a system of locks and dams devised to control flooding and facilitate navigation. Nineteen such riverine manipulations operate along the river's length from Pittsburgh to Cairo, Illinois. The five in Indiana between Switzerland and Posey Counties are managed by the Corps's Louisville District.

By the time the Ohio enters Hoosier territory at its confluence with the Great Miami River at the intersection of Ohio, Kentucky, and Indiana, the beautiful river has traveled almost five hundred miles from downtown Pittsburgh, where the Monongahela and Allegheny Rivers join to form the headwaters. And the journey to the Mississippi is just about half over. Where the two waterways meet at Cairo, the Ohio is clearly the more substantial.

When Native Americans canoed the Ohio in pre–European settlement days, a series of shallow rapids known as the Falls of the Ohio at Louisville left the river impassable for most of the

Mouth of Blue River Nature Preserve, O'Bannon Woods State Park, Harrison County.

year. Over a stretch of two and a half miles, the limestone bedrock that forms the riverbed there dropped twenty-six feet. The
water was shallow enough for ancient bison herds to cross by
hoof on annual journeys from Northern Kentucky salt licks to
the prairies of Western Indiana and Illinois. Their route, known
as the Buffalo Trace, roughly follows U.S. 150 from New Albany
to Vincennes.

The Ohio Tributaries

Four rivers drain Southern Indiana in their entirety and feed
the Ohio—the Whitewater River, Blue River, Little Blue River
(Crawford County), and Anderson River—along with numerous
creeks with names like Fourteenmile, Indian, Pigeon, Potato
Run, Knob, Mill, and Turtle.

In *The Rivers of Indiana,* Richard Simons dubbed the Ohio and
the 101-mile Whitewater "highways of settlement" for the roles
they played in Indiana's human settlement patterns throughout the ages. Of the Whitewater he wrote: "There is something
about the majestic, wooded hills of the Whitewater River Valley
that draws men to them. . . . It has been thus for centuries, going
back to the earliest Indians who lived in the valley and left burial mounds behind them on the highest, most scenic hills" (92).

The Whitewater rises at two forks, one north of Richmond
on the east and the other northeast of New Castle on the west.
The twin streams roughly parallel each other, about ten miles
apart, through deep valleys in the Dearborn Upland before con-
verging at Brookville.

Though the Whitewater has no rapids, it is reputed to be
the state's swiftest river, dropping an average of six feet per
mile over a rocky bed on the way to its rendezvous with the
Great Miami River, across the state line in Ohio, just north of
the Ohio River. The U.S. Army Corps of Engineers dammed the
Whitewater at Brookville in 1974 to create the fifteen-mile-long
Brookville Reservoir, the state's deepest man-made lake.

Another product of Wisconsin Glacial meltwaters, the
Blue River flows some ninety miles from north of Salem in

Washington County through Harrison County hill and cave country—with its underground caves, streams, and springs—on a path to the Ohio at the crossroads town of Leavenworth, population 236. With no cities or major development on its banks, the multiforked, unpolluted Blue River flows through relatively pristine landscape and is widely recognized as one of the state's most scenic waterways.

Known in pioneer days as the Great Blue, this wilderness river begins its journey on the western edge of Southern Indiana knob country and crosses the undulating Mitchell Plain into the rugged Crawford Upland at the Harrison county line. In its first 9 miles, the West Fork drops 160 feet through steep, rocky hills. The two forks and their tributaries become one at Fredricksburg. The forty-five-mile stretch from there to O'Bannon Woods State Park was the first waterway protected under the state's Natural Scenic and Recreational River System Act of 1973.

The Little Blue River—not to be confused with the Little Blue River that rises near New Castle and ultimately feeds the East Fork of the White River—rises near English and winds through the Hoosier National Forest to the Ohio River at Alton. It offers abundant bank fishing and wildlife watching.

The fifty-mile Anderson River rises in the wilds of the Hoosier National Forest in southwestern Crawford County, crosses through southeastern Dubois County, and serves as the county line between Spencer and Perry. Flowing over a rock-strewn bed through the unglaciated Crawford Upland, this short, narrow, shallow river empties into the Ohio at Troy.

The Wabash River

The 475-mile Wabash is indeed "The Essence of Indiana," as Simons dubbed it back in 1985 in *The Rivers of Indiana*. "To Hoosiers the number one river is the Wabash," he wrote in the opening lines to the book's opening chapter. "And to non-Hoosiers the Wabash is Indiana."

The official state river drains 90 percent of the state's landmass—thirty-three thousand of its thirty-six thousand total square miles—from its source a couple miles east of the state line near Fort Recovery, Ohio, to its discharge into the Ohio River in Posey County at the tristate junction of Indiana, Illinois, and Kentucky.

The Wabash bears northwest from its rise through Bluffton and Huntington, turns west through Peru and Lafayette, and then runs south just past Logansport. With nearly a dozen major tributaries, its watershed drains four-fifths of the state's counties.

The Wabash breaches the Southern Indiana territorial divide in the Wabash Lowland at Terre Haute, where it's greeted by the Wabashiki Fish & Wildlife Area, which spans I-70 on the river's western bank. The river and wildlife area names are derived from the Native American term *wah-bah-shik-ki*, which means "pure white." The French renamed it Ouabache, which the English shortened to Wabash. Its primary Southern Indiana tributaries are the White River and Patoka River.

Flowing south from Terre Haute to Vincennes, the Wabash follows a broad, partially filled, preglacial valley through fertile farmland. South of Vincennes, as Simons put it, the river "meanders, shifts, and wiggles" through land that is sometimes "wild and barren" (4).

Aside from East Mount Carmel, historic New Harmony is the only town on the Indiana side of the Wabash from Vincennes to its confluence with the Ohio some eighty miles south. The town is the site of two early nineteenth-century utopian communities, and its population is roughly eight hundred. The population for East Mount Carmel, which lies just south from the Patoka River's confluence with the Wabash River, isn't included on the Census Bureau website. Estimates range from fifty to eighty-six.

The White River

At its terminus in Southwestern Indiana, where the White River forms the border between Knox and Gibson Counties and meets the Wabash at the Illinois state line, the White's flow has been bloated by the merger of its East and West Forks some thirty miles to the east.

Both forks' watersheds originate near one another in Henry and Randolph Counties, east and a little north of Indianapolis not far from the Ohio state line. Following divergent paths to the southwest and their junction north and east of Petersburg in Gibson County coal country, the twin White forks carry Southern Indiana precipitation and runoff from five other rivers and their tributaries.

All told, the White River and its forks drain a third of the state of Indiana.

While the East Fork of the White River is shorter than the West Fork in terms of river miles, the East drains a larger area, 5,700 square miles versus 5,300.

East Fork

The East Fork is by far the more complex ecosystem of the two. Its basin begins in the till plain northeast of New Castle in Henry County, where the Big Blue River and Flatrock River rise just a few miles apart. Each flows some 100 miles south to Columbus, where they converge and form the 192-mile East Fork's headwaters.

Along the way south, the Big Blue River is joined by the Little Blue River. The name changes to the Driftwood River where the Big Blue and Sugar Creek converge at the Atterbury Fish & Wildlife Area. Through the years, some argued, to no avail, that the Big Blue–Driftwood stretch should be renamed to reflect its geographic reality as the East Fork's upper stream.

From Columbus, the East Fork traverses the flat, sandy, agricultural Scottsburg Lowland past Seymour to and through the unglaciated Norman Upland, Mitchell Plateau, and Crawford Upland, past Bedford and Shoals on its path to Petersburg and the Wabash Lowland.

On the Jackson-Washington county line, where the lowlands meet the uplands, the East Fork merges with its largest tributary, the Muscatatuck River. Due to its torturously twisted route, the Muscatatuck was known in the early 1800s as "the stream of many turns."

East Fork of the White River, Martin County.

The muddy-colored river with mud banks and silt bottom has two branches, the shorter one variously referred to as the Muscatatuck and the East Fork of the Muscatatuck. Regardless of the name, its journey west begins near Paris Crossing in northwestern Jefferson County, where Graham Creek and Big Creek meet. From there it flows some fifty miles to the East Fork of the White River.

West of Austin in Scott County, the East Fork merges with seventy-seven-mile Vernon Fork, which has passed just east of North Vernon and through the Selmier State Forest, Calli Nature Preserve, and Muscatatuck National Wildlife Refuge.

From that junction, the Muscatatuck River journeys west across the Scottsburg Lowland and crosses into the Norman Upland to meet the East Fork of the White River on the Jackson-Washington county line north and a little west of Salem.

At the Martin-Dubois county line, the White collects the mysterious Lost River, which flows through the Mitchell Plain in Southern Indiana karst country. The Lost rises near Orleans in Orange County and flows for twenty-three of its eighty-five miles underground through a system that has been called a "subterranean Grand Canyon."

Most of the East Fork's path flows over unglaciated, rocky terrain, through which the river has painstakingly carved narrow, oftentimes spectacular valleys with cliffs and canyons. As it passes through and out of the Crawford Upland past Shoals in Martin County before finally reaching the more compliant, glaciated Wabash Lowland, the East Fork's sandstone bluffs and ridges can loom a couple hundred feet or more.

West Fork

The 312-mile West Fork, by contrast, flows exclusively through glaciated terrain, and its valley, with brief exceptions in parts of Owen and Greene Counties, is mostly broad and flat.

The West Fork rises a few miles southwest of Winchester in Randolph County near the Ohio state line and bisects the industrial cities of Muncie, Anderson, and Indianapolis. On its way to meet the East Fork, the West Fork skirts the towns of Spencer and Washington.

In Greene County near Worthington, the West Fork absorbs the Eel River, whose flow originates 115 miles to the north of Indianapolis in Boone County. The Eel that flows through Western Indiana is known in some circles as Big Walnut Creek. It is not related to the historic river of the same name in Northeastern Indiana.

Upstream from Greencastle, the only city on its route, the Eel lazily crosses the flat, glaciated Tipton Till Plain. South of the college town it crosses the Wisconsin Glacial boundary and enters the Crawford Upland. Near the Putnam-Owen county line, the Eel merges with Deer Creek.

Just upstream, Deer Creek is joined by Mill Creek, which flows over and through Cataract Falls State Recreation Area. Mill Creek was dammed in 1953 to create fourteen-hundred-acre Cagles Mill Lake, also known as Cataract Lake.

The Patoka River

By the time the Patoka River meets the Wabash River just a mile south of the White River in Gibson County at a point known as Hells' Neck, it has completed a 167-mile journey that began on a ridge southeast of Paoli. Along the way to that meeting across from Mount Carmel, Illinois, in the Wabash Lowland, the river drops three hundred feet in its first twenty-five miles through the Crawford Upland and passes through Jasper, Huntingburg, and Princeton.

Formed by glacial activity some three hundred thousand years ago, the Patoka River initially flowed a tortuous two hundred miles or so. Much of the reduction came in the 1920s, when a winding, thirty-seven-mile channel was dredged and straightened into an eighteen-mile line.

Before the river was channelized, according to the *Fifth Annual Report of the Geological Survey of Indiana, Made during the Year 1873*, the Patoka at the village of Kirksville in Gibson County was "a foul, stinking, rotten river—in summer a solution of decaying vegetable matter, reeking with malarial poison . . . thick enough to bear up small animals" (397).

On its eastern reaches, the Patoka's flow is dammed in Dubois County, just west of the Orange county line, to create the eighty-eight-hundred-acre Patoka Lake. Along thirty miles of river in the center, the Patoka National Wildlife Refuge permanently protects eight thousand acres of forests, grasslands, wetlands, ponds, sloughs, and swamps.

Southern Indiana Physiography

Over billions of years, the geologic forces of rock, ice, and water transformed the southern part of the state into seven distinct physiographic units that were first detailed in W. N. Logan and colleagues' *Handbook of Indiana Geology* in 1922. "The Physiography of Indiana" chapter, written by Indiana University geology professor Clyde Mallott, divided the region into three uplands, two plateaus, and a pair of lowlands. These characterizations have withstood scientific rigor for almost a century and remain the framework through which geologists still see the region, with only minor modifications.

DEARBORN UPLAND

Underlain by the oldest bedrock in Indiana, the Dearborn Upland is the easternmost physiographic unit in Southern Indiana, occupying all of Ohio and Switzerland Counties, most of Dearborn, and significant portions of Franklin and Jefferson, while touching on Fayette and Decatur.

The Dearborn Upland features Southern Indiana's highest elevations, peaking at the state's sixth highest—1,140 feet—in Union County northeast of the Whitewater Memorial State Park. Indiana's highest elevation—1,257 feet—is not far north in Wayne County in the New Castle Till Plain. By comparison, Weed Patch Hill in Brown County State Park, the highest elevation in that world-famous hill country, is 1,058 feet.

The Dearborn Upland, an ancient, dissected plateau underlain by limestone and shale, mostly from the Ordovician period, is nearly five hundred million years old. Formed by the Wisconsin ice sheet, the area is covered by thick glacial deposits. It divides the watersheds of the west-flowing tributaries of the East Fork of the White and Muscatatuck Rivers from the south- and east-flowing Indian-Kentuck Creek, Laughery Creek, and Whitewater River.

MUSCATATUCK REGIONAL SLOPE

The Muscatatuck Regional Slope, now called the Muscatatuck Plateau, spreads across seven counties, spanning significant chunks of Decatur, Ripley, Jennings, Jefferson, and Clark. Its northeastern boundary bleeds over into small sections of Franklin and Dearborn.

The Muscatatuck Plateau's bedrock is predominantly limestone and dolomite, which formed during the Devonian period some four hundred million years ago. The landscape is so flat in places that water stands and leaves the soils saturated much of the year, creating seasonally wet forests called flatwoods.

Clifty Falls State Park, Jefferson County.

The Muscatatuck slope's gently undulating, glaciated landscape is downcut in places—like the Calli Nature Preserve on the Vernon Fork of the Muscatatuck River—where rivers and streams carved stark canyons through the solid bedrock as they wended their ways to the White and Ohio Rivers. Some of Southern Indiana's most spectacular bluffs, gorges, and canyons are found where the Muscatatuck slope meets the Ohio River, at Clifty Falls State Park, for example.

SCOTTSBURG LOWLAND

The likewise glaciated Scottsburg Lowland is a relatively flat landscape that includes large sections of Bartholomew, Jackson, Scott, and Clark Counties, with peripheral acreage in Johnson, Shelby, Jennings, and Washington. More recent physiographic designations have subdivided this region into the Scottsburg Lowland and Charlestown Hills, with most of the latter in Clark County.

The underlying shale bedrock, formed during the Devonian and Mississippian periods 408 million to 320 million years ago, offered little resistance to the Wisconsin ice sheets that covered it an estimated 13,600 years ago. The only place where the Ohio River's bed is stone from one side to the other is where the Scottsburg Lowland meets the Ohio at Jeffersonville.

The region is drained by the East Fork of the White River to the north and the Muscatatuck River to the south.

NORMAN UPLAND

The Norman Upland is a narrow, serpentine landform with steep hills and valleys that stretches across eleven counties, from Putnam and Morgan south to Floyd on the Ohio River. The largest blocks are in Putnam, Morgan, Monroe, and Brown Counties, with substantial pieces in Lawrence, Jackson, Washington, and Floyd and smaller sections in Owen, Johnson, and Scott.

The resistant Mississippian period bedrock, 360 million to 320 million years old, that underlies this scenic region is mostly siltstone.

This slice of uplands, also known as the Knobstone Escarpment, forms the eastern boundary of the state's unglaciated region. From the dramatic hills of Brown County to the scenic knobs of Floyd County, this rugged topography was formed by glacial meltwater that eroded the region's less-resistant rock to form the East Fork of the White River and Muscatatuck basins.

MITCHELL PLAIN

The unglaciated Mitchell Plain, also called the Mitchell Plateau, spans seven counties from north to south, occupying substantial portions of Owen, Monroe, Lawrence, Orange, Washington, and Harrison Counties, as well as a small slice of western Floyd.

This low-relief area is underlain with Mississippian era limestone that formed 360 million to 320 million years ago, when it was the floor of a shallow, inland sea. The Mitchell Plain is Indiana karst country and is characterized by sinkholes and underground drainage and cave systems, which were formed by stream erosion and limestone dissolution.

From north to south, the Mitchell Plain is drained by the West Fork of the White River, which skirts the northern boundary at McCormick's Creek State Park in Owen County; the East Fork of the White River, which flows south of Bedford in Lawrence County; the Lost River through Orange County karst, where most surface water disappears into swallow holes, sinkholes, and cracks in the rock; and Indian and Buck Creeks, which feed the Ohio.

CRAWFORD UPLAND

The Crawford Upland, which forms the unglaciated region's western boundary, slices through eleven Southern Indiana counties: Owen, Monroe, Greene, Lawrence, Martin, Washington, Orange, Dubois, Harrison, Perry, and Spencer. Unlike the Dearborn Upland, its landforms are the result of erosion, not glacial deposition.

This hill country expanse is composed of alternating layers of limestone, shale, and sandstone from the late Mississippian period, as well as some sandstone from the Pennsylvanian period, some three hundred million years ago. Reliefs of 300 to 350 feet are common.

This rugged upland area is drained by the West Fork of the White River, the East Fork of the White River, the Lost River, the Anderson River, and the Ohio River.

WABASH LOWLAND

The Wabash Lowland is by far Southern Indiana's largest physiographic unit, spanning fifteen counties: Parke, Clay, Vigo, Greene, Sullivan, Martin, Daviess, Knox, Dubois, Pike, Gibson, Spencer, Warrick, Vanderburgh, and Posey.

The Wabash Lowland averages about 500 feet above sea level and is more than 350 feet lower than the crest of the Crawford Upland. The dominant rock type is relatively nonresistant siltstone and shale formed 320 million to 266 million years ago during the Pennsylvanian period.

A thin layer of glacial materials from the Illinoian ice sheets some 220,000 to 70,000 years ago blankets the bedrock in places, but the glacial tills are too thin to have a noticeable effect on the landforms.

As its name suggests, this vast section of Southwestern Indiana is drained by the Wabash River, which is fed by the White and Patoka Rivers.

The Natural Regions

Ecologically speaking, the southern half of Indiana is divided into six *natural regions,* as defined in 1985 in the *Proceedings of the Indiana Academy of Science.* Led by Michael A. Homoya, who has served as the Indiana Department of Natural Resources' chief botanist / plant ecologist since three years before that landmark paper, a team of researchers defined *natural region* as: "A major, generalized unit of the landscape where a distinctive assemblage of natural features is present. It is part of a classification system that integrates several natural features, including climate, soils, glacial history, topography, exposed bedrock, presettlement vegetation, species composition, physiography, and flora and fauna distribution to identify a natural region." Natural regions can be subdivided into *sections* if "sufficient differences are evident such that recognition is warranted" (245).

Four of the six distinct natural regions between Interstate 70 and the Ohio River—Southwestern Lowland, Southern Bottomlands, Shawnee Hills, Highland Rim, Bluegrass, and Big Rivers—are subdivided into eleven sections.

BIG RIVERS NATURAL REGION

The Big Rivers Natural Region, which includes major waterways with average flows of seven thousand cubic feet per second or greater, drains all of Southern Indiana's other five natural regions and more. Big Rivers includes the two-hundred-mile Lower Wabash River, from Fountain County south to the Ohio River; the thirty-mile Lower White River, from the confluence of its forks at the intersection of Daviess, Pike, and Knox Counties to the Wabash on the Gibson-Knox county line; and the entire Ohio River bordering Indiana, from the Oxbow at Lawrenceburg to the Wabash River southwest of Hovey Lake.

The state's largest waterways trace their origins to the end of the Wisconsin glacier, when massive ice sheets began melting and the water started seeking new routes south. Today, the paths they've carved lead the precipitation that falls on the Switzerland Hills in Union County south and west to the Big Rivers, west to the Mississippi River, and on to the Gulf of Mexico.

The Big Rivers Natural Region supports aquatic life not found in smaller rivers, creeks, and streams, including shovelnose sturgeon, shortnose gar, skipjack herring, smallmouth buffalo, goldeye, mooneye, and blue sucker. Bottom-dwelling freshwater mussels (freshwater clams) can live up to fifty years and include the federally endangered fat pocketbook.

SOUTHWESTERN LOWLANDS NATURAL REGION

The Southwestern Lowlands Natural Region encompasses all or part of fourteen counties, from southern Parke south along the Wabash River to Posey, east along the Ohio River to the eastern edge of Spencer, and then back north to Parke.

As the name implies, much of this natural region's landscape is broad, low, and largely level valleys that were formed by glacial activity and deposition from the Wabash and White Rivers. In presettlement times, it was largely lowland forest with some uplands and prairies.

Over a little more than two centuries, the vast majority of the region's flat, poorly drained valleys were cleared and ditched for agriculture and mined for coal. What remnants of pre–European settlement landscape remain today include a variety of lowland forest types, including floodplain, flatwoods, and some dry flatwoods.

But the region is also home to significant chunks of upland barrens, some of which, near the Wabash and White Rivers,

Goose Pond Fish & Wildlife Area, Greene County.

feature deep, windblown sand deposits with remnants of dry oak barrens.

The Southwestern Lowlands is divided into three sections—Plainville Sand, Glaciated, and Driftless. The first two were formed by pre–Wisconsin Glacial activity. The Driftless Section was untouched by the last ice sheet, which retreated from Indiana some 13,600 years ago.

Plainville Sand Section

The Plainville Sand Section is a small but unique area of windblown sand dunes east of the Wabash and White Rivers with sandy, acidic soils. The barrens natural community type, which dominated the ridges and well-drained sites when the white settlers arrived, has essentially vanished from the landscape. Swamps, marshes, and wet prairies occupied the swales. Barrens vegetation consisted mostly of prairie species, along with a collection of sand-dwelling species of western and southern affinities.

Glaciated Section

By far the Southwestern Lowlands' flattest, the Glaciated Section occupies the northern two-thirds of this natural region, the bulk of it north of the White River. A narrow slice extends south of the White, along the Wabash and into northwestern Posey County.

This section was covered and shaped by ice during the Illinoian Glacial period, which took place between 220,000 and 70,000 years ago. The soils are mostly acid to neutral silt loams, with thick layers of loess—windblown sedimentary deposits.

While presettlement natural communities were mostly lowland forests, this section appears to have had the most prairie south of the Wisconsin glacier's boundary, which roughly corresponds to the Southwestern Lowlands Natural Region's northern edge. Several types of prairie are understood to have existed, but little is known of their composition.

Flatwoods are the most common remnant community type in the Glaciated Section. Other natural communities are swamp, marsh, pond, and relatively flat waterways, such as the Eel River, which merges with the West Fork of the White River in northern Greene County, or Busseron Creek, which empties into the Wabash in far northwestern Knox County.

Driftless Section

The Driftless Section occupies the unglaciated, far southern portion of the Southwestern Lowlands Natural Region. It is characterized by low hills and broad valleys in the part of the state with the most annual sun exposure and highest average summer temperature. Since the landscape was directly unaffected by glaciation, this section's topography is more varied than the rest of the region's and supports a wider variety of natural communities.

The natural communities are largely upland forests on well-drained slopes atop soils that were formed in loess and weathered bedrock. Southern flatwoods occupy the old Wabash and Ohio river lake plains and river terraces and feature predominantly moist, acidic soils. The post oak flatwoods' barrens support fewer typical prairie plants than other barrens communities. Other natural communities include marsh, swamp, sandstone cliff, and at least one acid seep spring.

Streams are low to medium gradient.

SOUTHERN BOTTOMLANDS NATURAL REGION

The Southern Bottomlands Natural Region includes the rich, fingerlike floodplains that follow Southwestern Indiana's rivers and larger streams as they flow southwest to the confluence of the Ohio and Wabash Rivers. The waterways include the Lower Ohio, Lower Wabash, White, and Patoka Rivers.

Unlike other lowland regions in Indiana, the Southern Bottomlands' primary natural communities—floodplain forest and forested swamps—in places support plant and animal species more commonly found in the Lower Mississippi River Valley and Gulf Coastal Plain, including the state threatened bald cypress. Contrary to their Deep South appearance, the swamps do not support alligators.

The Southern Bottomlands are subject to frequent flooding, now and historically, and the soils are mostly neutral to acid silt loams. The natural communities are primarily bottomland forest, with swamp, pond, and slough.

In addition to bald cypress, southern species that thrive in the swamps and sloughs include overcup oak and spider lily, both state watch list species, state threatened featherfoil, giant cane, and some rare sedges. The Southern Bottomlands' southern influence is also found in the region's fauna, which includes swamp rabbit and yellow-crowned night heron, both on the state endangered list.

The Patoka River typifies the type of silt-bottomed, low-gradient streams that drain this region. Other aquatic features include large bottomland ponds, especially along the Wabash River.

The Wabash, Ohio, and White Rivers themselves are not part of the Southern Bottomlands Natural Region. They are classified separately as the Big Rivers Natural Region. (See the Big Rivers Natural Region section above.)

A GUIDE TO NATURAL AREAS OF SOUTHERN INDIANA

Hemlock Cliffs, Hoosier National Forest, Crawford County.

SHAWNEE HILLS NATURAL REGION

The Shawnee Hills Natural Region forms a rugged, narrow swath of uplands that runs through twelve Indiana counties, from Putnam on the north to Harrison and Perry on the south. The Indiana slice is part of a larger natural region that extends south across the Ohio River into Kentucky and west into Southern Illinois.

According to Homoya and colleagues' 1985 paper "The Natural Regions of Indiana," the Shawnee Hills are also the most unspoiled: "This region appears to represent general pre-settlement conditions better than any other terrestrial region in the state" (258).

The region is named after the Shawnee Indians, who lived in the area in the late eighteenth and early nineteenth centuries after European encroachment had driven them from their homelands in Southern Ohio, West Virginia, and Western Pennsylvania.

This sparsely populated region's natural communities are primarily upland forests, though sandstone and limestone glades, gravel washes, and barrens are also present.

Except for some small areas of till in the north, the Shawnee Hills are unglaciated and sit atop bedrock from the Pennsylvanian and Mississippian periods—mostly sandstone in the west and limestone in the east. The region features some of the state's most spectacular cliffs and rockhouses, which in turn provide habitat for several unique plant and animal species.

The Shawnee Hills Natural Region is divided into two sections: the Crawford Upland to the west and the Escarpment to the east. Bedrock primarily dictates the difference. Sandstone dominates the Crawford Upland Section, limestone the Escarpment Section.

Crawford Upland Section

The Crawford Upland Section extends south from Putnam County to Perry and Crawford Counties on the Ohio River and is characterized by rugged hills with sandstone cliffs and rockhouses. In a chapter he contributed to *The Natural Heritage of Indiana*, Homoya says it is here that "we find some of our state's most massive and spectacular sandstone cliffs" (172).

Carved by millions of years of erosion, these cliffs assume a variety of forms, including sheer faces, detached blocks, and canyons. The sandstone cliff and rockhouse communities support several wildflower and fern species with Appalachian origins, including mountain laurel, a state watch list species.

While they are rare in Indiana, a few examples of bog-like acid seep springs are found in the Crawford Upland Section. Also rare are the section's high-quality barrens communities, which are similar to the glades and barrens in the Highland Rim Natural Region, minus many of their distinctive glade species. Two small sandstone glades, which are nearly nonexistent in the state, occur in this section.

Escarpment Section

The Escarpment Section, an even thinner slice of hill country than the Crawford Upland, includes portions of eight counties from southern Putnam to Harrison. This section is unglaciated and features large limestone cliffs along the Ohio River and smaller streams. Some karst features are present, especially in the lower and middle elevations.

While this section features sandstone bedrock, cliffs and rockhouses are virtually nonexistent. Most of the hills are covered by sandstone and sandstone-derived soils, with limestone and limestone-derived soils on the lower elevations.

The Escarpment Section's natural communities consist of various upland forest types and moist cove environments. Limestone cliff communities occur mostly at the section's southern end. Limestone glades and barrens are found, but they are not as common as in the Highland Rim Natural Region.

Some of Indiana's largest caves—Marengo and Wyandotte, for example—are located in the Escarpment Section, where the cave communities support some unique fauna, including the northern cavefish, which is on the state endangered list. Some caves support large populations of hibernating bats, the federally endangered Indiana bat among them.

Waterways in the Escarpment Section include normally clear, medium- and high-gradient streams, springs, and sinkhole ponds.

Limestone gravel wash communities are present.

HIGHLAND RIM NATURAL REGION

Southern Indiana's Highland Rim Natural Region is the northern extension of a discontinuous belt of mostly forested hills that stretch from southern Morgan County south, across the Ohio River, through Kentucky and Tennessee, and into Northern Alabama. The landscape is rugged and biologically rich. Its landforms are unique, not only to Indiana but also to the United States.

Named because the ridgetops form rims around their surrounding landscapes, the Highland Rim offers some of the wildest land east of the Rockies. The region is unglaciated, except for areas on its far northern and eastern edges. The northern boundary approximates the Wisconsin glacier's southern reach.

The bedrock, predominantly Mississippian with Pennsylvanian in places, shapes the land. Rock outcroppings are neither as big nor as frequent as in the Shawnee Hills Natural Region.

A distinctive feature of the Highland Rim is the large expanse of karst topography, which shares the region with cliffs, rugged hills, and other major topographic features. The western half is underlain by limestone, the eastern half by sandstone, shale, and siltstone, all of which support a variety of landforms, vegetation, and soil types.

In presettlement times, most of the region was forested, with large areas of chert barrens, along with smaller areas of limestone, siltstone, glade, and gravel wash communities.

The Highland Rim Natural Region is divided into three sections: the Mitchell Karst Plain Section, the Brown County Hills Section, and the Knobstone Escarpment Section.

Buddha Karst Cave, Lawrence County.

Mitchell Karst Plain Section

The Mitchell Karst Plain Section traverses Southern Indiana cave country through nine counties, from a small strip in far southeastern Putnam County south and east to Harrison and Floyd Counties. As the name implies, this section's signature feature is the karst plain, which, while relatively level, also features limestone cliffs and rugged hills.

Several natural communities are present, including caves, sinkhole ponds and swamps, flatwoods, chert barrens, limestone glades, and upland forests. But as Michael A. Homoya and Hank Huffman from the Indiana Division of Nature Preserves cowrote in a chapter they contributed to *The Natural Heritage of Indiana*, these surface features represent only the *seen* piece of the Mitchell Plain. An equally—if not more—spectacular world exists in the *unseen* beneath the surface.

Water—including a river—disappears from the karst plain's surface into a subterranean world that has been described as Grand Canyon–like in its immensity. Surface and groundwater are constantly working on the area's soluble limestone bedrock, creating underground drainage routes through sinkholes, joints, fractures, caves, and rivers. The world-famous Lost River in Orange County flows twenty-three miles underground.

Karst wetland communities are the section's major aquatic features. Springs and spring caves are found along major streams and in the walls of some sinkholes. When plugged, funnel-shaped sinkholes can form ponds or swamps, which in turn support biologically rich natural communities. Sinkhole pond communities generally have open water and marshy borders. Sinkhole swamp communities include some Gulf Coastal Plain swamp species, including Virginia willow (a.k.a. Virginia sweetspire), which is on the state endangered species list, and rare netted chainfern.

Underground wildlife that inhabits the karst section includes federally endangered Indiana bat and state-endangered northern cavefish, as well as northern cave crayfish, ghost crayfish, cave salamander, long-tailed salamander, northern cave isopod, stygian cave cricket, and southern cave cricket.

Untouched by glacial activity, the Mitchell Karst Plain's soils are generally well-drained silt loams derived from loess and weathered limestone. Surface streams are few and typically medium and high gradient with rocky bottoms.

The Mitchell Karst Plain Section contained the largest area of prairie-like chert barrens in Indiana, due in part to the dry soils left behind by sinks that drain most of the surface precipitation.

Most of the state's limestone glades occur in this section's more rugged areas, particularly in Harrison and Washington Counties. Glades are defined as naturally occurring forest openings where the bedrock is at or near the surface. They tend to be on steep, south-facing slopes, typically above cliffs. Sun exposure and thin soils make them hot and dry in summer and fall.

Most stream borders feature gravel wash communities with limestone and chert gravel.

Several forest communities are present in the Mitchell Karst Plain, but the predominant is the western mesophytic forest type, which requires moderate water. The glade communities feature some very dry forest types.

Brown County Hills Section

The Brown County Hills Section occupies the northeastern part of the Highland Rim Natural Region, following a line of forested uplands through six counties, from Morgan to Jackson. It includes all of Brown County and is contiguous until the East Fork of the White River Valley in western Jackson County. A separate section called the Brownstown Hills looms on the valley's east side.

The Brown County Hills—with their steep, V-shaped ravines and valleys—boast one of the largest forested landscapes in the Midwest. Moist cove forest communities occupy the north-facing slopes.

While early ice sheets covered some of this section, the Wisconsin glacier only skirted its northern boundary. The Brown County Hills are underlain by siltstone, shale, and sandstone, with soils that are well-drained acid silt loams and some loess.

The bedrock, which is near the surface but seldom crops out, has been deeply downcut through the ages by the erosive power of flowing water. The sharpest reliefs occur in the unglaciated areas, particularly in central and southern Brown County.

Small, high-gradient, ephemeral streams are common. Larger streams tend to be low to medium gradient.

The state-endangered green adder's mouth orchid and state threatened yellow ladies' tresses (a.k.a. yellow nodding ladies'-tresses) are limited to this geographic area. This section doesn't support many other threatened plant species, aside from state threatened purple flowering raspberry, which accompanies several patches of hemlock on steep slopes along waterways like Guthrie Creek.

Some siltstone glades are found on southwest-facing slopes in the Brownstown Hills. One acid seep spring community was known in the area, but it was covered in 1965 when the U.S. Army Corps of Engineers dammed the Salt Creek to create Monroe Lake.

Tribbett Woods Nature Preserve, Jennings County.

Knobstone Escarpment Section

The Knobstone Escarpment Section begins at the East Fork of the White River where Washington County meets Lawrence and Jackson Counties, directly across the water from the Brown County Hills. Its wooded uplands form a narrow rim that cuts east across northern Washington County and then south, spanning the Washington-Clark county line to Floyd County and the Ohio River.

This section is similar to the Brown County Hills in terms of vegetation, bedrock, and rugged, knobby topography. The hills are steep, precipitous in places, with narrow ravines. Rock outcrops are few and restricted to ridgetops. The knobs' forest communities support a different mix of flora and fauna.

American chestnut, historically a dominant until it was decimated by the chestnut blight of the late nineteenth and early twentieth centuries, has been replaced by the chestnut oak. American chestnut is present today only as stump sprouts.

In addition to the scrub pine (a.k.a. Virginia pine), other plant and animal species that distinguish the Escarpment from the Brown County Hills include several that are on the state endangered species list, including cucumber magnolia, rosette goldenrod (a.k.a. stout-ragged goldenrod), red salamander (a state endangered species), scarlet snake, and southeastern crowned snake. Painted sedge, which is common in the Brown County Hills, is rare in the Knobstone Escarpment, as is the state-endangered Harvey's buttercup.

While rare, siltstone glades are found on south-facing slopes and are more common here than in any other part of the state.

Small, high-gradient, ephemeral streams are the major aquatic features of the Knobstone Escarpment Section.

BLUEGRASS NATURAL REGION

The Bluegrass Natural Region is the easternmost of Southern Indiana's six and includes all or part of seventeen counties, from Wayne in the northeast to Clark in the southwest. The name is derived from similarities between the region's physiography and natural communities and those of the Bluegrass Region of North-Central Kentucky. Some bluegrass species are native to this natural region. Kentucky bluegrass is not.

Natural features include rugged hills with some of the state's highest elevations, acidic flatwoods, limestone canyons and cliffs, floodplain forests, and a few forested fens.

The entire Bluegrass Region was covered by at least one, perhaps more, of the early glaciers. The northern boundary approximates the Wisconsin ice sheet's southern reach and the northern limit for several southern plant species in this region, as well as many reptiles and amphibians. The bedrock is covered with a relatively thin layer of glacial drift.

While most of the region was forested when the Europeans arrived, a few glade, cliff, barrens, and nonforested aquatic habitats also occurred.

Charles C. Deam, Indiana's first state botanist whose early twentieth-century work is still the foundation for species identification today, observed in his *Flora of Indiana* in 1940 that the Bluegrass Region contained flora of Appalachian origins and poorly drained flatwoods.

The Bluegrass Natural Region is divided into three sections: the Scottsburg Lowland Section, Muscatatuck Flats and Canyons Section, and Switzerland Hills Section.

Scottsburg Lowland Section

The Scottsburg Lowland Section is a thin band of riverine lowlands that stretch through seven counties, from Johnson and Shelby on the north to Clark and the Ohio River on the south. Its main features are wide plains bordering the section's major streams and tributaries, particularly the Muscatatuck River, the East Fork of the White River, and Silver Creek.

The glaciated section sits atop nonresistant shale of the late Devonian and early Mississippian periods. Soils are acid to neutral silt loams, with a sizable area of windblown sand deposits just east of the East Fork of the White River. Bedrock outcrops are rare, despite the section's thin soils.

The Scottsburg Lowland's natural communities are primarily floodplain forest and swamp, with a few forested fens. Some upland forests occur where it meets the Muscatatuck Flats and Canyons Section.

The eastern ribbon snake and southern tubercled orchid (a.k.a. pale green orchid) are geographically restricted to this section. Nearly all records of northern studfish in Indiana are in the Scottsburg Lowland.

Wetland features in this section include swamps, acid seep springs, and ponds. Aquatic habitats include silt-bottomed, slow-flowing streams, rivers, and ponds.

Muscatatuck Flats and Canyons Section

The Muscatatuck Flats and Canyons Section is a relatively flat, west-sloping plain that encompasses parts of fifteen counties, from Johnson and Rush on the north to Clark on the south. The terrain features southern flatwoods, steep-walled canyons, and moderately deep valleys that have been downcut by major streams.

The section's most characteristic natural community is the flatwoods. Geographically restricted flatwoods species include dwarf ginseng, a state watch list species, fox grape, and Oneida grape-fern.

Compared to the flatwoods, the canyons, cliffs, and slopes are comparatively rich floristically, with a predominantly mixed mesophytic forest composition. Canada violet and long-spurred violet are more common here than elsewhere in Southern Indiana.

Nonforested community types include small areas of limestone gravel wash and limestone glades.

Bedrock consists of Silurian and Devonian age limestone and dolomites. Minor areas of karst topography with caves and sinkholes occur along valley borders.

The major aquatic features include medium-gradient streams with pavement-like limestone beds.

Switzerland Hills Section

The Switzerland Hills Section occupies the state's far south-eastern edge in nine counties, from Wayne to Jefferson and Switzerland. It is characterized by deeply dissected uplands—reliefs reach 450 feet in places—underlain by chalky shale and limestone. While the Ordovician age bedrock, the oldest in the state, is near the surface in this section, cliffs are rare.

The Switzerland Hills Section is the highest in Southern Indiana and includes some of the highest points in the state. Defined on the west by the Laughery Escarpment, with an average elevation of 1,100 feet, the escarpment divides the Wabash River and Ohio River watersheds. West-flowing streams drain to the East Fork of the White River. The south- and east-flowing streams feed Indian Creek, Laughery Creek, and Whitewater River, all of which discharge into the Ohio.

Most of the natural communities are forested, with a few barrens. A mixed mesophytic forest type is well represented, especially in the ravines. Historical evidence indicates that this area, especially in the south along the Ohio River, may be the only location where black locust is native in the state.

The Switzerland Hills' aquatic features are typically rocky, gravel-bottomed, medium-gradient streams.

Part 3

DESTINATIONS

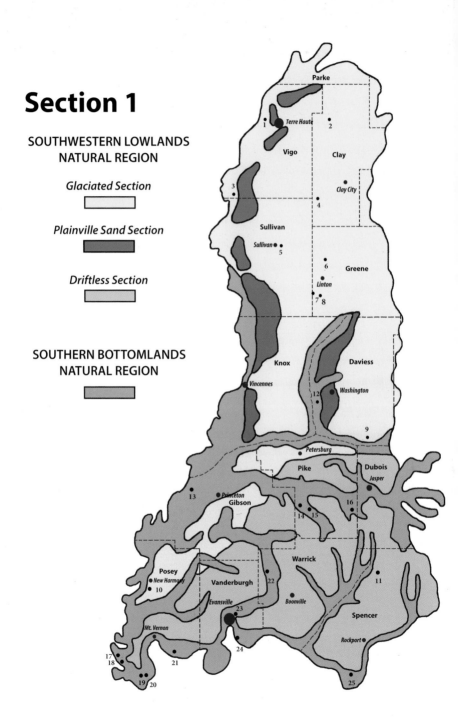

Section 1

SOUTHWESTERN LOWLANDS NATURAL REGION

Glaciated Section

Plainville Sand Section

Driftless Section

SOUTHERN BOTTOMLANDS NATURAL REGION

Parke

1
Terre Haute
2

Vigo

Clay

3

Clay City

4

Sullivan

Sullivan ●
5

6

Greene

Linton

7 8

Knox

Daviess

Vincennes

12
Washington

9

Petersburg

Pike

Dubois

Jasper

13
Princeton
Gibson

16

14 15

Warrick

Posey
New Harmony
Vanderburgh
22

11

10

Evansville

Boonville

Spencer

23

Mt. Vernon

Rockport ●

17
18

24

21

Spencer

19 20

25

Section 1

SOUTHWESTERN LOWLANDS NATURAL REGION

Glaciated Section

1. Wabashiki Fish & Wildlife Area
2. Chinook Fish & Wildlife Area
3. Fairbanks Landing Fish & Wildlife Area
4. Shakamak State Park / Shakamak Prairie Nature Preserve
5. Minnehaha Fish & Wildlife Area
6. Hillenbrand Fish & Wildlife Area
7. Greene-Sullivan State Forest
8. Goose Pond Fish & Wildlife Area
9. Glendale Fish & Wildlife Area
10. Harmonie State Park / Wabash Border and Harmonie Hills Nature Preserves

Driftless Section

11. Lincoln State Park / (Sarah) Lincoln Woods Nature Preserve

SOUTHERN BOTTOMLANDS NATURAL REGION

12. Thousand Acre Woods Nature Preserve
13. Saunders Woods Nature Preserve
14. Patoka River National Wildlife Refuge
15. Columbia Mine Preserve
16. Pike State Forest
17. Wabash Lowlands Nature Preserve
18. Section Six Flatwoods Nature Preserve
19. Twin Swamps Nature Preserve
20. Hovey Lake Fish & Wildlife Area
21. Goose Pond Cypress Slough Nature Preserve
22. Blue Grass Fish & Wildlife Area
23. Wesselman Woods Nature Preserve
24. Eagle Slough Natural Area
25. Kramer Original Woods Nature Preserve

SOUTHWESTERN LOWLANDS
NATURAL REGION

SOUTHWESTERN LOWLANDS NATURAL REGION

Glaciated Section

1. Wabashiki Fish & Wildlife Area

Owned by Indiana Department of Natural Resources,
Division of Fish & Wildlife

The twenty-six-hundred-acre Wabashiki Fish & Wildlife Area is composed of floodplain habitat along the western bank of the Wabash River between West Terre Haute and Terre Haute. Except for a couple of strip pits at the south end of Sixth Street in West Terre Haute, the area is a work in progress and is accessible primarily via the river.

The Dewey Point parking lot on National Road offers a beautiful, long-distance view of the wildlife area, with the Vigo County Courthouse as a backdrop, and features a walking/running/biking trail that follows the levee to the area's western perimeter. No trails lead into the wetlands from Dewey Point, though a trail system has been proposed.

Established in 2010, Wabashiki has a reputation as a bird-watching paradise, with the Wabash Valley Audubon Society having documented nearly two hundred bird species, including American bittern, golden-winged warbler, and black-crowned night heron, all on the state endangered species list, and sharp-shinned hawk, a state species of special concern. Other noteworthy species that live in or migrate through include cackling goose, American black duck, green-winged teal, pied-billed grebe, American white pelican, double-crested cormorant, cattle egret, American coot, pectoral sandpiper, American woodcock, ring-billed gull, Forster's tern, yellow-billed cuckoo, eastern screech owl, hairy woodpecker, blue-headed vireo, bank swallow, white-breasted nuthatch, gray-cheeked thrush, rose-breasted grosbeak, American finch, and American tree sparrow.

Game species include wild turkey, cottontail rabbit, white-tailed deer, American woodcock, raccoon, and red fox, along with various

(*Facing*) Wabashiki Fish & Wildlife Area, Vigo County.

species of duck and goose. Fish in the river, a seven-acre gravel pit, and several ponds include bluegill, crappie, bass, and catfish.

Long-term plans were announced in 2010 to protect forty-three thousand acres of river wetlands over a ninety-four-mile stretch from Shades State Park on Sugar Creek in Montgomery County to Fairbanks Landing Fish & Wildlife Area on the Wabash at the Vigo-Sullivan county line.

Activities
Boating (electric motors only), biking, fishing, hiking, hunting, nature study, photography, wildlife watching.

Directions to Dewey Point Trail and parking area
GPS coordinates: 39.467098, -87.442437
From I-70
- West on I-70 from the Wabash River to Darwin Road, 2.0 miles
- North on Darwin Road to U.S. 150 / West National Avenue in West Terre Haute, 0.8 mile
- East on U.S. 150 to Dewey Point Trail and parking area, 1.3 miles

Directions to Sixth Street strip pits
GPS coordinates: 39.455432, -87.449769
- West on I-70 from the Wabash River to Darwin Road, 2.0 miles
- North on Darwin Road to U.S. 150 / West National Avenue in West Terre Haute, 0.8 mile
- East on U.S. 150 to Sixth Street, 0.9 mile
- South on Sixth Street to strip pits, 0.7 mile

2. Chinook Fish & Wildlife Area
Owned by Indiana Department of Natural Resources,
Division of Fish & Wildlife
The 2,141-acre Chinook Fish & Wildlife Area features rolling grasslands and wooded areas on old surface mine land in western Clay County. Located immediately north of Interstate 70 just south of Staunton, the area has about eighty acres of water—mostly old strip pits.

Studies conducted by Indiana State University's Department of Ecology suggest the reclaimed grasslands—estimated at 61 percent of Chinook's acreage—provide productive breeding habitats for prairie birds and species typical of savanna and brushland habitats.

The National Audubon Society identifies Chinook as a Global Important Bird Area that supports state-endangered species American bittern, king rail, least bittern, northern harrier, short-eared owl, Virginia rail, and, most notably, a breeding population of more than three hundred Henslow's sparrows.

Other noteworthy species that live in or migrate through include common moorhen, dickcissel, grasshopper sparrow, and northern bobwhite. Common species include eastern meadowlark, common yellowthroat, field sparrow, and horned lark. Relatively large populations of raptors are present during the winter months.

Other Chinook wildlife include various species of deer, turkey, waterfowl, shorebird, quail, dove, rabbit, woodcock, duck, goose, raccoon, coyote, and fox. Fish species include bluegill and redear sunfish and various bass, trout, crappie, and catfish.

The strip pits range in size from three to thirty-three acres, with boat ramps on six of them: Little George, Scheister, Worm, Daredevil, Stump Jumper, and Hawg Pits.

Blackberries, raspberries, morels, and black walnuts may be gathered at Chinook.

Opened in 1997, the Chinook Fish & Wildlife Area was initially leased as a Public Fishing Area in 1982.

Activities

Berry picking, boating (electric motors only), fishing, hiking, hunting, nature study, photography, trapping, wildlife watching.

Directions

GPS coordinates: 39.446375, -87.214531

From I-70

- South on State Road 59 to State Road 42, 0.2 mile
- West on State Road 42 to Cory Staunton Road, 4.3 miles
- North on Cory Staunton Road to wildlife area, 0.1 mile

3. Fairbanks Landing Fish & Wildlife Area

Managed by Indiana Department of Natural Resources, Division of Fish & Wildlife, under an agreement with Indiana Michigan Power

The eight-thousand-acre Fairbanks Landing Fish & Wildlife Area is a complex of bottomland woods with adjoining farmland along eight miles of the Wabash riverbank. With no trail system, access is limited to old seasonal county roads that can be hiked but hold water in places. Some are private industrial roads marked with No Trespassing signs.

While the site map says the mission is to provide quality hunting and fishing, the emphasis at Fairbanks is on hunting. The ponds are few and situated mostly off the access roads. The brochure says fishing is limited. But the area provides habitat for nongame species, such as state-endangered osprey, bald eagle (a state species of special concern), and various songbird, hawk, and owl. Game species include white-tailed deer, wild turkey, northern bobwhite, cottontail rabbit, mourning dove, and American woodcock.

Blackberries, raspberries, walnuts, and mushrooms may be gathered. Spring mushroom hunting is limited to non-turkey-hunting hours.

Activities

Fishing, hiking, hunting, nature study, photography, wildlife watching.

Directions

GPS coordinates: 39.219246, -87.554380

From I-70

- South on U.S. 41 at Terre Haute to West Johnson Drive, 0.4 mile
- West on Johnson to State Road 63 / Prairieton Road, 1.1 miles
- South on State Road 63, through Prairieton, to West County Road 925N at Fairbanks, 15.8 miles
- West on 925N to wildlife area, 1.8 miles

From State Road 67

- West on State Road 46 at Spencer to State Road 246 at Vandalia, 6.6 miles

Shakamak Prairie Nature Preserve, Shakamak State Park, Sullivan County.

- West on State Road 246 to State Road 63 at Prairie Creek, 37.1 miles
- South on State Road 63 to West County Road 925N at Fairbanks, 4.1 miles
- West on 925N to wildlife area, 1.8 miles

4a. Shakamak State Park
Owned by Indiana Department of Natural Resources,
Division of State Parks & Reservoirs
The 1,766-acre Shakamak State Park surrounds three man-made lakes with four hundred acres of surface water and features a unique, twenty-seven-acre, moist-prairie nature preserve on the southwestern side. Shakamak is located where Clay, Sullivan, and Greene Counties meet.

The lakes—Kickapoo, Shakamak, and Lenape—offer fishing and boating, as well as wildlife watching for species that have adapted to life in the forest and water. Species include white-tailed deer, raccoon, eastern squirrel, and red fox, as well as northern cardinal, blue jay, red-headed woodpecker, and a variety of nuthatches and waterfowl.

Shakamak is a Native American name given to the park when the State Conservation Commission created it in 1929. Its meaning and origin are uncertain. The forest and abandoned coal mines were donated to the state by the three counties.

New Deal–era Civilian Conservation Corps workers developed much of the park in the 1930s, planting trees and implementing erosion control measures. Many of the brick buildings and structures they constructed are still used today. Brick was plentiful and manufactured locally at the time.

4b. Shakamak Prairie Nature Preserve

Located along the road in the park's southwestern corner by Lake Kickapoo, this preserve is the only protected example of a moist-prairie natural community type in the Southwestern Lowlands Natural Region. It's believed that in presettlement times this region contained the greatest amount of prairie in Indiana south of the Wisconsin glacier. Only remnants of prairie landscapes exist today, primarily along railroad lines and in isolated prairie patches in a few pioneer cemeteries.

Activities

Hiking Trails: Four, moderate, 1.4 to 3.95 miles.

Camping: 122 electric sites, 42 nonelectric sites, 10 sites with 2 paved accessible sites, youth tent area, dumping station, camp store.

Group Camps: One that accommodates 270, seven that sleep six, electricity in buildings, picnic table, fire ring, parking spur, drinking water supply in area, modern restrooms, and showers.

Group Camp Cottages: Twelve (reservations).

Cabins: Thirty (reservations), occupancy limited to fourteen consecutive nights.

Other Activities: Boating (electric trolling motors only), boat ramps, boat rentals (paddleboat, rowboat), fishing / ice fishing, nature center / interpretive naturalist services (seasonal), picnicking, play field, recreation building (rental), shelters (reservations), tennis, swimming pool / water slide.

Directions

GPS coordinates: 39.176435, -87.234199

From I-70

- South on State Road 59, through Clay City, to State Road 246 split, 13.9 miles
- West on State Road 246 to State Road 159, 6.7 miles
- South on State Road 159, through Coalmont, to State Road 48 and the park, 5.7 miles

From State Road 67

- West on State Road 46 at Spencer to State Road 246 at Vandalia, 6.6 miles
- West on State Road 246, through Patricksburg and Clay City, to State Road 159, 23.3 miles
- South on State Road 159, through Coalmont, to State Road 48 and the park, 5.7 miles

5. Minnehaha Fish & Wildlife Area

Leased and managed by the Indiana Department of
Natural Resources, Division of Fish & Wildlife

The thirty-five-hundred-acre Minnehaha Fish & Wildlife Area features grasslands, hills, pastures, woodlands, and lakes, with more than 125 acres of water, mostly on old strip mines. The landscape is composed of reclaimed surface mines that are leased from American Land Holdings of Indiana, a Peabody Coal subsidiary.

Minnehaha today is a fraction of its original size due to portions being removed from the lease. In the summer of 2014 the office by the hunter check-in on County Road 525E was closed. Maps and information should be available at the check-in kiosk. The wildlife area is marked only by boundary signs. There are no signs on State Road 54.

The National Audubon Society has identified ten thousand acres at Minnehaha and the nearby Dugger Unit of the Greene-Sullivan State Forest as a State Important Bird Area. Among the species that live in or migrate through are state-endangered Henslow's sparrow, American bittern, northern harrier, and short-eared owl. Other noteworthy species include eastern meadowlark, grasshopper sparrow, northern bobwhite, Bell's vireo, willow flycatcher, and dickcissel.

During the nonbreeding season, the area supports one of the state's largest populations of raptors, including rough-legged hawk.

This landscape's unique mix of rolling grasslands and hills with marshes, ponds, and lakes—due to its having been operated as large surface coal mines—resembles a prairie pothole habitat. More than three thousand acres of grasslands were created in the mine reclamation process, which involved planting cool-season grasses to meet erosion-control guidelines.

Common wildlife species at Minnehaha include American woodcock, white-tailed deer, wild turkey, cottontail rabbit, raccoon, coyote, and red fox, along with various species of waterfowl, songbird, raptor, duck, goose, and squirrel.

Predominant fish species include bluegill and redear sunfish and various bass, crappie, and catfish.

Activities
Berry, nut, and mushroom picking, boating (electric motors only), dog training, fishing, hunting, nature study, photography, wildlife watching.

Directions
GPS coordinates: 39.075608, -87.311291
From I-70
- South on U.S. 41 at Terre Haute to State Road 54 south of Sullivan, 25.7 miles
- East on State Road 54 to County Road 525E, 5.6 miles
- North on County Road 525E to kiosk at intersection with Center Road, 0.7 mile

From State Road 67
- West on State Road 54 at Switz City, through Linton and Dugger, to County Road 525E, 15.8 miles
- North on County Road 525E to kiosk at intersection with Center Road, 0.7 mile

Hillenbrand Fish & Wildlife Area, Greene County.

6. Hillenbrand Fish & Wildlife Area

Owned by Indiana Department of Natural Resources,
Division of Fish & Wildlife

The thirty-four-hundred-acre Hillenbrand Fish & Wildlife Area is composed of upland and wetland habitat and roughly two dozen lakes and shallow impoundments just east of the tiny, northwestern Greene County town of Midland. A reclaimed surface mine, Hillenbrand is managed for hunting and fishing.

The National Audubon Society identifies Hillenbrand as a Global Important Bird Area, citing high breeding concentrations of Henslow's sparrow and the presence of other state endangered species, including northern harrier, sedge wren, short-eared owl, and Virginia rail. Other noteworthy species that live in or migrate through include red-shouldered hawk, a state species of special concern, and dickcissel, eastern meadowlark, willow flycatcher, prairie warbler, yellow-billed cuckoo, yellow-breasted chat, American woodcock, Bell's vireo, field sparrow, grasshopper sparrow, Kentucky warbler, prothonotary warbler, red-headed woodpecker, whip-poor-will, and wood thrush.

Other wildlife at Hillenbrand includes deer, rabbit, dove, quail, and turkey. Fish include various species of bass, bluegill, sunfish, crappie, and catfish.

Purchased by the state in 1995 and named after Hoosier businessman and natural resource advocate John A. Hillenbrand II, this area is 60 percent grasslands, 36 percent mixed forest and shrublands, and 4 percent wetlands. Impoundments create 125 acres of wetland habitat and nearly twenty lakes and ponds, including the 127-acre Horseshoe Lake, so named for its shape.

The property has sections on both sides of State Road 59, is subdivided by multiple county roads, and has ample parking. The interior lands are laced with old mine roads, some with coal chunks embedded in their surfaces. Some lakes have roads leading to them.

The property has several kiosks with maps and information. The closest one to State Road 59 is a short distance east on County Road 700N.

Activities
Berry and mushroom picking, boat ramps (12-volt electric motor only), dog training area, fishing, hunting (handicap accessible), nature study, photography, wildlife watching.

Directions
GPS coordinates: 39.126354, -87.175910
From I-70
- South on State Road 59, through Clay City, to County Road 700N at Midland, 27.1 miles
- East on County Road 700N to wildlife area kiosk, 0.5 mile
From State Road 67
- North on State Road 157 (Jefferson Street) at Worthington to State Road 48, 3.1 miles
- West on State Road 48 to State Road 59 before Jasonville, 10.4 miles

Greene-Sullivan State Forest, Greene County.

- South on State Road 59 to County Road 700N at Midland, 2.5 miles
- East on County Road 700N to wildlife area kiosk, 0.5 mile

7. Greene-Sullivan State Forest

Owned by Indiana Department of Natural Resources,
Division of Forestry

The nine-thousand-acre Greene-Sullivan State Forest west of Linton, with more than 120 strip mines turned lakes, sits among the rolling, serene, wooded hills that span the county line in both directions. It is more than two-thirds reclaimed strip mines and one of the most unique landforms in Indiana. The Dugger Unit is located west of Dugger and south of State Road 54.

While the Greene-Sullivan landscape is one of the largest forest blocks in that part of the state, the water bodies—with names like T Lake, Ladder Lake, Corky Lake, Cottonwood Lake, and Reservoir 26—are by far the dominant natural feature. The property is well signed and crisscrossed with paved, gravel, and access roads, each leading to water bodies that resemble everything from long, narrow strings to fairly large reservoirs holding acid water that doesn't support fish. Sizeable tracts of private property lie within the forest boundary.

Greene-Sullivan's diverse ecosystems feature wildflowers and wildlife, with fossils in the rocky edges along the lakes. Hiking/bridle trails and fire lanes lead from one water overlook to another through woodlands with red maple, northern red oak, eastern cottonwood, sugar maple, sassafras, flowering dogwood, and other tree species. Pines have been planted around many of the shorelines.

Greene-Sullivan abuts the Goose Pond Fish & Wildlife Area, which is designated by the National Audubon Society as a Global Important Bird Area. Among the noteworthy species that live in or migrate through Greene-Sullivan is state-endangered golden-winged warbler, along with northern saw-whet owl, whip-poor-will, chuck-will's-widow, olive-sided flycatcher, Canada warbler, and other species of vireo, thrush, and warbler.

The National Audubon Society has also designated the Dugger Unit and nearby Minnehaha Fish & Wildlife Area as a Global Important Bird Area. (See no. 5, Minnehaha Fish & Wildlife Area, for details.)

Greene-Sullivan wildlife includes white-tailed deer, wild turkey, red fox, and raccoon.

Most lakes are stocked with largemouth bass, bluegill, and redear sunfish, with channel catfish, warmouth, and crappie species found in some. Airline Lake is stocked with rainbow trout.

The forest was established in 1936 when coal companies donated the strip-mined land to the state. At that time, the industry was not required to reclaim the land following mining. The water bodies are old strip pits and reservoirs created during the mining process.

Activities

Camping: One hundred primitive sites with pit toilets, seasonal drinking water, picnic tables, and grills; twenty horse camp sites; one wheelchair-accessible campsite; dumping station; and playground.

Cabins: Fifteen Rent-a-Camp Program cabins available year-round, with porch and swing, two small rooms, small table with bench seats, corner shelf, chair, rocking chair, loft, bunk bed (single), and double bed (no linens or mattress provided); dumping station; and playground.

Other Activities: Canoeing, fishing, hiking, horseback riding, hunting, mushroom hunting, nature study, photography, picnicking, shelter houses, wildlife viewing.

Directions

GPS coordinates: 39.044738, -87.259454

From I-70

- South on State Road 59 through Clay City to State Road 54, 30.0 miles
- West on State Road 54 to State Road 159, 4.1 miles
- South on State Road 159 to forest office, 1.7 miles

From State Road 67

- West on State Road 54, through Linton, to State Road 159, 12.9 miles
- South on State Road 159 to forest office, 1.7 miles

8. Goose Pond Fish & Wildlife Area

*Owned by Indiana Department of Natural Resources,
Division of Fish & Wildlife*

The 8,064-acre Goose Pond Fish & Wildlife Area south of Linton and east of Greene-Sullivan State Forest is one of the largest wetlands restoration projects in U.S. history and is home to a dazzling array of plants and animals. A 2010 biodiversity survey conducted by the Indiana Academy of Science identified nine hundred plant and animal species on the property.

Also known locally as Bee Hunter Marsh (one section is called Bee Hunter Marsh), Goose Pond is dedicated to hunting,

Goose Pond Fish & Wildlife Area, Greene County.

trapping, and wildlife watching. Its thirteen hundred acres of planted prairie and nearly five thousand acres of shallow water wetlands, created by thirty-plus miles of earthen dikes, are critical habitat for migrating birds, whose species have more than doubled since the 2010 survey, from 122 to more than 260.

The National Audubon Society has designated Goose Pond a Global Important Bird Area for providing "critical migrating and wintering waterfowl habitat." Its location between the Wabash and White Rivers "makes it an ideal area to receive migratory bird flights using the eastern portion of the Mississippi Flyway."

Among the species that have been identified there are federally endangered whooping crane and several state endangered species, including king rail, American bittern, least bittern, northern harrier, short-eared owl, sedge wren, and Henslow's sparrow. State species of special concern include sandhill crane and Wilson's phalarope. Other noteworthy species that live in or migrate through include northern pintail, greater white-fronted geese, black-necked stilt, little blue heron, northern bobwhite, grasshopper sparrow, and dickcissel.

Other wildlife species at Goose Pond include wild turkey, red bat, little brown bat, Virginia opossum, eastern chipmunk, woodchuck (a.k.a. groundhog), fox squirrel, beaver, muskrat, coyote, red fox, bobcat, raccoon, least long-tailed weasel, mink, striped skunk, white-tailed deer, cottontail rabbit, and eastern mole.

Described by early nineteenth-century surveyors as marsh, prairie, forest, and brushy ponds, the Goose Pond landscape has poorly drained clay soils that were ditched and drained for agriculture beginning in the late 1800s. Its last owner enrolled seventy-two hundred acres in the federal Wetlands Reserve Program, granting a permanent conservation easement to the Natural Resources Conservation Service. The last crops were harvested in 2000, and restoration to the land's original condition as wetland, prairie, and woodland began. The state purchased the property and the easement in 2005.

Goose Pond is bisected by State Road 59, which has periodic pull offs and parking lots on the roadside, as well as an informational kiosk on the ninety-degree curve west of the office. Other refuge areas and parking lots are located on other nearby roads.

Activities
Hiking: More than thirty miles of trails, mostly along the dikes.
Other Activities: Berry, mushroom, and nut picking, boating (12-volt electric motors only), canoeing, fishing, hunting, kayaking, nature study, photography, wildlife watching. Accessible hunting and wildlife-watching opportunities are available.

Directions
GPS coordinates: 38.994663, -87.177712
From I-70
- South on State Road 59, through Jasonville and Linton, to office, 35.0 miles

From State Road 67
- West on State Road 54 at Switz City to State Road 59 in Linton, 6.0 miles
- South on State Road 59 to office, 3.0 miles

A public information booth is located 0.6 mile west of the office.

9. Glendale Fish & Wildlife Area

Owned by Indiana Department of Natural Resources,
Division of Fish & Wildlife

The 8,060-acre Glendale Fish & Wildlife Area south of Washington is situated on the East Fork of the White River and features upland habitat, twenty-two ponds and marshes, a fourteen-hundred-acre lake, and small woodlots, all of which are managed for hunting and fishing.

The area surrounds the sprawling Dogwood Lake, which averages eight feet in depth and was created in 1963 by a dam on Mud Creek. The Himsel Bottoms Marsh sits just above the river on the property's southern tip, adjacent to the Flat Rock Public Access Site.

Glendale game species include white-tailed deer, northern bobwhite, cottontail rabbit, mourning dove, ring-necked pheasant, American woodcock, and wild turkey. The ponds and lakes are stocked with bluegill, redear sunfish, and largemouth bass and various catfish and crappie species.

Bird species that frequent Glendale include state-endangered osprey, bald eagle, a state species of special concern, red-tailed hawk, and a wide variety of waterfowl, songbirds, and woodpeckers.

Activities

Camping: Sixty-seven electric sites, fifty-four nonelectric (some have fire rings), no reservations, comfort station with heated showers and flush toilets, water fountains.

Other Activities: Boating (10 mph limit on Dogwood Lake, trolling motors only on other water bodies), boat ramps, boat rental, dog training, fishing (accessible piers), hiking, hunting, nature study, nut and berry picking, photography, picnicking, wildlife watching.

Directions

GPS coordinates: 38.552632, -87.051314

From I-70

- South on State Road 59 through Clay City, Jasonville, Linton, and Sandborn to State Road 58, 43.8 miles
- East on State Road 58 to I-69, 8.4 miles
- South on I-69 to U.S. 50 at Washington, 14.0 miles
- West on U.S. 50 at Washington to State Road 257, 1.8 miles
- South on State Road 257 to Glendale Road, 4.6 miles
- East on Glendale Road to Sportsman Road, 3.5 miles
- South on Sportsman Road to headquarters, 1.2 miles

From I-69

- West on U.S. 50 at Washington to State Road 257, 1.8 miles
- South on State Road 257 to Glendale Road, 4.6 miles
- East on Glendale Road to Sportsman Road, 3.5 miles
- South on Sportsman Road to headquarters, 1.2 miles

10a. Harmonie State Park

Owned by Indiana Department of Natural Resources,
Division of State Parks & Reservoirs

The 3,465-acre Harmonie State Park overlooks the Wabash River and features a varied topography, from flat floodplains to rolling hills and ravines that are reminiscent of Brown County. In addition to magnificent river views, the park offers two protected state nature preserves (which do not appear on park maps) and towering specimens of oak and maple, lush greenery, and hanging vines.

Harmonie State Park represents the natural side of the riverine area's broader historical context. It is located four miles south of New Harmony, which was the site of two early nineteenth-century utopian settlements, one religious based, the other knowledge based.

Led by Father George Rapp, the Rappite Community resettled from Harmony, Pennsylvania, to the banks of the Wabash in 1814 after having fled Germany to escape religious oppression. They sought to lead simple lives working the land in their new Indiana home, also called Harmony.

Wabash River, Harmonie State Park, Posey County.

In 1825 the Harmonists sold the land to Robert Owen, a Scottish industrialist and social reformer with a utopian vision based on education and equality. Over the next two years, Owen brought a stream of scientists and philosophers to the area to establish a new moral world through education. One January 1826 trip down the Ohio from Pittsburgh was dubbed the "boatload of knowledge" for the group of intellectuals on board. Owen's vision produced many of the nation's social firsts, including the first free public school, the first kindergarten, the first free public library, and equal education for boys and girls.

10b. Wabash Border and Harmonie Hills Nature Preserves

The park's two nature preserves—255-acre Wabash Border Nature Preserve and 355-acre Harmonie Hills Nature Preserve—both protect large, wild portions of the park and border the

Wabash River. Their natural communities contain area-sensitive, forest-interior plants and animals that depend upon large, unfragmented forest ecosystems.

Wabash Border protects three forest types on the park's north side: mature, dry–moist upland; moist ravine; and wet floodplain. Trail 3 passes through this preserve.

Harmonie Hills is located on the park's south side and supports one of the Southwest Lowlands' largest tracts of mature, moist-upland forest. Road Brook is home to several rare fish species. Trail 4 passes through Harmonie Hills.

Activities

Hiking Trails: Eight, 0.25 to 2.6 miles, easy to moderate.
Bridle Trails: One, 4 miles.
Bike Trails: Two, 3.5 to 4 miles, beginning to intermediate; one, self-guided.
Camping: Two hundred electric sites (reservations), youth tent areas, camp store, dumping station.
Other Activities: Boat launch ramp on Wabash River, fishing, nature center / interpretive naturalist services (seasonal), nature study, photography, picnicking, shelters (reservations), swimming pool / waterslide, wildlife watching.

Directions

GPS coordinates: 38.089845, -87.941875

From I-70

- South on U.S. 41 to I-64, 92.7 miles
- West on I-64 to State Road 69, 20.6 miles
- South State Road 69 to State Road 269, 9.2 miles
- West on State Road 269 to park, 1.0 mile

From I-69

- West on I-64 to State Road 69, 25.1 miles
- South State Road 69 to State Road 269, 9.2 miles
- West on State Road to 269 to park, 1.0 mile

Lincoln State Park, Spencer County.

Driftless Section

11a. Lincoln State Park

Owned by Indiana Department of Natural Resources,
Division of State Parks & Reservoirs

The 1,747-acre Lincoln State Park is a memorial established in 1932 to honor President Abraham Lincoln's mother, Nancy Hanks-Lincoln, who is buried in the U.S. Park Service's Lincoln Boyhood Memorial directly to the north. The sixteenth president's sister, Sarah Lincoln-Grigsby, is buried at the Little Pigeon Creek Baptist Church and Cemetery, located on the park property.

Born in 1809 in Kentucky, Lincoln spent fourteen years of his youth—from 1816 to 1830—in the woods and fields of the park region after his family moved from across the Ohio River. A one-mile trail known as Mr. Lincoln's Neighborhood Walk highlights the park's Lincoln-era sites, such as Noah Gorden's Mill and the graves of Sarah and her husband, Aaron Grigsby.

The adjacent Lincoln Boyhood Memorial is located on the

original Lincoln family farmstead. A trail connects the park with the memorial across State Road 162.

The New Deal–era Civilian Conservation Corps, a national make-work program that provided jobs for unemployed men during the Great Depression, planted many of Lincoln State Park's trees. The workers also built Lake Lincoln, the Lakeside Shelter House, the boat rental building (formerly a ranger cabin), and many of the trails.

Another historic Lincoln site is the Federal-style brick farmhouse of merchant, farmer, politician, and Union Army colonel William Jones, who also employed Abe Lincoln. The site includes a restored log barn that was moved there in 1995.

The park is mostly moist-upland forest that is dominated by eastern hardwoods—various oak, hickory, maple, walnut, sycamore, elm, and other species. Eastern red cedar, along with rare white pine and other pines, are the dominant conifers. The pines were also planted. The understories include dogwood, redbud, and immature oak and hickory stands. Runoff from steep slopes accumulates in the ravines, creating seasonal ponds and swampy areas in the bottomlands. Old fields occupy many park areas, often with early successional forest.

These ecosystems produce diverse habitat for birds and other wildlife. A 2011 survey by the National Park Service found forty-two bird species in the park, including twelve breeding species of continental importance.

Lincoln State Park is known for the Mississippi kite, a state species of special concern that has nested there since the 1990s. It's also home to osprey, cerulean warbler, and golden-wing warbler, all state endangered species, as well as worm-eating warbler and bald eagle, both state species of special concern. Other noteworthy species include yellow-throated warbler, prairie warbler, Kentucky warbler, Connecticut warbler, Canada warbler, barred owl, black-billed cuckoo, common loon, least flycatcher, wild turkey, Acadian flycatcher, summer tanager, eastern kingbird, and various species of heron, egret, thrush, and finch.

11b. (Sarah) Lincoln Woods Nature Preserve

The 110-acre (Sarah) Lincoln Woods Nature Preserve is located in the southernmost portion of the park and protects a rare Southern Indiana plant community called "oak barrens," which feature small populations of prairie plants growing in open oak woodlands on dry, sandy soil. Early surveyors described these sandy, ridgetop clearings as "barrens, some oak, hickory, grassy."

Activities

Hiking Trails: Eight, easy to moderate, 0.8 to 3.7 miles.

Camping: 150 electric sites, 88 nonelectric sites, 31 primitive sites, group camp that accommodates 155, youth tent areas, dumping station.

Cabins: Pine Hills Group Cottages, fifteen; Blue Heron Family Cabins, ten.

Other Activities: Amphitheater, basketball court, boating (electric motors only), boat launch ramp, boat rental (canoe, paddleboat, rowboat), canoeing, fishing, general store, nature center, interpretive naturalist services, nature study, photography, lookout tower, picnicking, public plaza honoring President Abraham Lincoln's two hundredth birthday, shelters (reservations), swimming.

Directions

GPS coordinates: 38.112534, -86.998053

From I-69

- East on I-64 to U.S. 231, 27.0 miles
- South on U.S. 231 to State Road 162, 5.9 miles
- West on State Road 162 to park, 1.2 miles

From State Road 37

- West on I-64 at St. Croix to U.S. 231, 22.1 miles
- South on U.S. 231 to State Road 162, 5.9 miles
- West on State Road 162 to park, 1.2 miles

(*Facing*) Thousand Acre Woods Nature Preserve, Daviess County.

SOUTHERN BOTTOMLANDS
NATURAL REGION

SOUTHERN BOTTOMLANDS NATURAL REGION

12. Thousand Acre Woods Nature Preserve

Owned by The Nature Conservancy

The Thousand Acre Woods Nature Preserve north of Washington straddles Prairie Creek's North and South Forks and supports remnants of two natural communities—flatwoods and bottomland forest—that in presettlement times covered large areas of Southwestern Indiana. Over its three-mile length, the 943-acre preserve's elevation rises and falls by only a foot.

The creek forks converge inside the preserve, but, like the miles of surrounding farmland, they have been impacted by a century and a quarter of agriculture. The nearby fields have been drained since the late 1800s. At least one ditch bisects the preserve. Prairie Creek and both of its forks have been straightened.

Still, forests this size are rare in Daviess County, and the Thousand Acre Woods bottomland hardwood forest supports a variety of plant and animal species, including one of the few remaining silver maple and elm forests in Indiana.

Spring floods and the flat landscape provide habitat for turtles, crayfish, frogs, and various fish species. Spring and summer wildflower species include purple fringeless orchid, a state watch list species, blue phlox, swamp milkweed, and hispid swamp buttercup.

Green ash, black ash, sweet gum, silver maple, red maple, box elder, sycamore, eastern cottonwood, and American elm tree species dominate, with smaller populations of black willow, hackberry, slippery elm (a.k.a. red elm), white basswood, mulberry, and sugarberry. Stands of swamp white oak, pin oak, and various species of maple and hickory also thrive throughout the preserve.

The understory is composed of the rare ostrich fern, along with sensitive fern, buttonbush, Virginia creeper, trumpet creeper, hairy spicebush, and deciduous holly (a.k.a. swamp holly), the latter a state watch list species found in only a few Indiana sites.

Mosquitoes and poison ivy thrive in Thousand Acre Woods during the hot summer months.

While there is no trail system, the preserve's level land provides easy hiking. A path follows a ditch from the intersection of County Roads 300E and 550N through the preserve to the North Fork of the Prairie Creek.

Thousand Acre Woods is a dedicated State Nature Preserve.

Activities
Hiking, nature study, photography, wildlife watching.

Directions
GPS coordinates: 38.735452, -87.111014
There is no parking lot. Please be careful where you leave your car.

From I-70
- South on State Road 59 through Clay City, Jasonville, Linton, and Sandborn to State Road 58, 43.8 miles
- East on State Road 58 to State Road 57 at Elnora, 5.3 miles
- South on State Road 57 through Plainville to County Road 400N, 12.8 miles
- East County Road 400N to County Road 75E, 0.7 mile
- South on County Road 75E to County Road 350N, 0.5 mile
- East on County Road 350N to the T at County Road 250E, 1.9 miles
- North on County Road 250E, becoming County Road 450N, 0.7 mile
- East on County Road 450N to County Road 300E, 0.4 mile
- North on County Road 300E to the preserve, 1.0 mile

From I-69
- West on U.S. 50 to State Road 57, 4.0 miles
- North on State Road 57 through Washington to County Road 400N, 6.3 miles
- East County Road 400N to County Road 75E, 0.7 mile
- South on County Road 75E to County Road 350N, 0.5 mile
- East on County Road 350N to the T at County Road 250E, 1.9 miles
- North on County Road 250E, becoming County Road 450N, 0.7 mile

Saunders Woods Nature Preserve, Gibson County.

- East on County Road 450N to County Road 300E, 0.4 mile
- North on County Road 300E to the preserve, 1.0 mile

13. Saunders Woods Nature Preserve

Owned by The Nature Conservancy

The 1,160-acre Saunders Woods is the largest block of bottom-land hardwood forest in Indiana and features mature tree species that are more commonly found in the deep soil deposits of the Mississippi and Illinois Rivers. This flatwoods forest sits on a secondary terrace near the Wabash River, whose ancient floods left behind the level layer of silts the preserve now occupies.

A rare remnant and the best remaining example of the Wabash wet–moist floodplain, the Saunders preserve's soupy soils hold water and become saturated in spring, leaving much of it underwater. The undulating landscape, which is bisected by State Road 64, is intermixed with lush green sedges and grasses, southern wildflowers, vines, and woods.

The forest canopy is dominated by overcup oak, a state watch list species, pin oak, swamp white oak, pecan, and a variety of hickories and other hardwoods at the northern limit of their natural ranges. Rare plants include creeping bracted sedge (a.k.a. social sedge), a state rare species, deciduous holly (a.k.a. swamp holly), a state watch list species, and climbing dogbane.

The forest is home to a variety of wildlife, including several species of frog and owl, along with pileated woodpecker and Appalachian brown eye butterfly.

While Saunders Woods has no developed trails, the relatively flat terrain makes for easy hiking, although poison ivy can be chest-high in places. Mosquitoes are thick.

The older-growth trees are located in the preserve's southwestern portion about a quarter mile south of State Road 64 through an old field that was planted with three hundred thousand acorns in 1998.

Saunders Woods is a dedicated State Nature Preserve.

Activities

Hiking, nature study, photography, wildlife watching.

GPS coordinates: 38.370234, -87.706751
The preserve is bisected by State Road 64 and can be accessed
from either direction on County Road 100N.
From I-70
- South on U.S. 41 at Terre Haute to State Road 64 in
  Princeton, 79.6 miles
- West on State Road 64 to County Road 100N and the
  preserve, 6.9 miles

From I-69
- West on State Road 64, through Princeton, to County Road
  100N and the preserve, 18.4 miles

14. Patoka River National Wildlife Refuge
Owned by U.S. Fish & Wildlife Service
The 8,800-acre Patoka River National Wildlife Refuge sprawls
along a thirty-mile stretch of the Patoka River in Pike and
Gibson Counties, with a potential to grow to more than twen-
ty-two thousand acres. It's divided into three sections: Western,
between Wheeling and Oakland City; Central, between Oakland
City and Winslow; and Eastern, between Winslow and Pikesville.
The U.S. Fish & Wildlife Service Patoka office is in Oakland City.

The refuge consists of a patchwork of tracts that are not contiguous, are interspersed with private property, and sometimes
are inaccessible. Boundaries are not always marked due to on-
going acquisition activity. The roads are often unmarked and
sometimes flooded and impassable.

Popular Patoka refuge destinations include the Patoka
River's South Fork, Snakey Point Marsh, Hugh Boyd Fishing Pier
& Wildlife Observation Deck, Maxey Birding Trail, Otter Run
Trail, Columbia Mine, Gray Woods Swamp, and Houchin's Ditch.

Established in 1994 as Indiana's second national wildlife refuge, Patoka's landscape is predominantly bottomland hardwood
forests and wetlands, which include shallow ponds, backwater
sloughs, and deepwater swamps, as well as some upland forest

and grassland. The long-term management goal is to create a contiguous, thirteen-thousand-acre belt of bottomland forest along the river's banks.

Federal law allows Fish & Wildlife to acquire up to 22,472 acres of land—7,000 acres of it rare bottomland forest wetlands—from willing sellers. Within the refuge purchase area are almost 5,500 acres at Pike State Forest and the Columbia Mine Preserve, which are owned by the DNR and Sycamore Land Trust, respectively.

U.S. Fish & Wildlife staff at Patoka also manage two satellite Wildlife Management Areas called Cane Ridge and White River Bottoms. Cane Ridge's 463 acres are located twenty-four miles west of Oakland City. White River Bottoms' 219 acres are nine miles to the north.

Wildlife refuge management objectives on the Patoka refuge include providing resting, feeding, and nesting habitat for migratory birds; maintaining and increasing biodiversity; restoring, protecting, and managing the 162-mile river corridor; improving the river's water quality; developing public understanding and support for natural resources; and providing wildlife-related education and recreation opportunities.

Bottomland hardwood forest dominates the Patoka River refuge. More than half of the area's 12,700 acres of wetlands—55 percent—are bottomland forest. Another thousand-plus acres have been planted to help maximize species diversity.

Bottomland forest ecosystems support tree species that can survive waterlogged soils for parts of the year and include overcup oak, a state watch list species, black willow, sweet gum, river birch, silver maple, eastern cottonwood, sycamore, pin oak, Shumard's oak (a.k.a. Schneck red oak), basket oak (a.k.a. swamp chestnut oak), swamp white oak, big shellbark hickory, green ash, and red maple.

A critical and unique component of the bottomland forest is giant cane, on which a variety of wildlife species—including the state-endangered swamp rabbit—rely for all aspects of their lives. A bamboo native to the United States, giant cane grows in dense stands known as "canebrakes." Its presence has been reduced an estimated 98 percent since European settlement in the Midwest. U.S. Fish & Wildlife has been actively restoring canebrakes at the Patoka refuge.

The upland forests support northern red oak, white oak, black oak, tulip poplar, wild black cherry, American beech, and black gum, as well as various hickory and walnut species.

The wetlands, shallow ponds, deepwater swamps, and old river oxbows are home to American lotus, a state watch list species, buttonbush, broad-leaved cattail, halberd-leaved rose mallow, lizard's tail, common water plantain, and coontail, all of which provide vital habitat and food for many animal species.

The Patoka refuge also includes more than one thousand acres of restored grasslands and savannas, which are reclaimed coal mine sites. Under federal law, coal companies must restore surface mines to the land's approximate premining contours, replace the topsoil, and reestablish vegetative cover. Another four thousand acres of grassland may eventually be added to the Patoka refuge.

The National Audubon Society has designated the Patoka River National Wildlife Refuge and Cane Ridge Wildlife Management Area as Global and State Important Bird Areas, respectively. The area "boasts one of the most rich and abundant bird communities in the state," the society's website says.

As one of the most significant bottomland hardwood forests in the Midwest, the refuge area supports large populations of birds that rely on various types of wetland habitats, including forested, shrubland, and herbaceous. The mature forests support healthy populations of neotropical migratory songbird species, which thrive in this rich ecosystem along the historically important north–south Wabash River Basin flyway.

The Patoka refuge area supports least terns and whooping cranes, both federally endangered, and several state endangered species, including cerulean warbler, king rail, short-eared owl,

Patoka National Wildlife Refuge, Pike County.

barn owl, northern harrier, American bittern, Henslow's sparrow, and yellow-crowned night heron, as well as bald eagle and great egret, both state species of special concern. Patoka is one of the few breeding areas for the yellow-crowned night heron in Indiana. Surveys show that at least one thousand pairs of prothonotary warblers nest along the Patoka River.

The Patoka bottomlands have some of the most productive wood duck nesting and brood-rearing habitat in the state, and they support several nesting colonies of great blue herons. The bottomlands also are vital stopover sites for migratory shorebirds and waterfowl, with state record numbers of northern shoveler, northern pintail, lesser yellowleg, and pectoral sandpiper species documented on the refuge.

Among the 250-plus species that live in or migrate through the refuge are dickcissel, red-headed woodpecker, Kentucky warbler, American woodcock, wood duck, great horned owl, red-tailed hawk, rough-legged hawk, northern bobwhite, wild turkey, grasshopper sparrow, blue grosbeak, and American kestrel.

The Cane Ridge / Gibson Lake area's IBA designation is due in part because it "supports the one of only two known 'interior' least tern nesting colonies east of the Mississippi River," Audubon says on its website. Least terns are federally endangered, and in 2005 a restoration project began on an isolated and protected island adjoining the Cane Ridge management area. Other noteworthy bird species include bald eagle, peregrine falcon, and Wilson's phalarope, all state species of special concern. Black-necked stilt, cattle egret, snowy egret, tri-colored heron, northern wheatear, and stilt sandpiper have been recorded at Cane Ridge.

Patoka supports nearly four hundred species of wildlife, among them the federally endangered Indiana bat, federally threatened northern long-eared bat, and state-endangered swamp rabbit. Other species include beaver, bobcat, coyote, mink, muskrat, Virginia opossum, river otter, northern bobwhite, raccoon, white-tailed deer, wild turkey, and various species of frog, squirrel, turtle, and snake, including northern water snake (a.k.a. midland water snake), rat snake, racer, and copperbelly water snake, all of which are nonvenomous.

A 2009–10 study documented nine salamander species on the Patoka, including the reclusive marbled salamander, which conceals itself under rocks and logs and in the burrows of small animals. This amphibian relies on permanent ponds on the forest floor for reproduction.

In the summer and fall the wetlands teem with forty-two species of dragonflies and damselflies, including the commonly seen Halloween pennant. Named for its orange and black wings, this dragonfly frequents the refuge's oxbows and wetlands from mid-June through early October.

Fish in the rivers, marshes, swamps, and ponds include bass, bluegill, and crappie.

Historic activities on the Patoka River National Wildlife Refuge property, including farming and strip mining, have left the landscape with lakes; ditches; successional fields; exposed rock;

rows of long, steep hills of barren rock; and jagged, rock-edged, straight-up-and-down highwalls.

The 459-mile Wabash & Erie Canal from Toledo to Evansville crossed the Patoka near the town of Dongola. Remnants from the nation's longest canal, which closed in 1874, include a canal berm set back in the woods on the Western Section Scenic Auto Tour, which follows State Road 57 and county roads. The local roads can be gravel and curvy, with one-lane bridges and missing road signs. Some flood and are closed during parts of the year.

Activities
Boat ramps (four), canoeing, environmental education, fishing, self-guided hiking, hunting, nature study, photography, wildlife watching.

Directions to the Patoka Office
GPS coordinates: 38.333691, -87.352218
The Patoka River National Wildlife Refuge is located in Pike and eastern Gibson Counties, running generally north of State Road 64 between the towns of Oatsville, Velpen, Pikeville, and Francisco. The office is located at 510½ West Morton Street in Oakland City, just east of I-69 and south of the refuge.
From I-69
• East on State Road 64 to office in Oakland City, 2.6 miles
From State Road 37
• West on State Road 64 to office in Oakland City, 42.9 miles
Information kiosks are located on north–south roads through the refuge, including the Oatsville Station on County Road 850E, Miller Bridge and Monty's Stations on County Road 1050 East, Dongola Station on State Road 57, Boyd's Station on County Road 25S, and Old Ben and McClure's Stations on State Road 257.

15. Columbia Mine Preserve
Owned by Sycamore Land Trust
The 1,043-acre Columbia Mine Preserve adjoins the Patoka River National Wildlife Refuge just east of Oakland City to form a

Columbia Mine Preserve, Pike County.

contiguous block of five thousand protected acres south of the Patoka River. The preserve is jointly managed with the U.S. Fish & Wildlife Service under an agreement with its original owner, Peabody Coal.

Columbia Mine is located just east of the Patoka refuge's Snakey Point Marsh and Hugh Boyd and Maxey Marsh Trail Areas. A portion of Snakey Point is inside Columbia Mine's western boundary. A portion of the Patoka's South Fork passes through the preserve's northwestern section.

The landscape includes eleven lakes, along with marsh and forested wetlands. With upland tree and prairie plantings, Columbia Mine provides diverse habitat for federally endangered Indiana bat, state-endangered cerulean warbler, along with copperbelly water snake, bobcat, river otter, coyote, whitetailed deer, and wild turkey.

The Patoka refuge, which stretches thirty miles along the river in Pike and Gibson Counties, is recognized by the National

Audubon Society as a Global Important Bird Area. (See no. 14, Patoka River National Wildlife Refuge, for more details.) A pair of bald eagles, a state species of special concern, has nested at Columbia Mine since 2001. An area close to the nest is closed to protect it from disturbance.

The Patoka River passes through the property and includes a portion of Snakey Point Marsh. Most of the wetland is Core Area Habitat for the copperbelly water snake.

Before Sycamore purchased the land in 2012, roughly seven hundred acres were surface mined for coal in the 1990s and then reclaimed as natural wildlife habitat. The reclamation emphasized habitat diversity, with native tree, shrub, and prairie plantings, as well as food plots, boulder piles, brush piles, and the lakes.

A Driving Route through the site leads to parking lots for the Indian Hill and Overlook Trails, old gravel roads, and mowed trails that provide access for hiking.

State-endangered Henslow's sparrows are now heard in the grassland habitat where Sycamore Land Trust and U.S. Fish & Wildlife conducted a controlled burn after Columbia Mine's official opening in October 2013. This was the first of several planned rotational burns to maintain the habitat.

Activities

Fishing (limited), hiking, hunting (not until approved by the federal government), nature study, photography, wildlife watching.

Directions

GPS coordinates: 38.354756, -87.299712
From I-69
- East on State Road 64 at Oakland City to County Road 1275E, 3.8 miles
- North on County Road 1275E to County Road 1300E, 0.5 mile
- North on County Road 1300E to County Road 175W, 1.2 miles
- East on County Road 175W/475S to County Road 125N, 0.8 mile
- North on County Road 125W to the preserve, 0.8 mile

Pike State Forest, Pike County.

From State Road 37

- West on State Road 64 at Eckerty to County Road 1275E before Oakland City, 39.7 miles
- North on County Road 1275E to County Road 1300E, 0.5 mile
- North on County Road 1300E to County Road 175W, 1.2 miles
- East County Road 175W/475S to County Road 125N, 0.8 mile
- North on County Road 125W to the preserve, 0.8 mile

16. Pike State Forest

Owned by Indiana Department of Natural Resources, Division of Forestry

The Pike State Forest is a 4,444-acre patchwork of wooded hills that loom a hundred feet above the Patoka River, which flows through the forest on its way to the Wabash River some thirty miles to the west. Pike's mature upland and bottomland forests are surrounded by the Patoka River National Wildlife Refuge on the federal property's east end between Winslow and Velpen.

Because of its ecological diversity, Pike supports a variety of plant and animal species. A popular birding area, the property provides habitat for migrant and nesting thrushes, wrens, vireos, warblers, and sparrows. Noteworthy species identified by the Indiana Audubon Society that live in or migrate through include Mississippi kite, worm-eating warbler, and hooded warbler, all state species of special concern, as well as pine warbler, Kentucky warbler, and red crossbill, which is a rare visitor.

Animal species that roam Pike State Forest include white-tailed deer, wild turkey, red fox, and raccoon.

Tree species include sugar maple, white ash, and eastern cottonwood.

A lookout tower with scenic views of the Southwest Indiana landscape has been closed for safety reasons.

Pike is popular with horse riders, who flock there on weekends.

The land that makes up Pike State Forest was purchased between the 1930s and 1950s. Most of the buildings were built in the 1930s by the News Deal–era Civilian Conservation Corps using local timber.

Activities

Hiking Trails and Bridle Trails: More than thirty miles.

Camping: Eleven primitive sites, twenty-five in the horse campground, available on a first-come, first-served basis, self-registration, pit toilets, seasonal drinking water, picnic table, and grill on each site.

Other Activities: Fishing, horseback riding, hunting, nature study, photography, picnicking, playground, shelter, wildlife watching.

Directions

GPS coordinates: 38.355595, -87.160309

From I-69

- East on State Road 64 at Oakland City to State Road 61, 8.7 miles
- North on State Road 61 to State Road 364, 1.5 miles
- East on State Road 364 to the state forest, 3.7 miles

From State Road 37

- West on State Road 64 near Eckerty to State Road 61, 36.9 miles
- North on State Road 61 to State Road 364, 1.5 miles
- East on State Road 364 to the state forest, 3.7 miles

17. Wabash Lowlands Nature Preserve

Owned by Indiana Department of Natural Resources,
Division of Nature Preserves

The 430-acre Wabash Lowlands Nature Preserve is located about a mile due east of the Wabash River, adjacent to the Halfmoon Pond, just upriver from the Wabash River's confluence with the Ohio. The landscape includes southern terrace flatwoods, bottomland forest, several ponds, and habitat for a number of rare plant and animal species. It also supports one of but a few remnants of dry flatwoods left in the state.

The nature preserve is just south of the Halfmoon Pond and is part of a Wildlife Management Area complex known as the Wabash Lowlands Tract, which is managed by the state Divisions of Nature Preserves and Fish & Wildlife, in cooperation with The

Nature Conservancy. Halfmoon Pond is private property but is viewable from the road.

The Evansville Audubon Society says the Halfmoon Pond / Wabash Lowlands area offers quality birding for shorebirds, ducks, and a wide variety of other birds, depending on the season. Great egret, a state species of special concern, is present in late summer. The variety of bird species passing through during migration is almost unlimited.

The preserve spans both sides of the road and is marked with signs. A parking lot with sign is located just past an operational oil pump jack on the same side of the road. Past the preserve, the roads are passable in both directions, though conditions are variable due to flooding.

While the nature preserve's southwestern boundary abuts the Section Six Flatwoods Nature Preserve, they are not connected by road.

Activities
Hiking, nature study, photography, wildlife watching.

Directions
GPS coordinates: 37.867752, -88.053222
From I-70
- South on U.S. 41 at Terre Haute, through Vincennes, to I-64 at Evansville, 92.7 miles
- West on I-64 to State Road 69, 20.7 miles
- South on State Road 69, through Mount Vernon, to Bonebank Road, 26.8 miles
- West on Bonebank Road to Spencer Ditch Road, 0.7 mile
- West on Spencer Ditch to the T at Halfmoon Pond Road, 4.5 miles
- Southwest on Halfmoon Pond Road to County Road 1115S, 0.5 mile
- South on County Road 1115S to the preserve, 0.6 mile
Parking lot is on the right.

From I-69
- West on I-64 to State Road 69, 25.1 miles

- South on State Road 69, through Mount Vernon, to Bonebank Road, 26.8 miles
- West on Bonebank Road to Spencer Ditch Road, 0.7 mile
- West on Spencer Ditch to the T at Halfmoon Pond Road, 4.5 miles
- Southwest on Halfmoon Pond Road to County Road 1115S, 0.5 mile
- South on County Road 1115S to the preserve, 0.6 mile

Parking lot is on the right.

18. Section Six Flatwoods Nature Preserve

Owned by Indiana Department of Natural Resources,
Division of Nature Preserves

The 403-acre Section Six Flatwoods Nature Preserve is located about a mile north of a deep, easterly bend in the Wabash River in southwestern Posey County. It is contiguous to the Wabash Lowlands conservation area to the west and consists of a remnant high-quality southern lowland flatwoods forest community. The preserve supports a variety of plant species that reflect this particular forest community's relatively undisturbed nature.

Many of the plant and animal species have southern roots and are found only in a few sites in Southwestern Indiana. The forest is dominated by southern red oak, a state watch list species, post oak, swamp white oak, pin oak, and big shellbark hickory.

Section Six is known for high rates of biodiversity and includes a number of rare or threatened species, such as state-endangered buffalo clover. It is an important habitat for a variety of mammals and birds, including woodpeckers.

The preserve, which is just a few miles north of the confluence of the Wabash and Ohio Rivers, has no established trails and is subject to flooding. Beyond the marked parking lot, Slim Pond Road dead ends at Slim Pond. Section Six is not connected via road to the adjacent Wabash Lowlands area.

Activities

Hiking, nature study, photography, wildlife watching.

Directions

GPS coordinates: 37.855213, -88.030093

From I-70

- South on U.S. 41 at Terre Haute, through Vincennes, to I-64 at Evansville, 92.7 miles
- West on I-64 to State Road 69, 20.7 miles
- South on State Road 69, through Mount Vernon, to Bonebank Road, 23.1 miles
- West on Bonebank Road to Slim Pond Road at the Township Church, 4.0 miles
- North on Slim Pond to the preserve, 1.6 miles

Parking lot is on the right.

From I-69

- West on I-64 to State Road 69, 25.1 miles
- South on State Road 69, through Mount Vernon, to Bonebank Road, 23.1 miles
- West on Bonebank Road to Slim Pond Road at the Township Church, 4.0 miles
- North on Slim Pond to the preserve, 1.6 miles

Parking lot is on the right.

19. Twin Swamps Nature Preserve

Owned by Indiana Department of Natural Resources,
Division of Nature Preserves

The 598-acre Twin Swamps Nature Preserve is located west of the Hovey Lake Fish & Wildlife Area in deep southwestern Posey County, less than two miles northeast of the confluence of the Wabash and Ohio Rivers. The preserve is named after its protected pair of swamps identified on signs as Cypress and Overcup Oak, which respectively support tree communities of swamp cottonwood–bald cypress and overcup oak.

The state threatened bald cypresses—relatives of the California redwoods—that dominate the swamp emerge from the water with reddish-brown bark and sloping, bell-bottom-shaped trunks. Their gnarly knees are modified roots that likewise rise from the water in stubby, surreal fashion. Their exact function has not been determined.

Twin Swamps Nature Preserve, Posey County.

The swamp cottonwoods that thrive in the cypress swamp are the most common trees in the twin-swamp environment and have large, heart-shaped leaves, furrowed barks, and trunks that bow and lean. They produce cottony seeds in spring that blanket the swamp.

The state threatened aquatic herb featherfoil lives in the cypress swamp. During flowering season, this underwater plant's spongy, inflated stems float on the surface of the water, which supports their flowers and helps transport seeds.

Among the reptile and amphibian species living in the swamps are copperbelly water snake, eastern gray tree frog, western chorus frog, and an eel-like salamander called lesser siren.

As its name also suggests, the overcup oak swamp was once dominated by this southern tree species, so named because the acorn cap nearly covers the entire nut. The overcup looks similar to other white oaks and is exceptionally tolerant of the sort of flooding this bottomland preserve experiences.

Some red maple, silver maple, and sweet gum are found on the twin swamps' fringes.

The swamps are fronted and separated by an area of southern flatwoods that is one of the few existing remnants of such communities in the state. In presettlement times, this forest type covered large portions of the Ohio and Wabash River Valleys.

The fragrant spider lily, a state watch list species, lives in the flatwoods and is so named because its long, white, narrow petals and anthers create a spidery appearance during their summer bloom. Tree species supported by the flatwoods ecosystem include cherrybark oak, a state watch list species, big shellbark hickory, shagbark hickory, post oak, swamp white oak, and pin oak.

The Twin Swamps Nature Preserve supports a variety of bird species normally associated with this type of wetland habitat, including the blue-gray gnatcatcher, prothonotary warbler, and state-endangered yellow-crowned night heron.

A well-marked, easy-to-follow, one-mile trail with boardwalks, bridges, and viewing platforms traverses the Twin Swamps preserve.

Activities
Hiking, nature study, photography, wildlife watching.

Directions
GPS coordinates: 37.831180, -87.984064
From I-70
- South on U.S. 41 at Terre Haute, through Vincennes, to I-64 at Evansville, 92.7 miles
- West on I-64 to State Road 69, 20.7 miles
- South on State Road 69 to Graddy Road at the Hovey Lake Fish & Wildlife Area, 31.4 miles
- West on Graddy Road to Raben Road (gravel), 1.3 miles
- North on Raben Road to the preserve, 0.9 mile

Parking lot is on the left.

From I-69
- West on I-64 to State Road 69, 25.1 miles
- South on State Road 69 to Graddy Road at the Hovey Lake Fish & Wildlife Area, 31.4 miles
- West on Graddy Road to Raben Road (gravel), 1.3 miles
- North on Raben Road to preserve, 0.9 mile

Parking lot is on the left.

20. Hovey Lake Fish & Wildlife Area
Owned by Indiana Department of Natural Resources,
Division of Fish & Wildlife

The 7,404-acre Hovey Lake Fish & Wildlife Area is located in the Ohio River and Wabash River floodplains that spread across Indiana's far southwestern tip. It includes five separate geographic units that stretch a little more than five miles to the west, from Hovey Lake to the Wabash Lowlands / Halfmoon Pond natural complex.

The Hovey Lake wildlife area's signature landforms include a 1,400-acre oxbow lake of the same name, smaller sloughs, marshes, and bottomland hardwood forests.

The easternmost section at the end of State Road 69 is roughly half the total, surrounds Hovey Lake, and borders the Ohio River. The main entrance features lakeside observation areas

Hovey Lake Fish & Wildlife Area, Posey County.

A GUIDE TO NATURAL AREAS OF SOUTHERN INDIANA

and a boat ramp from which to view the lake from the west. The bays and shallow areas are lined with bleached-white snags and attract a wide variety of songbirds, raptors, and waterfowl.

The unnamed road just south of County Road 1300S and north of the main entrance on State Road 69 leads to the area's easternmost boundary, the Ohio River, and access to the sloughs and wetlands on the riverside. The first road west of the main entrance leads south through more bottomlands and marshlands, with an access point on the Ohio River.

Game animals at Hovey include a variety of waterfowl, deer, turkey, and squirrel.

Human presence at Hovey Lake dates back several centuries. Archaeologists have identified a prehistoric Mississippian village on the lake's western bank that dates from AD 1400 to 1700. The land was initially ceded to Indiana by a series of treaties in the early 1800s, including the Treaty of Vincennes in 1804.

Initially designated as swampland in the 1803 and 1809 treaties that ceded it to the state, the Hovey Lake property eventually was granted to the Wabash & Erie Canal Company for the ill-fated Wabash & Erie Canal. After the nation's longest human-made canal failed in 1874, Hovey Lake was acquired by Charles Hovey in the 1880s.

Activities
Berry, mushroom, and nut picking, boating (10 mph limit enforced), fishing, hiking, hunting, nature study, photography, picnicking (restricted to designated areas at the lake), wildlife watching.

Directions
GPS coordinates: 37.818580, -87.959741
From I-70
- South on U.S. 41 at Terre Haute, through Vincennes, to I-64 at Evansville, 92.7 miles
- West on I-64 to State Road 69, 20.7 miles
- South on State Road 69 to the wildlife area, 31.4 miles

From I-69

- West on I-64 to State Road 69, 25.1 miles
- South on State Road 69 to the wildlife area, 31.4 miles

21. Goose Pond Cypress Slough Nature Preserve

Owned by The Nature Conservancy

The sixty-acre Goose Pond Cypress Slough southwest of Evansville in Posey County features natural abundance and beauty, with the look and feel of Louisiana and the Deep South. Stately bald cypresses, on the state threatened list, and their mysterious knees line this series of small sloughs—old side channels in the Ohio River floodplain—where many southern species have adapted to periodic river flooding. The preserve is unmarked.

Sloughs are wetland environments—either in channels or in series of shallow lakes—with water that is stagnant or flows slowly on a seasonal basis. The standing water at Goose Pond Slough, which forms a geographic curve about four miles long, supports bald cypress and swamp cottonwood trees.

Bald cypress is a deciduous conifer—hence the name—and a cousin to the California redwood. Its knees are root-system branches that rise from the ground into the mud or water; their purpose has not been scientifically determined. This swamp tree is at the northern limits of its natural geographic range here. Logging, draining, and other development have reduced the bald cypress community to only a few sites in the state, in far Southwestern Indiana.

On drier ground, the Goose Pond preserve's bottomland forest supports pecan, big shellbark hickory, and silver maple. The higher ground features dense patches of sedges and poison ivy.

The Goose Pond Slough ecosystem hosts a variety of wildlife, including bald eagle, a state species of special concern. Other species are copperbelly water snake, wild turkey, raccoon, beaver, white-tailed deer, and bobcat, as well as a variety of geese, turtles, frogs, and snakes. Despite the southern-swamp feel and occasional firsthand claims, there are no alligators at Goose Pond Cypress Slough.

Ohio River flooding contributes to siltation, which threatens the future at Goose Pond Slough. Much of the slough has already become choked with silt and invasive lily pads.

The preserve has no trails, but the terrain is good for hiking. While Goose Pond is perhaps the easiest place in Indiana to view the bald cypress and other southern trees that thrive here, exploring during wet periods can be challenging. When the Ohio's water levels rise in the spring, the road and the preserve itself are underwater or muddy much of the time.

Midsummer and autumn, when mud deposited from floodwaters has dried, are the best times to visit. Fall colors sport the rare-for-Indiana cypress gold, which blends with the bold red of maples for a unique color display. Winter offers an opportunity to walk upon a frozen cypress swamp.

Activities
Hiking, nature study, photography, wildlife watching.

Directions
GPS coordinates: 37.902504, -87.833759
From I-70
- South on U.S. 41 at Terre Haute, through Vincennes, to I-64 at Evansville, 92.7 miles
- West on I-64 to State Road 65 west of Evansville, 7.3 miles
- South on State 65 to State Road 66, 10.8 miles
- West on State Road 66 to University Parkway, 2.2 miles
- South on University Parkway to State Road 62, 5.0 miles
- West on State Road 62 to Indian Mounds Road, 9.3 miles
- South on Indian Mounds to the preserve, 2.9 miles
- Park along the road.

From I-69
- West on I-64 to State Road 65 west of Evansville, 11.7 miles
- South on State 65 to State Road 66, 10.8 miles
- West on State Road 66 to University Parkway, 2.2 miles
- South on University Parkway to State Road 62, 5.0 miles
- West on State Road 62 to Indian Mounds Road, 9.3 miles
- South on Indian Mounds Road to the preserve, 2.9 miles
- Park along the road.

22. Blue Grass Fish & Wildlife Area

Owned by Indiana Department of Natural Resources,
Division of Fish & Wildlife

The 2,532-acre Blue Grass Fish & Wildlife Area occupies upland habitat with six hundred acres of water northeast of Evansville. Strip-mined for coal by the Amax Coal Company between 1973 and 1993, the area features twenty-eight pits and lakes. When mining operations ceased, the land was revegetated with herbaceous cover and woody species.

Named after the nearby Blue Grass Creek, the area is managed for hunting, fishing, and wildlife watching. About 40 percent is set aside as a Waterfowl Resting Area, with no hunting permitted.

The Indiana Audubon Society has identified the following state endangered species at Blue Grass and the adjacent Ayrshire Mine: Henslow's sparrow, American bittern, black-crowned night heron, Virginia rail, king rail, northern harrier, short-eared owl, barn owl, and least bittern. State species of special concern include great egret, sandhill crane, and bald eagle. On rare occasions, sightings have included federally endangered least tern.

Other noteworthy species that live in or migrate through include cattle egret, little blue heron, sora, rough-legged hawk, dickcissel, grasshopper sparrow, blue grosbeak, Bell's vireo, red-throated loon, red-necked grebe, western grebe, Ross's goose, greater white-fronted goose, white-winged scoter, long-tailed duck, ferruginous hawk, Swainson's hawk, and marbled godwit.

Wildlife species that are common at Blue Grass include white-tailed deer, northern bobwhite, cottontail rabbit, and wild turkey.

Activities

Berry, nut, and mushroom picking, boating (outboards permitted, idle speed only on Blue Grass, Otter, and Loon pits, electric trolling motors only on all other pits), boat ramps, dog training, hiking, hunting (accessible areas require written permit), nature study, photography, wildlife watching.

Directions

GPS coordinates: 38.088689, -87.465741

From I-70

- South on U.S. 41 at Terre Haute, through Vincennes, to I-64 at Evansville, 92.7 miles
- East on I-64 to I-69, 4.4 miles
- South on I-69 to New Harmony Road, 5.8 miles
- East on New Harmony Road to the wildlife area, 0.5 mile

From I-69

- East on New Harmony Road (5.8 miles south of I-64) to the wildlife area, 0.5 mile

23. Wesselman Woods Nature Preserve

Owned by City of Evansville

The 197-acre Wesselman Woods Nature Preserve holds the state's largest stand of old-growth forest and, according to the Wesselman Nature Society, is the largest urban forest of its kind in the nation. This lowland forest supports roughly 125 trees per acre, some more than 150 feet tall and more than 300 years old. Managed by the nonprofit Wesselman Woods Nature Society, the preserve's forested wetlands and seasonal pond provide habitat for a variety of animal life, including mammals, reptiles, amphibians, and birds.

A dedicated State Nature Preserve and National Natural Landmark, Wesselman Woods is home to four of the state's largest trees: Biltmore ash, green hawthorne, Shumard's oak (a.k.a. Schneck red oak), and sweet gum, according to the DNR's 2010 Indiana Big Tree Directory. Trees are compared according to height, circumference, and crown spread. A 150-foot-plus Wesselman tulip poplar is a former state champion and is still the tallest of its kind in the state. Another tulip in Daviess County, while only 118 feet tall, has a more impressive circumference and crown spread.

Sweet gum and tulip poplar dominate the forest canopy but share it with a number of other tree species, including sugar maple, Shumard's oak, and green ash. Many indicate a southern

Wesselman Woods Nature Preserve, Vanderburgh County.

influence, including cherrybark oak and southern red oak, both state watch list species, and sugarberry.

Despite a moderate, twenty-foot change in elevation, the Wesselman Woods preserve supports a diversity of tree, shrub, and wildflower species. More than 125 plant species have been documented on its acreage.

Wildlife species at Wesselman Woods include the rare marbled salamander, as well as raccoon and white-tailed deer, with occasional sightings of red fox and coyote. Woodpeckers, owls, and other raptors, warblers, and songbirds inhabit or migrate through the preserve.

To support a greater diversity of wildlife, Wesselman Woods also includes a reconstructed prairie that is densely populated by native wildflowers, a seasonal pond, a man-made pond, and a grassy berm.

The property features a series of interconnected trails that include raised boardwalks over wetlands and pass by remnants of the Wabash & Erie Canal, two old railways, and seasonal and human-made ponds.

Wesselman Woods Nature Preserve is located in the city-owned Wesselman Park. The entrance is through an interpretive center that offers hands-on educational exhibits, a wildlife observation area, a gift shop, and two class/activity rooms.

Activities
Hiking Trails: Twelve, totaling more than six miles.
Other Activities: Interpretive center, nature study, photography, wildlife watching.

Directions
GPS coordinates: 37.983157, -87.516557
From I-70
- South on U.S. 41 at Terre Haute, through Vincennes, to I-64 at Evansville, 92.7 miles
- East on I-64 to I-69, 4.4 miles
- South on I-69 to State Road 62 / Morgan Avenue, 12.2 miles
- West on State Road 62 to Boeke Road, 2.9 miles
- South on Boeke Road to preserve, 0.6 mile

From I-69

- South from I-64 to State Road 62 / Morgan Avenue, 12.2 miles
- West on State Road 62 to Boeke Road, 2.9 miles
- South on Boeke Road to preserve, 0.6 mile

24. Eagle Slough Natural Area

Owned by Sycamore Land Trust

The 127-acre Eagle Slough Natural Area just north of the Ohio River in Evansville is bottomland forest, except for the northernmost part, which features lakes. Its wetland and mature bottomland forests feature some of the largest bald cypress trees in Indiana. On the state threatened list, bald cypress is a southern species and is rare this far north.

In addition to the bald cypress, Eagle Slough tree and plant species include red maple, mockernut hickory, pumpkin ash, swamp white oak, bur oak, Virginia dayflower, hog peanut, common bur sedge (a.k.a. Gray's sedge), false gray sedge, green-headed fox sedge, sugarberry, and buttonbush.

More than 150 bird species have been documented in its environs, including state-endangered osprey and various species of goose, duck, heron, hawk, vulture, eagle, sapsucker, gnatcatcher, sandpiper, owl, woodpecker, flycatcher, vireo, chickadee, warbler, tanager, sparrow, and finch.

Other animals include reptiles and amphibians such as red-eared slider, spiny softshell, and midland painted turtles; mammals such as beaver and muskrat; and fish such as the longnose gar and paddlefish.

Eagle Slough has a walking trail with interpretive signage along an old rail bed, observation decks overlooking the wetlands and open-water lakes, a nesting platform for bald eagles, a state species of special concern, and an outdoor education classroom.

Activities

Hiking, nature study, photography, wildlife watching.

Directions

GPS coordinates: 37.923138, -87.545941

From I-70

- South on U.S. 41 at Terre Haute, through Vincennes, to I-64 at Evansville, 92.7 miles
- East on I-64 to I-69, 4.4 miles
- South on I-69, through Evansville, to U.S. 41, 20.8 miles
- South on U.S. 41 to Waterworks Road, 1.2 miles
- East on Waterworks Road to preserve, 0.2 mile

From I-69

- South from I-64, through Evansville, to U.S. 41, 20.8 miles
- South on U.S. 41 to Waterworks Road, 1.2 miles
- East on Waterworks Road to preserve, 0.2 mile

25. Kramer Original Woods Nature Preserve

Owned by Indiana Department of Natural Resources,
Division of Nature Preserves

The 220-acre Kramer Original Woods Nature Preserve is an old-growth, southern hardwood, bottomland forest about a mile from the Ohio River southwest of Rockport. With two deep and steep-walled ditches, standing water, and no existing trails, this preserve is among the more challenging Indiana natural areas to visit anytime except winter.

Kramer Original Woods has one of the highest concentrations of old-growth trees per acre in the state, with dominant species including Shumard's oak (a.k.a. Schneck red oak), red oak, big shellbark hickory, pin oak, sweet gum, swamp white oak, silver maple, and hackberry. The lush shrub-and-herb understory features trumpet creeper, hairy spicebush, Canada wood nettle, lizard's tail, moonseed, and wild grape.

The property was part of the farmstead of state senator Henry Kramer, a Prussian whose family immigrated to the United States in 1854 when he was seven. Elected county treasurer in 1874 and state senator in 1878, Kramer died in 1905 at fifty-seven.

The senator's heirs protected the woods from major disturbance, and the National Park Service designated Kramer Original Woods as a National Natural Landmark in 1973. Kramer's grandchildren bequeathed the property to The Nature

Kramer Woods Nature Preserve, Spencer County.

Conservancy in 1998 to be protected as a memorial to their grandfather. The conservancy transferred the property to the Indiana Department of Natural Resources, and it was dedicated as a state nature preserve in 2003. The Nature Conservancy holds a reverter on the deed.

Activities
Hiking, nature study, photography, wildlife watching.

Directions
GPS coordinates: 37.843818, -87.134251
From I-69
- East on State Road 66 to State Road 161, 21.7 miles
- South on State Road 161 to County Road 300S, 4.0 miles
- West on County Road 300S to preserve, 1.3 miles

From State Road 37
- West on I-64 to U.S. 231, 22.4 miles
- South on U.S. 231 to State Road 66 at Rockport, 23 miles
- West on State Road 66 to State Road 161, 4.6 miles
- South on State Road 161 to County Road 300S, 4.0 miles
- West on County Road 300S to preserve, 1.3 miles

Section 2

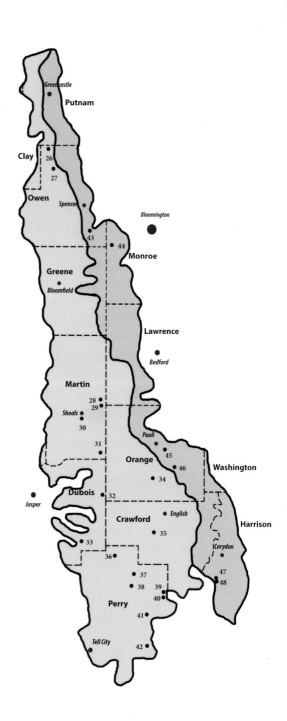

Section 2

SHAWNEE HILLS NATURAL REGION

Crawford Upland Section

26. Cagles Mill Lake / Lieber and Cataract Falls State Recreation Areas
27. Owen-Putnam State Forest
28. Martin State Forest
29. Tank Spring Nature Preserve
30. Bluffs of Beaver Bend Nature Preserve
31. Paw Paw Marsh Watchable Wildlife Site, Hoosier National Forest, Lost River Unit
32. Patoka Lake / Patoka Lake Hiking Area
33. Ferdinand State Forest
34. Springs Valley Recreation Area, Hoosier National Forest, Lost River Unit
35. Hemlock Cliffs, Hoosier National Forest, Patoka Unit
36. Haskins Tract Viewing Area, Hoosier National Forest, Tell City Unit
37. Indian-Celina Lake Recreation Area / Watchable Wildlife Site, Hoosier National Forest, Tell City Unit
38. Tipsaw Lake Recreation Area, Hoosier National Forest, Tell City Unit
39. Boone Creek Barrens Special Area, Hoosier National Forest, Tell City Unit
40. Buzzard Roost Recreation Area, Hoosier National Forest, Tell City Unit
41. Clover Lick Barrens / Clover Lick Special Area, Hoosier National Forest, Tell City Unit
42. German Ridge Recreation Area, Hoosier National Forest, Tell City Unit

Escarpment Section

(*Facing*) Cataract Falls State Recreation Area, Owen County.

SHAWNEE HILLS
NATURAL REGION

SHAWNEE HILLS NATURAL REGION

Crawford Upland Section

26. Cagles Mill Lake / Lieber and Cataract Falls State Recreation Areas

Owned by Indiana Department of Natural Resources, Division of State Parks & Reservoirs

The Cagles Mill Lake recreational complex sprawls over 8,075 acres of upland forest and limestone between Greencastle and Spencer, creating a landscape that an early settler described as "a sensitive display of rolling hills surrounded by numerous streams and creeks. The hills often rise into steep rock bluffs or furnish valleys with soil as rich as the prized river bottoms," according to the U.S. Army Corps of Engineers' website. It includes two State Recreation Areas—Lieber and Cataract Falls—and the fourteen-hundred-acre Cagles Mill Lake, also known as Cataract Lake.

Cataract Falls, the state's largest waterfalls, are located beneath limestone bluffs on the wide, shallow Mill Creek at the lake's headwaters. Crashing over flat limestone rocks, beds, and ledges, Upper Cataract Falls drop twenty feet. About a half mile downstream, Lower Cataract Falls drop another eighteen feet. While their roar is constant and soothing, the whitewater displays they create are wide-ranging in size and form.

The falls were formed during the Illinoian Glacial—which is estimated to have advanced and retreated in Indiana between 220,000 and 70,000 years ago—by glaciers that carved Mill Creek's channel through two bedrock ridges that had been buried beneath ancient lake sediments.

The state's first flood-control reservoir, Cagles Mill Lake was built in 1952 to protect the Eel River (a.k.a. Big Walnut Creek) and White River watersheds. Mill Creek feeds the lake and is named after a gristmill that operated downstream. The mill was destroyed and rebuilt several times before being destroyed by fire a final time in 1975. The old low-level dam is still in place.

The Cataract Falls Bridge, the only surviving covered bridge in Owen County, is listed in the National Register of Historic Places. One of only six bridges in the state using Smith trusses, its design is a simple latticework of crossing timbers. Smith bridges were built in Toledo and assembled onsite, which explains their white pine timbers' smooth, planed surfaces and uniform dimensions. This bridge may be the best surviving example of a Smith truss.

The lake has been home to a state species of special concern bald eagle's nest since the early 1990s.

Activities

Hiking Trails: Three, short, easy to moderate.

Camping: 120 electric sites, 96 nonelectric sites, dumping station.

Other Activities: Basketball court, boating (two launch ramps), boat rental (fishing boats, pontoons), fishing (pier), horseshoe pits, hunting, picnicking / shelter house, playground equipment, nature center / interpretive naturalist services, swimming beach, swimming pool, water safari boat tours, waterskiing.

Directions

GPS coordinates: 39.486942, -86.876095

From I-70 to Cagles Mill Lake / Lieber State Recreation Area
- South on State Road 243 to recreation area, 3.0 miles

From I-70 to Cataract Falls State Recreation Area
- South on U.S. 231 to Cataract Road, 6.8 miles
- West to Cataract Road to the falls recreation area, 3.2 miles

From State Road 67 to Cataract State Recreation Area
- North on U.S. 231 west of Gosport to Cataract Road, 6.5 miles
- West to Cataract Road to the falls recreation area, 3.2 miles

From State Road 67 to Cagles Mill Lake / Lieber State Recreation Area
- North on U.S. 231 to State Road 42, 10.9 miles
- West on State Road 42 to State Road 243, 5.6 miles
- North on State Road 243 to Lieber recreation area, 2.5 miles

Owen-Putnam State Forest, Owen County.

27. Owen-Putnam State Forest

Owned by Indiana Department of Natural Resources,
Division of Forestry

The sixty-five-hundred-acre Owen-Putnam State Forest north and west of Spencer features second-growth, hardwood-forested hills of oak, hickory, and walnut, with more than two dozen ponds interspersed throughout. All are managed for timber production and wildlife. Only two of the ponds are open to the public for fishing.

With 95 percent of the property forested and only primitive camping available, Owen-Putnam is not heavily used for recreation. Fire and forest access roads, mountain-biking trails, bridle trails, and one self-guided trail are open to the public.

Unlike most of Southern Indiana's public lands, Owen-Putnam State Forest, which is mostly cleared and cutover farmland, was not reclaimed by the New Deal–era Civilian Conservation Corps for public use after the Great Depression. It was not established until 1948, with most of the land acquired in the 1950s and 1960s.

In addition to the woods and wildlife—including deer, squirrel, rabbit, grouse, turkey, raccoon, and fox—Owen-Putnam features a seasonal waterfall, a fifty-foot sandstone bluff, and the old Pleasant Grove Cemetery.

The forest is composed of scattered, noncontiguous blocks in a north–south direction. Care should be taken to avoid trespassing.

Activities
Hiking Trails: One, self-guiding, 1.5 miles; hiking available on fire, forest-access, and bridle trails.
Bridle Trails: Three, from 1.7 to 10 miles.
Mountain Bike Trails: Six miles, bikes permitted only on designated trails.
Camping: Thirty-five primitive sites, including fifteen horse campsites, with vault toilets, picnic tables, grills, and parking spurs; no drinking water at the Horse and Rattlesnake Campgrounds, but it can be obtained at the Forest Office or Fish Creek Campground.
Other Activities: Fishing, hunting, nature study, photography, picnicking, playground, wildlife watching.

Directions
GPS coordinates: 39.321097, -86.845124
From I-70
- South on U.S. 231 to State Road 46 in Spencer, 18.5 miles
- West on State Road 46 to Fish Creek Road, 5.2 miles
- North on Fish Creek Road to forest, 0.8 mile

From State Road 67
- West on State Road 46 at Spencer to Fish Creek Road, 5.2 miles
- North on Fish Creek Road to forest, 0.8 mile

28. Martin State Forest
Owned by Indiana Department of Natural Resources,
Division of Forestry

The 7,863-acre Martin State Forest between Bedford and Shoals is composed of rugged hills and deep woods with a network of hiking and biking trails and fire lanes that lead to three lakes. A three-acre arboretum features a self-guided trail and signage identifying sixty tree species.

Established in 1932 when the state purchased 1,205 acres, most of the Martin forest was cutover and abandoned farmland. The New Deal–era Civilian Conservation Corps built picnic areas, shelter houses, and the fire tower that still exists today. Three fishing ponds—three-acre Martin Lake, four-acre Hardwood Lake, and three-acre Pine Lake—were added in 1957. Martin and Hardwood Lakes are near the main road. Pine Lake is accessible only by hiking fire lanes.

The Hoosier Woodland Arboretum, which is free and open year-round, was established in an existing wooded area along the main road not far from the forest entrance. It's traversed by an easy, self-guided trail of a quarter mile, with a shorter, gravel-covered path that is wheelchair accessible. Common Indiana woodland tree species—tulip poplar, red maple, sugar maple, white ash, American elm, sweet gum, and others—have been planted among the oaks and hickories that already flourished on the site. Interpretive signs identify tree species by common and scientific names, though some signs may be missing.

The Willow Valley Fire Tower, which stands one hundred feet tall, was built in 1932 as a lookout for forest fires. It is still maintained and used as an emergency lookout.

Elusive worm-eating warbler, a state species of special concern, and bobcat have been identified near Martin State Forest. Common wildlife species include white-tailed deer, wild turkey, gray squirrel, cottontail rabbit, and raccoon.

The forest's three ponds have catfish, bluegill, bass, crappie, and sunfish.

Activities
Hiking Trails: Five, including a self-guiding path through the Hoosier Woodland Arboretum, 0.25 to 1.25 miles, easy to moderate.

Bike Trails: Four, from 1.9 to 5 miles, mild to difficult.

Camping: Twenty-six designated primitive sites for a fee, toilets and drinking water available near sites, self-check-in station is located in the campground, no reservations—camping is available on a first-come, first-served basis.

Tank Spring Nature Preserve, Martin County.

Other Activities: Boating (electric trolling motors only), fire tower, fishing, hiking, hunting, nature study, photography, picnicking, shelters.

Directions
GPS coordinates: 38.690076, -86.728709
From I-69
- East on U.S. 50 at Washington, through Loogootee and Shoals, to forest, 23.5 miles

From State Road 37
- West on U.S. 50 south of Bedford, through Huron, to the forest, 16.1 miles

29. Tank Spring Nature Preserve
Owned by Indiana Department of Natural Resources,
Division of Nature Preserves
The sixty-acre Tank Spring Nature Preserve just south of Martin State Forest is named for a freshwater spring that continuously flows from a layer of limestone at the base of a sandstone cliff alcove. A smaller spring alcove is located on another bluff a quarter mile south.

A three-mile loop called the Tank Spring Hiking Trail journeys through the preserve and passes by the spring. The wooden DNR sign at the parking lot calls the trail "moderately rugged." The terrain is easy to negotiate, and the trail is well marked, even in the height of summer when undergrowth is at its peak. But it's a strenuous up-and-down trek.

The Tank Spring trail initially follows an old fire lane and features wildflowers—including false sunflower or oxeye in the summer—and colorful and multishaped fungi. Moss-covered sandstone outcrops are prevalent along the trail and can be slippery.

The Tank Springs preserve occupies the rich soils of moist-upland and bottomland forests. Various oak and hickory species dominate the uplands, along with tulip poplar, American beech, white ash, wild black cherry, and sugar maple.

The west side runs along Beaver Creek and contains typical bottomland hardwoods, including sycamore, eastern cottonwood, box elder, and black walnut. A two-acre wetland is situated between the railroad tracks and the upland area.

The broad ravine bottom on the south edge incudes honey locust and eastern red cedar.

Tank Spring was originally called Green Spring and supplied steam-powered locomotives on the adjacent railroad that runs parallel to U.S. 50. The water was piped to a tank near the former hamlet of Willow Valley.

Activities
Hiking Trail: One loop, three miles, moderate.

Directions
GPS coordinates: 38.690307, -86.707639
From I-69
- East on U.S. 50 at Washington, through Loogootee and Shoals, to State Road 650, 23.5 miles
- South on State Road 650 to the T at Deep Cut Lake Road (County Road 67), 0.8 mile
- North on Deep Cut Lake Road to Tank Spring Road, 0.3 mile

Bluffs of Beaver Bend Nature Preserve, Martin County.

- East on Tank Spring Road to preserve, 0.5 mile
- Parking on the north side.

From State Road 37

- West on U.S. 50 south of Bedford, through Huron, to State Road 650 East, 16.1 miles
- South on State Road 650 to the T at Deep Cut Lake Road (County Road 67), 0.8 mile
- North on Deep Cut Lake Road to Tank Spring Road, 0.3 mile
- East on Tank Spring Road to preserve, 0.5 mile
- Parking on north side.

30. Bluffs of Beaver Bend Nature Preserve

Owned by Indiana Department of Natural Resources,
Division of Nature Preserves

The 748-acre Bluffs of Beaver Bend Nature Preserve is a sheer, mile-long bluff on a bend of the White River at its confluence with the Beaver Creek a mile southwest of Shoals. Known as a crown jewel of Indiana's dedicated nature preserves due to its geologic rarities, Beaver Bend's principal natural features are the precipitous, 150-foot, multicolored, sandstone cliffs with rock shelters that run the property's length.

The Beaver Bend landscape supports moist and dry–moist forest communities from the riverbank to the blufftops, with the cliffs and hillsides sporting ferns and a variety of lower plants that produce a vivid array of earth-tone colors and sensual textures. This preserve is best known for the fern species it supports, including ebony spleenwort, pinnatifid spleenwort, marginal shield fern, walking fern, Christmas fern, and maidenhair fern.

Nearly forty tree species—tulip poplar, American beech, sugar maple, northern red oak, and white oak among them—have been identified at the Bluffs of Beaver Bend. So have roughly twenty shrubs and dozens of mosses, liverworts, lichens, and other understory plants.

Bald eagle, a state species of special concern, downy woodpecker, and red-bellied woodpecker live in and pass through Beaver Bend preserve.

Unique geologic formations are present where bedrock is exposed by sections of cliffs that have broken away.

The bluffs have been known by several other names, including White River Bluffs, Spout Springs, and Gormerly's Bluff (after a former owner).

Native Americans, who inhabited the area as far back as AD 750–1500, used the bluffs for shelter. They used the river below, with its large beds of freshwater mussels, for food. Hoosier outdoor writer Harold Allison wrote in *The Nature Conservancy's Guide to Indiana Preserves* (Jordan and Leonetti 2006) that early settlers reported three piles of mussel shells six feet high on the blufftops.

Moonshiners, bootleggers, and gangsters also played roles in the region's rich history, which includes historic French Lick and West Baden Springs, the next towns to the southeast on U.S. 150, also known as the Indiana Historic Pathway, South Spur.

According to Division of Nature Preserves literature on Beaver Bend, William Barnes, the first director of the Division of Nature Preserves, wrote of the Beaver Bend bluffs in a 1969 issue of the DNR magazine *Outdoor Indiana:* "The scenic quality of this unique area must not be overlooked. One may stand on several promontories about one hundred feet above the river. The view of the bend to the east is spectacular with churches and buildings in Shoals standing out in relief against the backdrop of distant hills. The view to the north reveals the tree-bordered river adjoining farmed bottomland with high hills beyond."

The Beaver Bend preserve occupies land along both sides of the road from the Spout Springs intersection past the small parking area, which provides access to the river where it meets the creek. There are no trails.

Activities
Hiking, nature study, photography, wildlife watching.

Directions
GPS coordinates: 38.658560, -86.806167
From I-69
- East on U.S. 50 at Washington, through Loogootee, to Water Street in Shoals (east of the river), 19.3 miles
- South on Water Street (becomes Spout Springs Road at 0.2 mile) to unmarked road just over bridge, 1.0 mile
- West to preserve, 0.1 mile

From State Road 37
- West on U.S. 50 south of Bedford to Water Street in Shoals (east of river), 20.1 miles
- South on Water Street (becomes Spout Springs Road at 0.2 mile) to unmarked road just over bridge, 1.0 mile
- West to preserve, 0.1 mile

31. Paw Paw Marsh Watchable Wildlife Site, Hoosier National Forest, Lost River Unit
The Paw Paw Marsh Watchable Wildlife Site is a frequently flooded, five-acre stand of bottomland trees along an oxbow of

the Lost River in southeastern Martin County near the Dubois and Orange county lines. The surrounding lowlands contain hardwood forest, a white pine plantation, and shrubby, old field areas.

Watchable Wildlife Sites are areas where the odds of seeing wildlife are high.

Beaver and muskrat are common at Paw Paw Marsh, though the beaver are mostly nocturnal and are usually only seen when they emerge from their lodges before sundown. Deer, herons, and egrets are among the wild creatures that inhabit the area. Winter songbirds frequent the pines and shrubby fields between the parking lot and the marsh.

See no. 86, Hoosier National Forest, for more details on the national forest.

Activities

Hiking, nature study, photography, wildlife watching.

Directions
GPS coordinates: 38.57685, -86.74313
From I-69
- East on U.S. 50 at Washington, through Loogootee, to U.S. 150 in Shoals, 19.5 miles
- Southeast on U.S. 150 to Butler Bridge Road, 3.1 miles
- South on Butler Bridge Road to Peggy Hollow Road, 2.9 miles
- East on Peggy Hollow Road, past H. Jones Road, to Paw Paw Marsh parking area, 1.3 miles

From State Road 37
- West on U.S. 50 south of Bedford to U.S. 150 in Shoals, 20.4 miles
- Southeast on U.S. 150 to Butler Bridge Road, 3.1 miles
- South on Butler Bridge Road to Peggy Hollow Road, 2.9 miles
- East on Peggy Hollow Road, past H. Jones Road, to Paw Paw Marsh parking area, 1.3 miles

32a. Patoka Lake
Owned by U.S. Army Corps of Engineers, managed by the Indiana Department of Natural Resources, Division of State Parks & Reservoirs

Patoka Lake, Orange County.

The 25,800-acre Patoka Lake complex is the DNR's largest property and includes Indiana's second largest lake, seven state recreation areas, and a thousand-acre roadless area set aside for hiking and backcountry camping. The landscape includes mature upland forests, sandstone rock shelters and outcrops, pine plantations, abandoned farm fields in various stages of succession, and panoramic lake views.

The 8,880-acre Patoka Lake sprawls across Dubois, Crawford, and Orange Counties and is surrounded by rolling topography, with heavy woods, deep draws, and a rustic, rural atmosphere. The lake, formed by a dam in eastern Dubois County, is 25 miles long and sits 118 miles upstream from the confluence of the Patoka and Wabash Rivers.

In 2011 *USA Today* called Patoka Lake one of the best places in the United States for wildlife watching, citing osprey, on the state endangered list, and bald eagle, a state species of special concern, as examples of creatures that can be seen "by car, boat or boots on the ground." Patoka Lake has been the site of successful threatened- and endangered-species restoration efforts for bald eagle, osprey, and river otter. Other wildlife at Patoka includes bobcat, deer, squirrel, rabbit, raccoon, and coyote.

Bird species that live in, nest in, or migrate through the lake area include American coot, field sparrow, grasshopper sparrow, eastern bluebird, eastern meadowlark, eastern kingbird, horned lark, northern oriole, orchard oriole, willow flycatcher, northern mockingbird, brown thrasher, indigo bunting, northern bobwhite, and turkey vulture, as well as various species of cuckoo, thrush, nuthatch, owl, duck, grebe, loon, hawk, woodpecker, dove, and warbler.

In addition to the various species of bass, bluegill, pike, walleye, and catfish stocked by the DNR, Patoka's waters also support freshwater jellyfish.

The bulk of the Patoka watershed is upland forest supporting oak-hickory and beech-maple forest communities. Eastern red cedars, which grow well in poor soils, are common in the area's abandoned, regenerating fields.

The property is managed for wildlife through use of sharecrop agreements, wildlife food plots, controlled burns, and other techniques.

State Recreation Areas at Patoka include Newton-Stewart, Jackson, Lick Fork, Little Patoka, Painter Creek, Walls Lake, and South Lick Fork. The interpretive services staff presents programs and events that feature the reconstructed mid-nineteenth-century Moery Cabin; nonreleasable raptors, such as bald eagle (a state species of special concern), red-tailed hawk, and eastern screech owl; and other aspects of the area's natural and cultural history.

The visitors' center is located in the Newton-Stewart State Recreation Area on the lake's south side in Birdseye.

Totem Rock, Patoka Lake Hiking Area, Orange County.

32b. Patoka Lake Hiking Area

The Patoka Lake Hiking Area occupies about a thousand acres of Patoka's watershed on a peninsula north of the visitors' center. "This area was set aside to provide visitors an opportunity to explore on foot a large roadless tract of Southern Indiana uplands," the DNR says in a brochure.

Geologically, the landscape crosses a sandstone boundary from Wickliffe to Mansfield Formations. It features several outcrops whose multihued overhangs and passages have been sources of utility and inspiration to humans for thousands of years.

The Mississippian period Wickliffe sandstone was laid down some 325 million years ago by a river that dumped sand and silt into the shallow tropical sea, known as the Devonian Sea, that covered Southern Indiana. The younger Mansfield stone dates to the Pennsylvanian period, which occurred some 320 million to 266 million years ago. The two formations meet near the Totem Rock, which displays the younger Mansfield.

The first Europeans to settle in the Totem Rock area found petroglyphs with three turtles carved into rocks and trees, assumed to be a totem from ancient humans who seasonally hunted the Patoka River Valley and camped there. While pot hunters dug up most of the artifacts, archaeologists have uncovered flint points, mussel shells, pottery shards, and stone tools on the site.

Settlers who also called it Saltpeter Cave found Totem Rock ideal for picnics and church gatherings. They farmed the surrounding land and used the Totem Rock formation—it's more than one rock—as a livestock pen. They also extracted saltpeter from the rocks and sediments below.

Today, the sandstone's honeycombed weathering and broad cross-bedding—colored red, brown, and white by iron, magnesium, gypsum, and saltpeter—inspire awe in nature lovers and stimulate the juices of creative souls.

A 6.5-mile trail—with shortcuts back—traverses the Patoka Lake Hiking Area and has a Birdwatching Spur at the north end.

Activities

Hiking Trails: Three loops in the Patoka Lake Hiking Area, short to 6.5 miles, moderate to rugged. One is a self-guided interpretive wildlife management demonstration trail that illustrates habitat requirements of wildlife and wildlife management techniques.
Bike Trails: More than six miles.
Camping: 455 electric sites, 45 primitive sites, dumping station.
Other Activities: Archery range, boating (ten launch ramps, including two majors in the Newton-Stewart State Recreation Area), cross-country skiing, disc golf course, fishing / ice fishing, hunting, interpretive/recreational programs, including walks and hikes, picnicking, shelter houses (reservations), swimming beach, waterskiing.

Directions

GPS coordinates: 38.384509, -86.646854
The Patoka Lake property is roughly bordered by North Cuzco Road on the west, State Road 56 on the north, State Road 164 on the south, and State Road 145 on the east. The office is located at 3084 N. Dillard Road in Birdseye.

Ferdinand State Forest, Dubois County.

From I-69 to Patoka Lake Office
- East on State Road 56 at Petersburg to State Road 164 at Jasper, 20.8 miles
- East on State Road 164 to Dillard Road, 17.2 miles
- North on Dillard Road through Birdseye to the office, 1.2 miles

From State Road 37 to Patoka Lake Office
- West on State Road 56 at Paoli to State Road 145 at French Lick, 10.8 miles
- South on State Road 145 to State Road 164, 13.9 miles
- West on State Road 164 to Dillard Road, 1.3 miles
- North on Dillard Road through Birdseye to the office, 1.2 miles

33. Ferdinand State Forest

Owned by Indiana Department of Natural Resources, Division of Forestry

The 7,640-acre Ferdinand State Forest in southeastern Dubois County on the Perry County line is primarily upland hardwood forest with four lakes, including the forty-three-acre Ferdinand

Lake, which has been described as the most beautiful forested lake in Indiana. The gravel drive to the lookout tower offers stunning treetop views of the wooded valley below.

The forest is dominated by various species of oak, hickory, maple, tulip, ash, sassafras, gum, and others. Cypress and an abundance of planted pine species are also present.

The topography is unglaciated and characterized by short, steep slopes that are often broken by relatively flat benches and rocky bluffs.

A variety of noteworthy bird species have been identified at Ferdinand State Forest through the years, including cerulean warbler, black-crowned night heron, osprey, and golden-winged warbler (a.k.a. Brewster's warbler), all on the state endangered list. Other species include hooded warbler, worm-eating warbler, bald eagle, and broad-winged hawk, all state species of special concern, along with various other warbler, cuckoo, waterthrush, owl, turkey, loon, chat, redstart, tanager, heron, oriole, vireo, swallow, flycatcher, and sparrow.

Ferdinand State Forest is known for deer and squirrel hunting. Other game species include wild turkey, red fox, gray fox, and raccoon.

The state forest property was purchased in 1933 by a local conservation club for hunting and fishing. The club transferred it the next year to the Indiana Department of Conservation, which established Ferdinand State Forest and a Civilian Conservation Corps (CCC) camp on the property. The New Deal–era CCC workers built the fire tower, roads, service buildings, and lakes.

Activities
Hiking/Bike Trails: Five, 1.2 to 2.6 miles, 8.8 miles total.
Camping: Sixty-nine primitive sites, available on a first-come, first-served basis, vault toilets, seasonal drinking water, picnic tables, and grills.
Other Activities: Boating (electric trolling motors only), boat launch ramp on Ferdinand Lake, canoe and rowboat rental, fishing, horseshoe pits, hunting, nature study, picnicking, pho-

tography, playground, shelter houses, swimming beach on Ferdinand Lake, wildlife watching.

Directions
GPS coordinates: 38.262881, -86.792712
From I-69
- East on I-64 to State Road 162, 33.4 miles
- North on State Road 162, through Ferdinand, to State Road 264, 2.2 miles
- East on State Road 264 to forest, 4.9 miles

From State Road 37
- West on I-64 to State Road 162, 15.6 miles
- North on State Road 162, through Ferdinand, to State Road 264, 2.2 miles
- East on State Road 264 to forest, 4.9 miles

34. Springs Valley Recreation Area, Hoosier National Forest, Lost River Unit

Owned by U.S. Forest Service

The Springs Valley Recreation Area southwest of Paoli is located on the northern end of the 141-acre Springs Valley Lake—once known as Tucker Lake—and offers scenic views of the lake and remnants of the Buffalo Trace, a path used by bison and other wildlife to migrate from Kentucky and the Falls of the Ohio across Southern Indiana to Vincennes and the Wabash River. Scenic hardwood forests surround the lake.

The 12.7-mile Springs Valley Trail is open to hikers, mountain bikers, and horse riders. Permits are required for horses and bikes.

Access to Springs Valley Recreation Area is free. Parking is available at the trailhead.

See no. 86, Hoosier National Forest, for more details on the national forest.

Activities
Hiking/Bike/Bridle Trails: One, 12.7 miles.
Camping: Primitive, vault toilets, no drinking water.
Other Activities: Boat ramp, picnicking, nature study, photography, wildlife watching.

Directions

GPS coordinates: 38.488389, -86.560000

From I-69

- East on U.S. 150 at Washington, through Loogootee and Shoals, to State Road 37 in Paoli, 41.7 miles
- South on State Road 37 to Unionville Road, 0.6 mile
- Southwest on Unionville Road to County Road 150S, 1.0 mile
- West on County Road 150S to County Road 225W, 1.3 miles
- South on County Road 225W to County Road 325S (bear right), 2.1 miles
- Southwest on County Road 325S to County Road 500W, 1.9 miles
- South on County Road 500W to County Road 550W, 0.9 mile
- South on County Road 550W to Springs Valley Lake, 0.9 mile

From State Road 37

- Southwest on Unionville Road (0.6 mile south of the stoplight in Paoli) to County Road 150S, 1.0 mile
- West on County Road 150S to County Road 225W, 1.3 miles
- South on County Road 225W to County Road 325S (bear right), 2.1 miles
- Southwest on County Road 325S to County Road 500W, 1.9 miles
- South on County Road 500W to County Road 550W, 0.9 mile
- South on County Road 550W to Springs Valley Lake, 0.9 mile

35. Hemlock Cliffs Special Place, Hoosier National Forest, Patoka Unit

Owned by U.S. Forest Service

Hemlock Cliffs is a remote, box-shaped canyon southwest of English with sandstone formations that feature a seasonal waterfall rivaling the best in the state, as well as rock outcrops, overhangs, cliffs, shelters, ravines, springs, small caves, and underground drainage conduits. The colorful Tar Springs Formation sandstone, which is honeycombed in places, overlies limestone.

The canyon's cool environs support some unique trees and plants, including the hemlock tree, a tall evergreen with short

Hemlock Cliffs, Hoosier National Forest, Crawford County.

needles and small cones, which thrives there. Lush vegetation occupies the cliffs, waterfalls, and floor, including mountain laurel, on the state watch list, rare French's shootingstar, spotted wintergreen, and wild geranium.

Archaeological excavations in the area indicate Native American occupation between ten thousand and six hundred years ago.

An at-times narrow and rugged 1.2-mile loop hiking trail leads into the canyon. Access is restricted in some areas for resource protection. Camping and campfires are not allowed in rock shelters. Rappelling is prohibited in areas designated for resource protection.

See no. 86, Hoosier National Forest, for more details on the national forest.

Activities
Camping, hiking, nature study, photography, wildlife watching.

GPS coordinates: 38.271660, -86.540359

From State Road 37

- East on West Bethany Church Road (3.0 miles south of State Road 64) to South Mifflin, 1.5 miles
- South on South Mifflin to Pleasant Ridge (gravel), 0.5 mile
- East on Pleasant Ridge to Hatfield Road, 0.7 mile
- South on Hatfield Road to National Forest Road, 0.6 mile
- North on National Forest Road to parking area, 0.4 mile

From I-65

- West on I-265 to I-64, 6.4 miles
- West on I-64 to State Road 37, 42.9 miles
- North on State Road 37 to West Bethany Church Road, 3.8 miles
- East on West Bethany Church Road to South Mifflin, 1.5 miles
- South on South Mifflin to Pleasant Ridge (gravel), 0.5 mile
- East on Pleasant Ridge to Hatfield Road, 0.7 mile
- South on Hatfield Road to National Forest Road, 0.6 mile
- North on National Forest Road to parking area, 0.4 mile

36. Haskins Tract Viewing Area, Hoosier National Forest, Tell City Unit

Owned by U.S. Forest Service

The 125-acre Haskins Tract in northern Perry County is maintained as an early successional habitat and native pollinator resource area. It's a former agricultural field that the U.S. Forest Service seeded with a native seed mixture of eighteen forbs and six grasses. It also contains two newly created ponds and adjacent fields planted with native hardwood trees.

The area provides a variety of wildflowers that are sources for pollinators such as bees, moths, butterflies, and other insects. Other wildlife that inhabit the Haskins Tract include turkeys, deer, bats, and songbirds.

Wildflowers bloom throughout the summer. Early summer bloomers include monkey flower, black-eyed Susan, butterfly weed, common milkweed, gray-headed coneflower, broad-leaved purple coneflower, rattlesnake master, marsh blazing star, and emerging clumps of warm-season grasses. In late summer and early fall, showy tickseed and golden cassia (a.k.a. partridge pea), scattered clumps of various species of goldenrod, native thistles, and mistflower dominate.

See no. 86, Hoosier National Forest, for more details on the national forest.

Activities
Hiking, nature study, photography, wildlife watching.

Directions
GPS coordinates: 38.262092, -86.619189
From State Road 37
- West on Doolittle Mills (1.2 miles north of I-64) to Okalona Road (junction at Bethel Church), 0.8 mile
- Northwest on Okalona Road from the church to the parking area, 1.3 miles

From I-65
- West on I-265 to I-64, 6.4 miles
- West on I-64 to State Road 37, 42.9 miles
- North on State Road 37 to Doolittle Mills, 1.2 miles
- West on Doolittle Mills to Okalona Road (junction at Bethel Church), 0.8 mile
- Northwest on Okalona Road from the church to the parking area, 1.3 miles

37. Indian-Celina Lake Recreation Area / Watchable Wildlife Site, Hoosier National Forest, Tell City Unit
Owned by U.S. Forest Service
The Indian-Celina Lake Recreation Area in northern Perry County surrounds two scenic lakes and offers a wide array of natural beauty and wildlife-viewing opportunities, observable from boat, trail, and road. Named after Celina Lake and Indian Lake—164 and 152 acres, respectively—the area also features the late nineteenth-century Rickenbaugh House and cemetery.

The sixteen-mile Two Lakes Loop Hiking Trail, which encircles the two fishing lakes and surrounding hills and valleys, features wildlife openings along its rugged path. The trail, which

Indian Lake Recreation Area, Hoosier National Forest, Perry County.

rises and falls along numerous steep slopes, has several access spurs with parking on the road. Four to five hours should be allotted to hike just half the trail. The spurs connect shorter day hikes.

The one-mile Rickenbaugh Interpretive Trail is located on Celina Lake behind the two-story, sandstone-block Rickenbaugh House. Built in 1874 by Jacob Rickenbaugh, a tanner by profession and self-sufficient farmer by necessity, the home has been renovated and is only open in summer when staff is available. From 1880 to 1951 the structure also served as the Celina Post Office.

The road from the gatehouse to Indian Lake has several pull-offs that offer scenic views.

Watchable Wildlife Sites are areas where the odds of seeing wildlife are high.

Deer, songbirds, quail, hawks, and vultures are among the creatures that inhabit the area's native hardwood forest, which is mixed with pine trees. Bald eagle, a state species of special concern, and osprey, on the state endangered list, are spotted occasionally.

April and May produce an abundance of spring wildflowers. Fall colors are spectacular.

Drinking water is available in the campgrounds and at the Celina boat ramp. Vault and flush toilets are also available.

A fee is charged for day use between April 15 and October 1. Annual permits are available.

See no. 86, Hoosier National Forest, for more details on the national forest.

Activities
Camping (campground and RV), hiking, boat ramps (electric motors only), fishing (accessible pier on Celina Lake), hunting, nature study, photography, wildlife watching.

Directions
GPS coordinates: 38.199080, -86.598249
From I-65
- West on I-265 to I-64, 6.4 miles
- West on I-64 to State Road 37, 42.9 miles
- South on State Road 37 at I-64 to entrance, 1.9 miles

From State Road 37
- South on State Road 37 at I-64 to entrance, 1.9 miles

38. Tipsaw Lake Recreation Area, Hoosier National Forest, Tell City Unit
Owned by U.S. Forest Service

The Tipsaw Recreation Area surrounds the 131-acre Tipsaw Lake on the Hoosier National Forest in Perry County amid a native hardwood forest mixed with pine. The area offers excellent wildlife-viewing opportunities, especially for woodland songbirds.

Wildlife species that inhabit the area include turkey vulture, white-tailed deer, and wild turkey. Deer are common along the roads and trails and at the lake in early morning. Hawks and vultures soar above the lake, while bald eagles, a state species of special concern, occasionally perch in shoreline trees during winter.

Spring delivers an abundance of wildflowers.

In addition to a variety of recreational activities, Tipsaw features a trail that traverses a variety of different forest types and features scenic overlooks of the lake and valley.

Tipsaw Recreation Area is operated by a concessionaire, and a day-use/vehicle fee is charged from April 15 to October 15. A parking fee is charged past the entrance gate, except for campground occupants. An annual pass is available at the gate.

See no. 86, Hoosier National Forest, for more details on the national forest.

Activities

Hiking/Bike Trail: A 5.9-mile trail for hiking or mountain biking runs from the day-use area around the lake. A trail permit is required for mountain bikers seventeen years of age or older.

Camping: Thirty-five electric or nonelectric sites, walk-in, single or extra large, centralized water, flush toilets, hot showers, recharge table for electric boat motors, open April 15 through October 15 (weather dependent).

Group Camping: Two, capacities of up to sixty-five people, water, vault toilets, showers in the main campground, open from April 15 through October 15, special arrangements may be made for groups to camp later in the fall.

Other Activities: Boat ramp (electric motors only), fishing, nature study, photography, picnicking, swimming beach (no lifeguards), shelter houses, horseshoes, open area for games, wildlife watching.

Directions

GPS coordinates: 38.131500, -86.639600
From State Road 37

- South on State Road 37 at I-64 intersection to Tipsaw entrance sign, 5.1 miles
- West to the recreation area, 2.8 miles

From I-65
- West on I-265 to I-64, 6.4 miles
- West on I-64 to State Road 37, 42.9 miles
- South on State Road 37 to Tipsaw entrance sign, 5.1 miles
- West to the recreation area, 2.8 miles

39. Boone Creek Barrens Special Area, Hoosier National Forest, Tell City Unit

Owned by U.S. Forest Service

The Boone Creek Barrens Special Area contains several rare barrens communities—openings surrounded by dry forests—with brilliant wildflowers that are viewable from short hikes and drives along south- and west-facing ridges. The colorful display begins in midsummer. The barrens occur mostly on the steep slopes and rocky outcrops, where caution should be observed.

The openings also feature a diversity of prairie forbs and warm-season grasses, with stunted post oak and blackjack oak the dominant tree species, and an assortment of plants that attract grassland insects, including moths, butterflies, and skippers.

Boone Creek Barrens Special Area does not have a developed trail system.

See no. 86, Hoosier National Forest, for more details on the national forest.

Activities
Hiking, nature study, photography, wildlife watching.

Directions
GPS coordinates: 38.142800, -86.469400
From State Road 37
- East on I-64 to State Road 66, 13.7 miles
- South on State Road 66 to Onido Road, 7.0 miles
- East on Onido Road to northwestern corner of special area, 1.25 miles
- Special area lies to the south side of Onido Road.

Buzzard Roost Recreation Area, Hoosier National Forest, Perry County.

From I-65

- West on I-265 to I-64, 6.4 miles
- West on I-64 to State Road 66, 29.5 miles
- South on State Road 66 to Onido Road, 7.0 miles
- East on Onido Road to northwestern corner of special area, 1.25 miles
- Special area lies to the south side of Onido Road.

40. Buzzard Roost Recreation Area, Hoosier National Forest, Tell City Unit

Owned by U.S. Forest Service

The eighty-acre Buzzard Roost Recreation Area is a scenic area in eastern Perry County featuring precipitous sandstone bluffs overlooking the Ohio River, with panoramic views of the river valley, picnicking, camping, and a hiking trail that leads to the water.

Buzzard Roost is named after the birds—mostly turkey vultures—that frequented the area in large numbers in the late nineteenth century. The Cherokee Nation called the buzzard "peace eagle" because it does not kill its prey.

These scavengers, whose systems are immune to the bacteria

and viruses they ingest, were attracted to animal carcasses piled at a smokehouse a couple miles to the south at the town of Magnet. The smokehouse is long gone, but the buzzards still frequent the cliffs and soar above the valleys, bluffs, and hikers who venture along the trail.

The half-mile trail begins at a roadside pond and follows the cliff face along, through, and by sandstone rock outcrops, bluffs, hardwood forests, and waterfalls, with an overlook on the Ohio River, before descending to the water. A sign at the beginning of the descent warns: "The trail is steep, rocky, and slippery in some places. Please watch your step."

Primitive pit toilets, picnic tables, and benches are provided. Primitive camping is allowed.

See no. 86, Hoosier National Forest, for more details on the national forest.

Activities
Hiking, camping, nature study, photography, picnicing, wildlife watching.

Directions
GPS coordinates: 38.119851, -86.465581
From State Road 37
- South on State Road 237 at English to State Road 66 at Sulphur, 10.2 miles
- West (right) on 66 to Onido Road / 182, 6.2 miles
- East on Onido Road to Buzzard Roost Road stop sign, 3.4 miles
- South (straight) on Buzzard Roost to marked entrance, 0.9 mile

From I-65
- West on I-265 to I-64, 6.4 miles
- West on I-64 to State Road 66, 35.7 miles
- South on State Road 66 to Onido Road / 182, 6.2 miles
- East on Onido Road to Buzzard Roost Road stop sign, 3.4 miles
- South (straight) on Buzzard Roost to marked entrance, 0.9 mile

41. Clover Lick Barrens / Clover Lick Special Area, Hoosier National Forest, Tell City Unit

Owned by U.S. Forest Service

The shallow soils and rocky outcrops of the Clover Lick Barrens along the eastern section of the Mogan Ridge East Trail support prairie-like, fire-dependent ecosystems and rare plant species not normally found in this part of Indiana. Located near the Ohio River just north of Derby in southeastern Perry County, this natural area features some exceptional remnant communities.

Barrens, where bedrock, thin soils, and other conditions limit or preclude tree growth, mostly occur on rocky, steep slopes and face south and west. The limestone barrens in the Clover Lick Special Area contain a variety of habitat, from moist forests and ponds to open communities of dry forest and fields. Stunted post oak and blackjack oak trees dominate.

This rare natural community also supports prairie forbs in small openings, along with spectacular wildflowers and grasses that more commonly grow in prairies. Midsummer to late fall are the best wildflower seasons.

Some of the more abundant barrens plant species are blazing star, rattlesnake master, prairie dock, rosin weed, rigid goldenrod (a.k.a. stiff goldenrod), obedient plant (a.k.a. false dragonhead), and various coneflowers, along with grasses such as little bluestem grass and Indian grass.

The plant diversity, in turn, attracts a variety of grassland insects, including moths and butterflies.

A variety of birds frequent the Clover Lick area, including prairie warbler, northern cardinal, Carolina chickadee, blue jay, eastern bluebird, and summer tanager.

Butterflies include giant swallowtail, zebra swallowtail, tiger swallowtail, question mark, red admiral, and painted lady. Skipper species include sachem, hoary edge, fiery, northern cloudy wing, and several duskywings.

Common animal species are white-tailed deer, wild turkey, and fox squirrel.

Follow the southern leg of the Mogan Ridge East Trail to the barrens.

See no. 86, Hoosier National Forest, for more details on the national forest.

Activities
Hiking, nature study, photography, wildlife watching.

Directions to Mogan Ridge East Trail
GPS coordinates: 38.050358, -86.520436
From State Road 37
- South on State Road 237 at English to State Road 66 at Sulphur, 10.2 miles
- West (right) on 66 to gravel road over bridge on Oil Creek, 17.5 miles
- North on gravel road to the Mogan Ridge East trailhead, 0.6 mile

From I-65
- West on I-265 to I-64, 6.4 miles
- West on I-64 to State Road 66, 35.7 miles
- South on State Road 66 to gravel road over bridge on Oil Creek, 18.5 miles
- North on gravel road to the Mogan Ridge East trailhead, 0.6 mile

42. German Ridge Recreation Area, Hoosier National Forest, Tell City Unit
Owned by U.S. Forest Service

The German Ridge Recreation Area southwest of Derby features a variety of recreational opportunities revolving around primitive camping, two hiking trails, and a scenic lake deep in the forested hills of Perry County.

The twenty-four-mile, multiple-use German Ridge Trail is accessible from a half dozen parking lots and has several interior connector trails that form shorter loops.

The 1.9-mile German Ridge Lake Trail is for hikers only. It encircles its namesake lake and passes by some scenic sandstone bluffs and outcrops. It includes stone steps that pass through a historic picnic area.

Established by the New Deal–era Civilian Conservation Corps, German Ridge also has several historic buildings.

German Ridge Recreation Area, Hoosier National Forest, Perry County.

See no. 86, Hoosier National Forest, for more details on the national forest.

Activities
Hiking Trails: 1.9 to 24 miles.
Camping: Twenty primitive sites.
Other Activities: Nature study, photography, picnicking, swimming (at your own risk), wildlife watching.

Directions
GPS coordinates: 37.955800, -86.587200
From State Road 37
- South on State Road 237 at English to State Road 66 at Sulphur, 10.2 miles
- West (right) on 66 to State Road 70 at Derby, 17.9 miles
- West on State Road 70 to Tiger Road (at German Ridge sign), 1.0 mile
- South on Tiger Road to the T at Gerald Road, 4.6 miles

- To German Ridge Trailhead, follow Gerald Road from the T to the parking lot, 0.9 mile
- To the campground and lake, follow German Ridge Road south of the T at Gerald Road, 4.0 miles

From I-65
- West on I-265 to I-64, 6.4 miles
- West on I-64 to State Road 66, 35.7 miles
- South on State Road 66 to State Road 70 at Derby, 19.5 miles
- West on State Road 70 to Tiger Road (at German Ridge sign), 1.0 mile
- South on Tiger Road to the T at Gerald Road, 4.6 miles
- To German Ridge Trailhead, follow Gerald Road from the T to the parking lot, 0.9 mileTo the campground and lake, follow German Ridge Road south of the T at Gerald Road, 4.0 miles

Escarpment Section

43. Green's Bluff Nature Preserve
Owned by The Nature Conservancy

The 563-acre Green's Bluff Nature Preserve between Spencer and Bloomington is a remote upland-ravine forest community that is among the most scenic in the state. It features tributary valleys, steep cliffs, karst features, and hemlock and floodplain forests. A precipitous, Mississippian-age sandstone bluff overlooks the Raccoon Creek about five miles upstream from its convergence with the West Fork of the White River.

The preserve's rugged loop trail follows a narrow, damp, pronounced ridge; a steep, rocky slope; and the northern bank of the emerald-green Raccoon Creek. The path traverses hardwood forest; a fern-encrusted cliff with karst features, including limestone outcrops with shelters and seeps; a great blue heron rookery; and a deeply carved riparian valley.

Dense stands of hemlock trees, considered glacial relics, cover the steep slopes and cliffs along the valley's south side, along with northern red oak, sugar maple, and white oak. Black oak and black gum occupy the upper, drier portions. Thick beech-maple woods grow in the rugged ravines, while sycamore trees tower over the tall scouring rushes (a.k.a. horsetails) that flourish along the creek.

Spring offers a vast array of wildflowers, including sharp-lobed hepatica, fire pink, and mayapple. The view from atop the sandstone bluff reveals a wooded landscape that feels like wilderness. The dark forest floor supports a variety of ferns and sedges, including maidenhair fern and plantain-leaved wood sedge. Marginal shield fern lives on the cliffs, painted sedge high on the slopes and ridges.

Unusual plants include cliff clubmoss (a.k.a. rock clubmoss) and hay-scented fern, both on the state watch list, pinesap, and spotted wintergreen.

In addition to herons, other nesting bird species at Green's Bluff include the wood thrush, red-eyed vireo, Acadian flycatcher, and scarlet tanager.

Riparian species include southern leopard frog, green frog, and banded water snake, which share the creek with a variety of mollusks, crustaceans, insects, and fish—sucker, bass, bluegill, darter, minnow, and shiner among them.

The remnants of a gristmill, operated by James Green from the 1840s until floods wiped him out in 1882, sit in a bend of Raccoon Creek, known as Big Raccoon Creek in Green's day.

Activities
Hiking, nature study, photography, wildlife watching.

Directions
GPS coordinates: 39.209312, -86.756988
From State Road 67
- East on State Road 46 at Spencer to State Road 43, 1.9 miles
- South on State Road 43, through Freeman, to Sherfield Road, 4.9 miles
- West on Sherfield to the T, 1.0 mile
- South to the preserve, 0.4 mile

From State Road 37

- West on State Road 46 at Bloomington, through Ellettsville, to State Road 43, 12.0 miles
- South on State Road 43, through Freeman, to Sherfield Road, 4.9 miles
- West on Sherfield to a T, 1.0 mile
- South to the preserve, 0.4 mile

44. Porter West Preserve
Owned by Sycamore Land Trust

The 190-acre Porter West Preserve west of Bloomington contains a combination of mature and young forest, early successional areas, small ponds, sandstone outcrops, and karst features, including sinkholes and a spring. A mowed trail from the parking lot splits, with one branch going north to the woods and the other continuing west through an open area to some ponds. A short trail spur in the open area leads to a small pioneer cemetery, which has two marked graves from 1816 and 1820.

The Porter West woods rises a hundred feet to the north, exposing a variety of geologic strata along the way. The loop trail that leads to the ridgetop passes by sinkholes. Sandstone outcrops are prominent near the top of the hill in the northwest section. The spring is located on the woods' south edge.

An open area that is reverting to nature on the southeast portion is the site of a former composting business operated by the land's former owner, David Porter. Ponds are located there and on the southwest section at the end of the trail's western spur as well. The preserve is bisected by a utility cut.

The trail is lined in places with wildflowers such as marsh fleabane (a.k.a. Philadelphia fleabane) and self-heal, as well as blackberries. Trout lily, cut-leaved toothwort, mayapple, and other ephemeral spring wildflowers thrive in the woods.

Parking is available in front of the first gate on Vernal Pike north of State Road 48.

Activities
Hiking, nature study, photography, wildlife watching.

Porter West Preserve, Monroe County.

Directions
GPS coordinates: 39.171016, -86.661566
From State Road 67
- East on State Road 46 at Spencer to State Road 43, 1.9 miles
- South on State Road 43 to State Road 48, 10.7 miles
- East on State Road 48 to Vernal Pike, 1.1 miles
- North on Vernal Pike to first gate on west side, 0.1 mile

Pioneer Mothers Memorial Forest, Hoosier National Forest, Orange County.

From State Road 37

- West on State Road 48 at Bloomington to Vernal Pike, 4.9 miles
- North on Vernal Pike to first gate on west side, 0.1 mile

45. Pioneer Mothers Memorial Forest, Hoosier National Forest, Lost River Unit

Owned by U.S. Forest Service

The 88-acre Pioneer Mothers Memorial Forest is the second largest stand of old-growth forest in the state, next to the 197-acre Wesselman Woods Nature Preserve in Evansville. The one-mile hike through the ancient upland hardwoods features startling views of giant black walnut, tulip poplar, white oak, and white ash trees. Some are more than fifty inches in diameter and tower sixty feet before their first limbs appear.

The trees have grown undisturbed since settlers Joseph and Mary Cox purchased 258 acres of land south of Paoli in 1816. The couple, who migrated from Tennessee in 1811, loved the trees and left their hillside uncut. After two generations of family preservation, however, their heirs sold the Cox Woods to a Louisville lumber company in 1943. The community, however, organized, persuaded the company to save and sell the virgin tract, and, with help from the U.S. Forest Service, raised the funds to buy it.

In the deal, the Forest Service retained ownership and, along with a 165-acre buffer, has always managed the property to protect its unique natural qualities. The undisturbed forest was renamed to recognize the Indiana Pioneer Mother's Club, which donated $5,900 to the cause.

Pioneer Mothers is a Research Natural Area, and no hunting, camping, biking, horseback riding, target shooting, or plant collecting is allowed.

The lowland below the old-growth trees along the Lick Creek was the site of a fourteenth-century Native American village from the Late Woodland period's Oliver phase. Archaeologists excavated the stockade village, estimating about a hundred people lived there.

See no. 86, Hoosier National Forest, for more details on the national forest.

Activities
Hiking, nature study, photography, wildlife watching.

Directions
GPS coordinates: 38.534328, -86.458343
From State Road 37
- South on State Road 37 from stoplight at U.S. 150 / State Road 56 in Paoli to parking lot, 2.0 miles

46. Lick Creek African American Settlement, Hoosier National Forest, Lost River Unit
Owned by U.S. Forest Service
The Lick Creek African American Settlement is the site of a nineteenth-century community of free blacks that predated Indiana statehood by five years. The property was settled by eleven North Carolina families who, beginning in 1811, traveled to Orange County, Indiana, in search of a home that outlawed slavery. As was a custom at the time, these migrants traveled with Quakers, who provided a level of security during their journey and the prospect of friendly neighbors once they settled. The area has also been called Little Africa, South Africa, and Paddy's Garden.

When Orange became a county in 1820, census records show ninety-six black citizens living at the biracial Lick Creek Settlement. In 1831 the first black purchased property there. Twenty-five years later, 260 called the county home, with black ownership at Lick Creek peaking in 1855 at 1,557 acres.

As happened at the dozens of black settlements throughout Indiana at the time, Lick Creek's population began to decrease at the end of the Civil War. By the early 1900s, African Americans were gone from Lick Creek and Orange County. While the reasons are unclear, the war, industrial growth in nearby cities, and increasing racial tensions in rural America are likely causes. The last black at the Lick Creek Settlement sold his land in 1902.

The 7.7-mile Lick Creek Trail passes near the Roberts and Thomas families settlement sites, which are unmarked to protect their cultural resources. Two trailheads lead through maturing hardwood forest to an inner loop. The Grease Gravy Road Trailhead is the shortest and easiest route to the settlement. Trail maps are provided at the trailheads.

See no. 86, Hoosier National Forest, for more details on the national forest.

Activities
Hiking, nature study, photography, wildlife watching.

Directions to Grease Gravy Road Trailhead
GPS coordinates: 38.492198, -86.410370
From State Road 37
- East on U.S. 150 from the Paoli Town Square to County Road 250E (Grease Gravy Road), 3.8 miles
- South on 250E to the trailhead, 2.3 miles

Directions to Valeene Road Trailhead
GPS coordinates: 38.487856, -86.425469
From State Road 37
- South on State Road 37 from stoplight in Paoli to County Road 450S (Valeene Marengo Road), 5.4 miles
- East on County Road 450S to the Lick Creek parking area, 0.9 mile

47a. Harrison-Crawford State Forest

Owned by Indiana Department of Natural Resources,
Division of Forestry

The twenty-four-thousand-acre Harrison-Crawford State Forest, established in 1932, borders the Ohio River between Leavenworth and Corydon, where the Shawnee Hills Natural Region
reaches its southernmost point in Indiana. The landscape has
been dissected by the Blue River and Potato Run Creek, whose
ancient, erosive meanderings are largely responsible for its
dramatic landscape of ridges and knobs, caves and sinkholes,
bottoms and bogs, limestone outcrops, scenic river bluffs, and
steep, secluded gorges.

Ensconced in Harrison-Crawford's southwestern edge, along
the Ohio between the Blue and the Potato Run, is the 2,294-acre
O'Bannon Woods State Park, formerly known as the Wyandotte
Woods State Recreation Area. (See no. 48a, O'Bannon Woods
State Park, for details.) In a unique partnership for Indiana, the
state forest's recreational facilities, including four hiking trails
and eighty miles of bridle trails, are operated by the state park.

Much of the 25.5-mile Adventure Hiking Trail, one of the
state's longest, passes through the forest and park. It has five
overnight shelters and is open for backpacking. The trail loops
through Harrison-Crawford from the northeast to the western-
most bend, where the forest and the park's northern boundary
meet the Blue River. From there the trail zigzags south through
O'Bannon Woods and back to the state forest at the Ohio River;
pursues a deep-southerly route that passes through and by the
Charles C. Deam Nature Preserve; and turns back to the northeast on the way to its easternmost point a few miles west of
Corydon.

The Blue River, which flows from north of Salem to the Ohio,
is a state Natural, Scenic, and Recreational River. Drawing its
name from the aqua color the water assumes when the river
level is low, this pristine waterway supports aquatic species that
require relatively pollution-free water, such as state-endangered

hellbender, a salamander that can reach a foot and a half in length, and a variety of mussels.

The Blue River features several canoe runs of various lengths that start north of the forest and end in the Ohio, with two access points in Harrison-Crawford. Often called the state's most beautiful river, the Blue has a few riffles and outstanding scenery.

Much of the Potato Run creekbed, which forms the state park's southeastern border, is dry. The creek also marks the southern border of the Post Oak–Cedar Nature Preserve.

Among the forest's more unique ecosystems is a healthy stand of state threatened bald cypress trees and a surrounding bog that are more suggestive of the South than the Midwest. The trees were planted by the New Deal–era Civilian Conservation Corps in the early 1930s.

Harrison-Crawford's upland forests support a diverse range of native wildlife, from fox, turkey, deer, grouse, squirrel, and raccoon to protected and threatened species, such as cerulean warbler and Allegheny woodrat (a.k.a. packrat), both on the state endangered list, bald eagle, a state species of special concern, eastern spadefoot toad, and bobcat.

The National Audubon Society has designated the Harrison-Crawford forest complex as a State Important Bird Area, in part due to its large, contiguous block of mature forest and the habitat it provides for one of the state's most diverse and abundant populations of nesting neotropical songbirds. Noteworthy species that live in or migrate through include cerulean warbler, on the state endangered species list; hooded warbler, broad-winged hawk, and red-shouldered hawk, all state species of special concern; and American woodcock, Kentucky warbler, Louisiana waterthrush, prairie warbler, and prothonotary warbler.

The forest also has a pioneer log cabin and fire tower. The tower, situated just inside the O'Bannon Woods gatehouse, provides a magnificent view of the surrounding Shawnee Hills, which extend across the Ohio River and into Kentucky.

47b. Post Oak–Cedar Nature Preserve

The 266-acre Post Oak–Cedar Nature Preserve spans two contrasting natural communities in the state forest on the park's eastern edge. The upper slopes of limestone and sandstone support outstanding examples of dry upland forest. The lower slopes and valley feature limestone and a moist forest.

The dry sites are covered with slow-growing trees, shrubs, and open glades, which support post oak, chestnut oak, white oak, blackjack oak, and black oak, mixed with eastern red cedar. Several openings, known as glades or barrens, support prairie plants that include big bluestem grass, little bluestem grass, and false dragonhead.

The moist lower slopes and valley sites have mixtures of maple, hackberry, oak, ash, and hickory.

A rugged, 0.8-mile, self-guiding nature trail passes through the preserve. The trailhead is on Cold Friday Road, 1.5 miles south of State Road 462. Turn left just before the O'Bannon Woods State Park gatehouse. Hikers must register at the trailhead before entering.

Activities

Hiking Trails: Four, one to 25.5 miles, moderate to rugged.
Bridle Trails: Ten, from two to seventeen miles, eighty total miles of marked loops.
Camping: Twenty-five primitive sites, pit toilets, fire rings, parking spurs, drinking water supply in area. Overnight backpack camping is permitted along the Adventure Hiking Trail. Trail shelters available.
Other Activities: Boating, canoe ramps on the Blue and Ohio Rivers, fishing, hunting, nature study, photography, wildlife watching.

Directions

GPS coordinates: 38.199358, -86.265846
From State Road 37

- South on State Road 237 at English to I-64, 8.9 miles
- East on I-64 to State Road 66, 6.0 miles

Post Oak–Cedar Nature Preserve, Harrison-Crawford State Forest, Harrison County.

- South on State Road 66 to State Road 62, 2.7 miles
- East on State Road 62 through Leavenworth to State Road 462, 8.2 miles
- South on State Road 462 to forest office inside O'Bannon Woods State Park gatehouse, 2.9 miles

From I-65
- West on I-265 to I-64, 6.4 miles
- West on I-64 to State Road 135, 16.5 miles
- South on State Road 135 to State Road 62 at Corydon, 1.7 miles
- West on State Road 62 to State Road 462, 6.9 miles
- South on State Road 462 to forest office, inside O'Bannon Woods State Park gatehouse, 2.9 miles

48a. O'Bannon Woods State Park
Owned by Indiana Department of Natural Resources,
Division of State Parks & Reservoirs
The 2,294-acre O'Bannon Woods State Park west of Corydon is about as rugged and wild as Indiana state parks get. In less than four miles, from the gatehouse to the Ohio River, the elevation

O'Bannon Woods State Park, Harrison County.

drops more than four hundred feet. Two-hundred-foot-plus limestone bluffs rim the riverbank and trail through the Mouth of the Blue River Nature Preserve. Its southwestern boundary follows the Blue to its confluence with the Ohio, where, it's said, the state's most beautiful river meets its mightiest.

O'Bannon Woods is surrounded by the thirty-seven-square-mile Harrison-Crawford State Forest. (See no. 47a, Harrison-Crawford State Forest, for details.) The two properties are managed separately, but park officials oversee some recreational activities on the forest. A brochure provided at the gatehouse has one map for both properties. The 25.5-mile Adventure Hiking Trail traverses O'Bannon Woods from north to south on the western end.

Established in 1980 as the Wyandotte Woods State Recreation Area and renamed in 2004 after former Indiana governor Frank O'Bannon, the park features rich biological, historical, and cultural resources. Its natural features mirror those of Harrison-Crawford, with deep ravines, scenic vistas, rocky slopes, escarpment bluffs, and dry creekbeds, all formed through the ages by the erosive power of the Ohio and its tributaries, especially the Blue River.

The National Audubon Society has designated the state forest / park complex as a State Important Bird Area. (See no. 47a, Harrison-Crawford State Forest, for more details.)

The Blue River, known in pioneer days as the Great Blue, originates in Washington County north of Salem and flows to the Ohio, with its last few miles bordering O'Bannon Woods on its western edge. A forty-five-mile stretch of the Blue north of the Ohio was the first waterway protected under the Indiana Natural Scenic and Recreational River Act of 1973.

The Potato Run Creek forms O'Bannon Woods' southeastern boundary. Its dry creekbed branches east through Harrison-Crawford, serving as the Post Oak–Cedar Nature Preserve's southern boundary.

In addition to O'Bannon Woods' unique natural beauty, the park also boasts a rich human history, relics of which remain intact.

For thousands of years before the European settlers arrived in the early 1800s, Native Americans mined and fashioned the bluish-gray Wyandotte chert, or flint, they found in caves and fields into spear points, knives, arrowheads, and other tools. Stone foundations, cemeteries, historic structures, a restored pioneer farmstead, and an oxen-powered, working hay press barn—all leftover from the days when riverboats plied the Ohio—are scattered among the hillsides.

The Department of Conservation, now the Department of Natural Resources, began purchasing the land for a state forest in 1932. Beginning in 1934, New Deal–era Civilian Conservation Corps (CCC) workers planted trees and built structures like a rock staircase, Shelter House 2, the property manager's residence, the service area, and numerous retaining walls.

The camp hosted one of Indiana's few African American CCC companies, which was located where the group camp is today.

48b. Mouth of the Blue River Nature Preserve

Created in 2012, the 470-acre Mouth of the Blue River Nature Preserve features knobs, deep ravines, and craggy, two-hundred-foot bluffs with caves, along with several high-quality natural communities. The preserve is home to two state-endangered animals, two state-endangered invertebrates, two state-endangered plants, and several other rare animals and plants.

Access is via hiking, biking, and bridle trails that pass through the Mouth of the Blue River preserve. Park at the Ohio River Overlook Shelter 2 parking lot—near one of the preserve's highest points—and follow the Ohio River Bluff Hiking Trail to the west.

Activities

Hiking Trails: Nine, 0.8 to 2 miles, easy to rugged. Part of the 25.5-mile Adventure Hiking Trail passes through the park.
Mountain Bike Trails: Two hike-bike trails, four miles total.
Camping: 281 electric sites, 47 nonelectric horse sites, 25 primitive sites.
Group Camping: One-hundred-bed, self-contained, group camp structures, dumping station.
Other Activities: Boating, family aquatic center, fishing, nature center / interpretive naturalist services, nature study, photography, picnicking, shelters, wildlife watching.

Directions

GPS coordinates: 38.199358, -86.265846
From State Road 37
- South on State Road 237 at English to I-64, 8.9 miles
- East on I-64 to State Road 66, 6.0 miles
- South on State Road 66 to State Road 62, 2.7 miles
- East on State Road 62 through Leavenworth to State Road 462, 8.2 miles
- South on State Road 462 to park gatehouse, 2.9 miles

From I-65
- West on I-265 to I-64, 6.4 miles
- West on I-64 to State Road 135, 16.5 miles
- South on State Road 135 to State Road 62 at Corydon, 1.7 miles
- West on State Road 62 to State Road 462, 6.9 miles
- South on State Road 462 to park gatehouse, 2.9 miles

Section 3

Mitchell Karst Plain

Brown County Hills Section

Knobstone Escarpment Section

63

Martinsville

Morgan

Johnson

64

65

49 50

51

74

Brown

66

75 76

Monroe

67

68

Bartholomew

Bloomington

71

77

Nashville

69 70

78

52

72 73

79

53

80 81 82

83 84

54

85

86 87 88

55

89

Jackson

Lawrence

Brownstown

90 91

92

Bedford

56

93

57 58

Washington

Paoli

Salem

Scott

Orange

59

94

95

60

Clark

Floyd

Harrison

New Albany

61

97

Corydon

96

62

Section 3

HIGHLAND RIM NATURAL REGION

Mitchell Karst Plain Section

49. McCormick's Creek State Park / McCormick's Cove Nature Preserve / Wolf Cave Nature Preserve
50. Powell Preserve
51. Beanblossom Bottoms Nature Preserve / Muscatatuck National Wildlife Refuge, Restle Unit
52. Wayne Woods
53. Leonard Springs Nature Park
54. Cedar Bluffs Nature Preserve
55. The Cedars Preserve
56. Spring Mill State Park / Mitchell Karst Plains Nature Preserve / Donaldson Cave Nature Preserve / Donaldson Woods Nature Preserve
57. Orangeville Rise of the Lost River Nature Preserve
58. Wesley Chapel Gulf, Hoosier National Forest, Lost River Unit
59. Twin Creek Valley Nature Preserve and Henderson Park
60. Big Spring Nature Preserve
61. Hayswood Nature Preserve
62. Harrison County Glades

Brown County Hills Section

63. Fred and Dorothy Meyer Nature Preserve
64. Morgan-Monroe State Forest / Scout Ridge Nature Preserve / Morgan-Monroe Back Country Area / Low Gap Nature Preserve
65. Atterbury Fish & Wildlife Area / Driftwood State Fishing Area
66. Lake Lemon Woods
67. Griffy Lake Nature Preserve
68. Scarlet Oaks Woods
69. Latimer Woods

70. Dan Willard Woods
71. Campbell Preserve
72. Pizzo Preserve
73. Stillwater Marsh / Northfork Waterfowl Resting Areas, Monroe Lake
74. Trevlac Bluffs Nature Preserve
75. Yellowwood State Forest
76. Hitz-Rhodehamel Woods
77. Selma Steele State Nature Preserve
78. Brown County State Park
79. Laura Hare Nature Preserve at Downey Hill
80. Austin and Mary Ann Gardner Memorial Woods
81. Middlefork Waterfowl Resting Area, Monroe Lake
82. Crooked Creek Marsh, Monroe Lake
83. Maines Pond Watchable Wildlife Site, Hoosier National Forest, Pleasant Run Unit
84. Sundance Lake, Hoosier National Forest, Pleasant Run Unit
85. Monroe Lake
86. Hoosier National Forest
87. Charles C. Deam Wilderness Area, Hoosier National Forest, Pleasant Run Unit/ Hickory Ridge Lookout Tower
88. Southfork Waterfowl Resting Area, Monroe Lake
89. Hardin Ridge Recreation Area, Hoosier National Forest, Pleasant Run Unit
90. Jeremy K. Oakley Preserve
91. Hemlock Bluff Nature Preserve
92. Jackson-Washington State Forest, North Unit / Knobstone Glade Nature Preserve / Starve Hollow State Recreation Area
93. Jackson-Washington State Forest, South Unit

Knobstone Escarpment Section

94. Clark State Forest / Virginia Pine–Chestnut Oak
    Nature Preserve / White Oak Nature Preserve
95. Deam Lake State Recreation Area
96. Minton Nature Preserve

BIG RIVERS NATURAL REGION

97. Falls of the Ohio State Park

HIGHLAND RIM
NATURAL REGION

HIGHLAND RIM NATURAL REGION

Mitchell Karst Plain Section

49a. McCormick's Creek State Park

Owned by Indiana Department of Natural Resources,
Division of State Parks & Reservoirs

Indiana's oldest state park, the 1,924-acre McCormick's Creek State Park surrounds a mile-long limestone canyon with deep woods, clear streams, and scenic waterfalls along a flowing creek named after John McCormick, the area's first settler. He homesteaded nearly one hundred acres there in 1816, the year Indiana was granted statehood.

McCormick's Creek's natural features include classic karst topography—sinkholes, rock shelters, intermittent streams over limestone bedrock, outcrops, a cave with arches—surrounded by lush, beech-maple forest, with outstanding stands of beech, oak, hickory, elm, walnut, and giant sycamore along the river. More than 350 wildflowers have been documented on the park's floor, which they share with ferns and a variety of woody species.

The park's canyon and ravines are steeped in history, dating from presettlement times to their inclusion in the state's first state park exactly one hundred years after statehood.

Located on the West Fork of the White River, the area provided prime hunting and fishing grounds for the Miami Indians, who dominated the region and state when the settlers arrived. Native Americans found the landscape far too craggy to use for anything other than hunting deer, squirrel, and grouse.

The settlers initially survived by logging the land, grazing their livestock on the steep, timbered slopes, and farming the flat spots on the ridgetops. But aside from some mills operated on the creek by McCormick's sons, most development plans for the unforgiving land failed. The creek's water level and force weren't sufficient to make sawmills profitable. The inability to

(*Facing*) Wolf Cave Nature Preserve, McCormick's Creek State Park, Owen County.

transport stone to the railroads on the opposite side of the river ruled out quarrying, at least initially.

The property's scenic and restful qualities, however, caught the attention of Frederick Denkewalter, a physician and minister who purchased it in 1880 to build a sanitarium for the wealthy and weary to recuperate and get away from it all. He also ran a hotel and orphanage on the site. The park's Canyon Inn sits on the original sanitarium's foundations.

Local residents likewise found the creek and canyon ideal picnicking and hiking grounds, and when Dr. Denkewalter passed away in 1914, the "father of Indiana state parks," Richard Lieber, seized the moment. The state of Indiana purchased 350-plus acres at auction for $5,250 and established McCormick's Creek as Indiana's first state park on May 25, 1916.

Like most public lands in Southern Indiana, the bulk of the park's improvements came in the 1930s, when workers for President Franklin D. Roosevelt's Civilian Conservation Corps reclaimed the land and built improvements like roads, trails, shelter houses, bridges, and a fire tower.

Improving technology eventually enabled quarrying on the river's south shore. And the park today features remnants of the historic Statehouse Quarry on McCormick's Creek just up from its confluence with the White. The operation, which began in 1878, was so named because it produced limestone for the Indiana Statehouse in Indianapolis.

49b. McCormick's Cove Nature Preserve

What is now the 177-acre McCormick's Cove Nature Preserve was recognized as a significant natural area in the 1969 book *Natural Areas in Indiana and Their Preservation* by Alton A. Lindsey, Damian Vincent Schmelz, and Stanley A. Nichol. A 1985 inventory of Owen County described it as "probably the best mesic [moist] and dry-mesic forest seen in the county."

The preserve's north-facing slopes contain high-quality moist and wet–moist floodplain forests with old-growth forest conditions. Wildflowers, ferns, and woody species abound.

49c. Wolf Cave Nature Preserve

Wolf Cave was created by a small underground water passage that enters from a wet-weather stream and emerges in a secluded valley below on the Litten Branch, which empties into the White River. Where the flow emerges, a limestone ceiling collapse created the two Twin Bridges arches, which rank among the largest such openings in the state. Visitors are allowed to walk through the cave from the entrance to the arches.

The 214-acre preserve's cool slopes feature American beech, northern red oak, white ash, tulip poplar, sugar maple, and hackberry. Sycamore, slippery elm (a.k.a. red elm), and black walnut thrive in the narrow valleys, with chinquapin oak, northern red oak, white oak, and shagbark hickory on the drier uplands. Mosses, liverworts, and ferns are common.

Activities

Hiking Trails: Nine, easy to rugged, from 0.6 to 3 miles.

Camping: Electric, primitive, and youth tent sites; campground with modern restrooms, hot water, and showers; occupancy limited to fourteen consecutive nights; reservations available.

Group Camping: Camp McCormick and Camp NaWaKwa, four sleeping barracks each, capacity twenty-five people each; a large-capacity dining hall / kitchen accommodating one hundred people in each camp and a modern shower house located in the center of both camps. Reservations available.

Lodging: Canyon Inn's guest rooms feature private bath, telephone, coffee pot, hair dryer, television, and air conditioning. Restaurant is open to the public and serves three meals, seven days a week, year-round. Outdoor pool is open to inn guests only. No pets. Guest and meeting rooms equipped with wireless Internet service. Reservations available.

Other Activities: Basketball, game room, handball, interpretive naturalist service, nature study, open shelters, photography, picnicking, playfields, playground equipment, racquetball, recreation buildings, recreation center, shuffleboard courts, swimming pool with concession stand, volleyball, wildlife watching.

Powell Preserve, Monroe County.

Directions

GPS coordinates: 39.283281, -86.726173

From State Road 67

- East on State Road 46 to park entrance, 1.7 miles

From State Road 37

- West on State Road 46 to park entrance, 12.3 miles

50. Powell Preserve

Owned by Sycamore Land Trust

The sixty-seven-acre Powell Preserve features a one-hundred-foot relief with a diverse mix of ecosystems, from forested hills, bottomland woods, and wet meadow to a prairie area with native wildflowers and grasses. The property borders Beanblossom Creek, a tributary of the West Fork of the White River.

Sycamore Land Trust volunteers planted trees, while a contractor planted the native wildflowers and grasses in the field. The latter provide brilliant colors and butterfly habitat in the late summer and fall. Among the wildflower species growing there are American bellflower (a.k.a. tall bellflower), cut-leaved coneflower, yellow coneflower (a.k.a. prairie coneflower, gray-headed coneflower), and wild bergamot.

A mowed trail starts at the Powell Preserve's north end at the bottom of the Brighton Road hill, leads along a feeder creek to the field, and then loops around the prairie planting. A spur from the loop leads up the hill to another gate at the top.

The preserve is named after the Powell family, which has lived in the area for more than a century and still lives nearby. The family had owned the preserve land since the mid-1960s and donated it to Sycamore Land Trust.

Parking is available at the edge of the field along Brighton Road, at the bottom of the hill by the creek. A small gravel ramp on the south side leads off the road for parking in the grass. A pull-off for one car is present at the trailhead near the top of the hill.

Activities
Hiking, nature study, photography, wildlife watching.

Directions
GPS coordinates: 39.328163, -86.634146
From State Road 67
- East on State Road 46 at Spencer to Matthews Road in Ellettsville, 8.7 miles
- North on Matthews to Mt. Tabor Road, 1.2 miles
- East, then north on Mt. Tabor to Brighton Road, 5.3 miles
- West on Brighton to preserve, 0.5 mile

From State Road 37
- West on State Road 46 at Bloomington to Matthews Road in Ellettsville, 5.3 miles
- North on Matthews to Mt. Tabor Road, 1.2 miles
- North on Mt. Tabor to Brighton Road, 5.3 miles
- West on Brighton to preserve, 0.5 mile

51. Beanblossom Bottoms Nature Preserve / Muscatatuck National Wildlife Refuge, Restle Unit
Owned by Sycamore Land Trust / U.S. Fish & Wildlife Service
The 750-acre-plus Beanblossom Bottoms Nature Preserve, a complex of protected wetlands on the Beanblossom Creek northwest of Bloomington, features a diverse combination of

Beanblossom Bottoms Nature Preserve, Monroe County.

lowland ecosystems, from wet bottomland hardwood forest to shrub wetlands, sedge meadows, and successional fields. The creek is a tributary of the West Fork of the White River.

The bulk of the Beanblossom bottoms—596 acres—is owned by Sycamore Land Trust. The U.S. Fish & Wildlife Service owns an adjacent 78 acres known as the Restle Unit, which is part of the Muscatatuck National Wildlife Refuge. (See no. 103, Muscatatuck National Wildlife Refuge, for more details.) The rest is private property that Sycamore and the federal government protect through voluntary land easements.

A 2.5-mile trail follows an elevated boardwalk with four observation decks, allowing visitors to stop and experience natural beauty that would otherwise be inaccessible due to the marshy conditions.

The Indiana Department of Natural Resources has designated 336 acres of the Beanblossom Bottoms property as a dedicated state nature preserve. The preserve is roughly one mile of land along the creek, which meanders off in places and forms sloughs that are often bordered by the wetland wildflower lizard's tail. The diversity of wetland flora is extensive throughout the property.

Eighty bird species have been identified at Beanblossom Bottoms. The National Audubon Society recognizes the preserve as a State Important Bird Area for its "overall ornithological diversity." Great blue herons have had a rookery at Beanblossom Bottoms, and a pair of bald eagles, a state species of special concern, nest there. Species on the state endangered list include American bittern, cerulean warbler, Virginia rail, Henslow's sparrow, and king rail. State species of special concern include black-and-white warbler, bald eagle, and red-shouldered hawk.

Other noteworthy species that live in or migrate through include Acadian flycatcher, American woodcock, eastern wood-pewee, great crested flycatcher, Kentucky warbler, Louisiana waterthrush, northern bobwhite, prairie warbler, prothonotary warbler, red-headed woodpecker, summer tanager, willow flycatcher, wood thrush, yellow-billed cuckoo, and yellow-breasted chat.

The preserve also serves as important habitat for other threatened and rare animal and plant species, including the state-endangered Kirtland's snake, bobcat, and purple fringeless orchid, a state watch list species.

Tree species include swamp white oak, pin oak, swamp cottonwood, sycamore, and silver maple.

Beanblossom Bottoms floods often and can be inaccessible for days at a time in the spring. The calls of spring peepers and other frogs can fill the springtime air. Evening primrose plants are on display in the fields in summer, along with turtleheads in the water and orchids in the woodland. Some orchids also occur in the sun. Common sunflower and common beggar's tick turn the fields into colorful palettes in the fall.

Activities
Hiking Trail: One, interpretive, elevated, with observation decks, easy, 2.5 miles.
Other Activities: Nature study, photography, wildlife watching.

Directions

GPS coordinates: 39.276827, -86.578497

From State Road 67

- East on State Road 46 at Spencer to Maple Grove Road, 7.8 miles
- East on Maple Grove Road to North Matthews Drive, 0.8 mile
- North on North Matthews Drive to Mt. Tabor Road, 0.5 mile
- North on Mt. Tabor Road to Delap Road (County Road 600N), 0.1 mile
- East on Delap Road to Woodall Road (County Road 250W), 2.4 miles
- North on Woodall Road to preserve parking lot, 1.4 miles
- To reach the Restle Unit, follow Woodall Road north to Bottom Road and turn east on Bottom.

From State Road 37

West on Bottom Road north of Bloomington to Muscatatuck National Wildlife Refuge, Restle Unit, 5 miles

West on Bottom Road to Woodall Road, 0.7 mile

Left on Woodall Road to preserve parking lot, 1.3 miles

52. Wayne Woods

Owned by Sycamore Land Trust

The thirteen-acre Wayne Woods on Bloomington's far west side is one of Indiana's smallest nature preserves and packs into a small space a variety of natural features, including mature hardwood trees that thrive in its moist conditions, a spectacular display of spring wildflowers, and several sinkholes typical of the karst area the woods lies in.

A trail begins along Duncan Road near the northeastern corner, north of the neighbors' mailboxes, and traverses the property. The path is unmarked and gets overgrown and sometimes hard to follow in summer. The preserve has no parking lot. Visitors must park on the shoulder of Duncan Road.

Activities

Hiking, nature study, photography, wildlife watching.

Directions

GPS coordinates: 39.128116, -86.596313

From State Road 67

- East on State Road 46 at Spencer to State Road 37 in Bloomington, 14.0 miles
- South on State Road 37 to State Road 45, 3.0 miles
- West on State Road 45 in Bloomington to Duncan Road, 1.5 miles
- South on Duncan to the preserve, 0.5 mile

From State Road 37

- West on State Road 45 in Bloomington to Duncan Road, 1.5 miles
- South on Duncan to the preserve, 0.5 mile
- Park on the shoulder. Don't be surprised if you are approached by a neighbor.

53. Leonard Springs Nature Park

Owned by City of Bloomington

The ninety-five-acre Leonard Springs Nature Park, named after one of two natural springs that drain into the wetland below, features a landscape formed by the forces of karst and humankind. The water that emerges from the large alcoves at Leonard Spring and Shirley Spring just southwest of Bloomington has flowed for miles through underground passages in the soluble limestone that underlies the region.

The 180-foot descent at Leonard Springs, aided by a stairway, features characteristic karst landforms, including alcoves, caves, sinkholes, and underground streams. In winter, Shirley Spring Cave *breathes,* releasing warm, moist air from the entrance that turns to steam. Shirley Spring never stops flowing—not in droughts, not in twenty-below-zero winters. Several smaller springs appear in times of high rainfall.

The springs release enough outflow to provide water for a community, which they did a century ago. The City of Bloomington dammed the creek below in 1917 to provide drinking water to its residents. But due to the underlying stone, Leonard Springs leaked and was abandoned as a water source in 1943.

Leonard Springs Nature Park, Monroe County.

In 1998, after a half century of natural succession back into a wetland, Leonard Springs was sold by the City of Bloomington Utilities to the City of Bloomington Parks Board, which established the nature preserve the next year.

In addition to the karst, the Leonard Springs Nature Park has a diverse mix of plant and animal life, fossils, chert, and historic structures. A variety of wildlife can be seen, including turtles, frogs, snakes, deer, beavers, muskrats, turkeys, ducks, herons, hawks, kingfishers, phoebes, and migrating and nesting songbirds. Red-headed woodpeckers use the trees killed by beaver dams as nest sites.

Activities

Hiking Trails: Two, 0.3 to 1.1 miles, easy and rugged, one accessible.

Other Activities: Nature study, photography, wildlife watching.

Directions

GPS coordinates: 39.119320, -86.591675

From State Road 67

- East on State Road 46 at Spencer to State Road 37 in Bloomington, 14.0 miles
- South on State Road 37 to Tapp Road, 4.0 miles
- West on Tapp Road south of Bloomington to Leonard Springs Road, 0.5 mile
- South on Leonard Springs Road to the nature park, 1.7 miles
- At 1.4 miles Leonard Springs Road turns ninety degrees south.

From State Road 37

- West on Tapp Road south of Bloomington to Leonard Springs Road, 0.5 mile
- South on Leonard Springs Road to the nature park, 1.7 miles
- At 1.4 miles Leonard Springs Road turns ninety degrees south.

54. Cedar Bluffs Nature Preserve

Owned by The Nature Conservancy

The twenty-three-acre Cedar Bluffs Nature Preserve south and a little west of Bloomington offers one of the most spectacular views the state of Indiana has to offer, with some equally stunning biology accompanying the vistas. The preserve surrounds a seventy-five-foot-high limestone bluff, cut by the Clear Creek below, with topside vistas of the creek valley and southern Monroe and northern Lawrence Counties.

With its gnarly red cedar trees growing from the cliffs, the Cedar Bluffs preserve provides what The Nature Conservancy calls on its website "a stunning display of species adaptation and survival in a harsh environment." With thin soils facing south, the bluffs support only life forms that can thrive in such extreme, dry conditions.

In addition to the red cedar, tree species include white oak, black oak, and scarlet oak, as well as plant species far more typical of dry prairies, such as flowering spurge, nodding wild onion, and hoary puccoon. In early spring, Virginia bluebell, celandine poppy (a.k.a. wood poppy), prairie trillium, blue phlox,

Cedar Bluffs Nature Preserve, Monroe County.

columbine, shooting stars, and other wildflower species create magnificent displays on the valley, cliff, and blufftop.

On the north side, the bluff drops into a rock-walled canyon, cut over time by a Clear Creek tributary, that sports some remarkable rock formations.

Cedar Bluffs is open to the public and has only one access route on Ketcham Road. The trail is extremely rugged, both along the creek and up to the bluff. A trail west from the blufftop to the road passes through private property and should be avoided. Visitors must remain on the trail to prevent erosion and avoid trampling the plants.

As at all nature preserves, rock climbing, rappelling, and campfires are prohibited at Cedar Bluffs.

Activities
Hiking Trails: One, rugged.
Other Activities: Hiking, nature study, photography, scenic views, wildlife watching.

Directions

GPS coordinates: 39.035297, -86.567758

From State Road 67

- East on State Road 46 at Spencer to State Road 37 in Bloomington, 14.0 miles
- South on State Road 37 to Smithville Road, 9.1 miles
- West on Smithville Road to Ketcham Road, turn left at the T and then immediately right, 0.5 mile
- West on Ketcham Road to nature preserve, sign on the left, 3.6 miles

From State Road 37

- West on Smithville Road to Ketcham Road, turn left at the T and then immediately right, 0.5 mile
- West on Ketcham Road to nature preserve, sign on the left, 3.6 miles

55. The Cedars Preserve

Owned by Sycamore Land Trust

The forty-four-acre Cedars Preserve south and a little west of Bloomington is a remote forest at the end of a dead-end road that features a twenty-acre stand of mature eastern red cedar trees, along with a seasonal creek and karst features.

A well-marked loop trail system follows the creek and ascends a hill around and through the cedar grove. Along the way it passes limestone outcrops, sinkholes, and remnants from a century-old limestone quarry, including an old shed with a rotting table and chair still inside.

The shreddy-barked cedars, which are widely distributed in Indiana due to birds eating and dispersing the trees' berries and seeds, thrive on limestone cliffs and bluffs. They are also among the first trees to grow on abandoned fields. Early spring wildflowers are prolific at the Cedars Preserve.

The shed and some large stone blocks along the creek are all that remain of the quarry, whose operations ended in 1912 when its owner reportedly died on the *Titanic*.

The Cedars is located at the end of a narrow, dead-end road with multiple ninety-degree turns. Sycamore Land Trust shares the driveway that is marked "private." Entry is permitted, with parking available in a small parking lot in front of the preserve sign. Visitors should not block the neighbor's bridge.

Activities
Hiking, nature study, photography, wildlife watching.

Directions
GPS coordinates: 39.023821, -86.579102
From State Road 67
- East on State Road 46 at Spencer to State Road 37 in Bloomington, 14.0 miles
- South on State Road 37 to Smithville Road, 9.1 miles
- West on Smithville Road to Ketcham Road—turn left at the T and then immediately right, 0.5 mile
- West on Ketcham Road, past the Cedar Bluffs Nature Preserve, to Thrasher Road, 5.4 miles
- West on Thrasher Road to the preserve, 1.3 miles

From State Road 37
- West on Smithville Road to Ketcham Road—turn left at the T and then immediately right, 0.5 mile
- West on Ketcham Road, past the Cedar Bluffs Nature Preserve, to Thrasher Road, 5.4 miles
- West on Thrasher Road to the preserve, 1.3 miles

56a. Spring Mill State Park
Owned by Indiana Department of Natural Resources,
Division of State Parks & Reservoirs

The 1,358-acre Spring Mill State Park west of Mitchell features old-growth forest and karst features so distinctive that nearly half of it is set aside as three contiguous but unique, dedicated state nature preserves. With old-growth forest, caves, underground streams, a human-made lake, and restored Pioneer Village, Spring Mill has one of the more eclectic natural and cultural offerings in the state, not to mention a colorful past.

The park is named for an eccentric nineteenth-century Scotsman named George Donaldson, who, while a world-traveling,

Donaldson's Woods Nature Preserve, Spring Mill State Park, Lawrence County.

big-game hunter, allowed neither logging nor hunting on his Indiana estate—he had five estates in the United States and Mexico. After he died without a will in 1898, Donaldson's property reverted to the state, first to Indiana University in 1915 and then to the Indiana State Department of Conservation in 1927 to form the core of what became Spring Mill State Park.

Flowing water from several cave springs at Spring Mill never freezes and, in the early 1800s, powered several gristmills, a woolen mill, a sawmill, and a distillery. Pioneer settlers then cleared the land around this industrial village for agriculture and timber. A pioneer cemetery is located a short hike from the village.

Spring Mill tree species include white oak, black oak, shagbark hickory, pignut hickory, American beech, maple, tulip poplar, black gum, white ash, and black walnut.

Wildlife species include white-tailed deer, coyote, red fox, gray fox, raccoon, striped skunk, wild turkey, great blue heron, kingfisher, and wood duck.

Prairie plants grow in several locations throughout the park and include hoary puccoon, stout blue-eyed grass, prairie dock, and New Jersey tea.

The twenty-seven-acre Spring Mill Lake, shelter houses, trails, and other structures were built by the New Deal–era Civilian Conservation Corps in the 1930s.

56b. Mitchell Karst Plains Nature Preserve

The 459-acre Mitchell Karst Plains Nature Preserve represents perhaps Indiana's largest block of undisturbed sinkhole plain in a natural forest community. It is classic karst, with a pronounced sinkhole plain bordering the Mill Creek Valley. It is dominated by sinkholes in various states of activity, including unobstructed swallow holes that quickly drain rainwater, other swallow holes that get plugged and pond for short periods of time, natural openings, and small cavern collapses.

The entrances to Bronson Cave and Twin Cave are examples of "karst windows," which occur when segments of cave roofs collapse and entrances are created at each end of the collapses. A boat tour ventures five hundred feet into Twin Caves and explores several cave features.

56c. Donaldson Cave Nature Preserve

Legend has it that George Donaldson used to sit above the entrance to his cave and shoot over the heads of visitors who dared to approach. Today, the state-endangered northern cavefish (a.k.a. blind cavefish) lives in the thirty-nine-acre Donaldson Cave Nature Preserve's ecosystem.

Creating one of the more picturesque scenes in the state, stream water flows from Donaldson's Cave and winds along the gorge bottom. The slopes support forest species typical of the Southern Indiana hill country, with white oak, black oak, and pignut hickory on the higher, drier portions. Beech-maple forest covers the lower, more shaded areas.

Of the few plants that can grow on the steep, dry slope above the cave, many are more commonly found in prairies, including hoary puccoon, stout blue-eyed grass, prairie dock, and New Jersey tea.

56d. Donaldson Woods Nature Preserve

This 145-acre preserve includes 67 acres of undisturbed, old-growth forest that George Donaldson refused to cut. It is arguably *the* most impressive stand of old-growth forest left in Indiana, third in size behind Wesselman Woods in Evansville and Pioneer Mothers Memorial Forest in the Hoosier National Forest south of Paoli. Some of its trees are estimated at three hundred or more years old and include an unusually high number of white oaks. A western, mesophytic forest type, Donaldson's Woods is in between beech-maple and oak-hickory types, with beech and maple assuming greater importance.

Activities

Hiking Trails: Eight, easy to rugged, 0.375 to 2.5 miles.
Bike Trails: One, two miles.
Camping: 187 electric sites, 36 primitive sites, youth tent areas, camp store, dumping station.
Other Activities: Bike rental, boating (electric trolling motors only), canoeing, dining, fishing, Grissom Memorial (to commemorate Mitchell native and original Mercury astronaut Virgil "Gus" Grissom), hayrides, inn, nature center / interpretive naturalist services, nature study, lodging, photography, picnicking, pioneer village, shelters, tennis courts, Twin Caves boat tour, picnic areas, swimming, wildlife watching.

Directions

GPS coordinates: 38.723307, -86.417000
From State Road 37

- East on State Road 60, south of Mitchell, to the park gate, 3.4 miles

From I-65

- West on U.S. 50 at Seymour, through Brownstown, to State Road 37 at Bedford, 40.3 miles
- South on State Road 37 to State Road 60 south of Mitchell, 10.6 miles
- East on State Road 60 south of Mitchell to the park gate, 3.4 miles

Orangeville Rise of the Lost River Nature Preserve, Orange County.

57. Orangeville Rise of the Lost River Nature Preserve
Owned and managed by The Nature Conservancy
and Indiana Karst Conservancy

The three-acre Orangeville Rise of the Lost River Nature Preserve in northern Orange County features Indiana's second-largest spring. Part of the Lost River Watershed, this artesian spring drains about thirty square miles of karst and scenic hills to the north and northeast of the town of Orangeville, including the town of Orleans.

The rise pool's extraordinary karst features have earned it recognition as a National Natural Landmark and dedicated state nature preserve. In honor of the federal recognition, a 1973 marker from the U.S. Park Service says: "This site possesses exceptional value as an illustration of the nation's natural heritage and contributes to a better understanding of man's environment."

The Lost River originates in Washington County and flows roughly eighty-five miles westward—twenty-three of them underground—emptying into the East Fork of the White River in southern Martin County. The underground portion runs between 60 and 150 feet below the ground surface. The river's watershed drains 355 square miles in five counties and is characterized by sinkholes, caves, underground streams, and other karst features. On its website, the U.S. Geological Survey calls the Lost "one of the most fascinating hydrologic systems in the state."

The Lost River is one of the largest sinking streams in the United States and has been referred to as a "subterranean Grand Canyon." It dips underground through a series of swallow holes on a ten-foot-wide riverbed by a farm field eight miles upstream from the nature preserve. A dry creekbed continues its former route for several miles, carrying water only during heavy precipitation.

The Lost River's underground ecosystem supports more than two dozen cave species, including state-endangered northern cavefish (a.k.a. blind cavefish), cave beetle, and southern cave cricket.

As suggested by the preserve's name, scientists used to believe the Orangeville Rise was the point where the Lost River reemerged from its underground journey. But dye tests have shown that the true rise is a 160-foot spring on privately owned land to the south. The water at Orangeville drains the karst to the northeast.

The flow at the Orangeville preserve emerges from a cave into a rock-walled pit 220 feet across at the base of a low limestone cliff. From there, it meanders southwest, above ground, to merge with the Lost River's main channel on the way to its confluence with the White.

The Orangeville Rise of the Lost River Nature Preserve is bordered by two roads and is directly across the street from a private dwelling.

Activities
Nature study, photography.

Directions
GPS coordinates: 38.631450, -86.556899
From I-69
- East on U.S. 50 at Washington to U.S. 150 at Shoals, 19.5 miles
- South on U.S. 150 to Orangeville Road, 14.6 miles
- North on Orangeville Road to Orangeville Rise, 5.0 miles

- West on West County Road 500N (2.4 miles south from the stoplight in Orleans) to the T at West County Road 510N, 5.3 miles
- South on County Road 510N to Orangeville Rise, 0.4 mile

58. Wesley Chapel Gulf, Hoosier National Forest, Lost River Unit

Owned by U.S. Forest Service

Designated a National Natural Landmark in 1972, Wesley Chapel Gulf is a collapsed, eight-acre sinkhole that provides a rare glimpse of the Lost River, which flows roughly twenty-three miles underground through the karst areas of western Orange County. In addition to the steep-walled gulf, other karst features present in or nearby include swallow holes, sinkholes, and caves.

The Nature Conservancy owns and protects an additional 213 acres of property adjacent to the Wesley Chapel Gulf known as the Blanton Tract, named after its former owners.

Named for the nearby 1858 Wesley Chapel, the gulf features abrupt, steep walls, ranging from twenty-five feet of slippery mud to a ninety-five-foot limestone cliff. At roughly 1,075 by 350 feet, Wesley Chapel Gulf is wider than any known section of Lost River.

Gulfs form when overhead rocks collapse on underground streams that wash away the debris, leaving deposits of clay, silt, sand, and gravel on the streambeds, at the same time exposing underground streams that rise and sink. An estimated 720,000 cubic yards of native limestone have been dissolved and removed through the ages at Wesley Chapel Gulf.

The Lost River, which begins its subterranean journey in a farm field five miles to the northeast, appears at the gulf's southern end from a 125-foot rise pool called Boiling Spring. The waters are forced up at least twenty feet during low-water periods and fifty feet or more during floods. During low-water periods, the Boiling Spring pool is twenty-five to thirty feet deep. The water flows for a short distance, then disappears at the base of the south wall, reappearing again at a rise south of Orangeville.

Since acquiring 187 acres of property surrounding Wesley Chapel Gulf in 1996, the Forest Service has practiced no active management there other than custodial care. A family farm since the early 1900s, the property has several sinkholes, most of which had been filled with trash, per the local custom. They were cleaned out and restored to natural conditions in the summer of 1999.

A trail leads from the parking lot to the gulf. The mud sides are slippery and difficult to negotiate.

See no. 86, Hoosier National Forest, for more details on the national forest.

Activities
Hiking, nature study, photography, wildlife watching.

Directions
GPS coordinates: 38.625797, -86.524916
From I-69
- East on U.S. 150 at Washington, through Loogootee and Shoals, to State Road 37 at Paoli, 42.0 miles
- North on State Road 37 to County Road 500N, 5.1 miles
- West on County Road 500N to County Road 350W, 3.6 miles
- South on County Road 350W to Wesley Chapel parking lot, 0.2 mile

From State Road 37
- West on County Road 500N (2.4 miles south from the stoplight in Orleans) to County Road 350W, 3.6 miles
- South on County Road 350W to Wesley Chapel parking lot, 0.2 mile

59. Twin Creek Valley Nature Preserve and Henderson Park
Owned by The Nature Conservancy and Salem Parks Department
The 240-acre Twin Creek Valley Nature Preserve is composed of remote, mature upland and floodplain forests, glades, and caves west of Salem. The state-dedicated nature preserve occupies the far northwest end of an 870-acre natural complex that is a mix of public and private lands, all managed to protect their natural characteristics by The Nature Conservancy (TNC).

Twin Creek Valley Nature Preserve & Henderson Park, Washington County.

The four-hundred-acre Henderson Park is owned by the City of Salem and managed by TNC through a conservation easement. The remaining 230 acres are privately owned but managed through the TNC's Forest Bank Program, which conserves "working woodlands while preserving opportunities for recreation, wildlife habitat, natural beauty, and solitude," according to its website.

While the site is open to the public, visitors must call or check in at the police station at Salem City Hall on the southeast corner of the downtown square.

A series of unmarked trails traverse the preserve's rolling, moderate hills. An old road follows a ridgetop from the Henderson Park Road parking lot and is open for hiking through the karst features and limestone glades down to the creeks' convergence not far from the Twin Creek preserve.

The Twin Creek ecosystem includes moist upland oak forest, with limestone glades and boulders, rock outcrops, scenic cove waterfalls, aquatic caves, and historic structures. Its habitat supports cave animals and spring wildflowers.

The federally endangered Indiana bat inhabits the forest, as, in summer, does the elusive hooded warbler, a state species of special concern.

The glades support a diverse mix of prairie grasses and wildflowers, including the grooved yellow flax and limestone adder's tongue, both rare.

While oak species dominate the woods, hickories are prominent as well. The understory features flowering dogwood, eastern redbud, deerberry, and maple-leaved arrowwood (a.k.a. mapleleaf viburnum).

Cove waterfalls are surrounded by a variety of spring wildflowers in April and May. The glades are particularly resplendent in mid- to late summer.

The creeks that give the preserve its name once provided water to the city of Salem.

Activities
Hiking, nature study, photography, wildlife watching.

Directions
GPS coordinates: 38.643891, -86.200438
From State Road 37
- East on State Road 60 south of Mitchell to Hitchcock Road west of Salem, 19.3 miles
- North on Hitchcock to the T at Henderson Park Road (unmarked), 1.8 miles
- West on Henderson Park Road to the preserve entrance, 1.5 miles

From I-65
- West on State Road 56 at Scottsburg, through Salem, to State Road 60, 19.9 miles
- West on State Road 60 to Hitchcock Road, 2.5 miles
- North on Hitchcock to the T at Henderson Park Road (unmarked), 1.8 miles
- West on Henderson Park Road to the preserve entrance, 1.5 mile

60. Big Spring Nature Preserve

Owned by Indiana Department of Natural Resources,
Division of Nature Preserves

The ten-acre Big Spring Nature Preserve due south of Salem features an alluviated cave spring—previously covered by stream sediments—whose minimum flow has been recorded at 650,000 gallons per day. It sits at the base of a precipitous spring alcove whose water originates from the sinkhole plain to the site's northeast. The rise pit is about fifteen feet in diameter and six to eight feet deep.

A small but high-quality old-growth forest occupies the adjacent hillside, which is bordered by a farm field. White oak, northern red oak, black oak, and chinquapin oak dominate the forest, with pawpaw, sugar maple, and hairy spicebush prevalent in the understory. Just off the trail, a fallen tree's roots envelop slabs of limestone from the bedrock it grew on.

A marked trail begins at the back of the Big Springs Church property, just a few feet from the church. Deference should be paid to church activities.

Activities

Hiking, nature study, photography, wildlife watching.

Directions

GPS coordinates: 38.484661, -86.113859

From State Road 37

- East on State Road 60 south of Mitchell to State Road 135 in Salem, 23.2 miles
- South on 135 to Big Springs Road, 8.6 miles
- West to Big Springs Church sign, ninety-degree turn at church sign, 0.6 mile
- South to Big Springs Church, trail sign in the parking lot at the edge of the woods, 0.3 mile

From I-65

- West on State Road 56 at Scottsburg to State Road 135 at Salem, 18.5 miles
- South on State Road 135 to Big Springs Road, 8.6 miles

Big Spring Nature Preserve, Washington County.

- West to Big Springs Road, ninety-degree turn at church sign, 0.6 mile
- South to Big Springs Church, trail sign in the parking lot at the edge of the woods, 0.3 mile

61. Hayswood Nature Preserve

Owned by Harrison County

The thirty-seven-acre state-dedicated Hayswood Nature Preserve just north of Corydon features scenic rock outcrops overlooking the Indian Creek some three hundred feet below. It is named after Dr. Samuel Hays, who donated 311 acres to Harrison County on the condition that 130 of them be preserved. The entire tract is county owned and known as the Hayswood Nature Reserve.

The county set aside the 130 acres—including the state preserve—as a protected conservancy that features nature trails, wildlife projects, birdhouses, and other conservation work but no electricity, modern restrooms, logging, motorized vehicles, hunting, trapping, or harvesting of natural-grown vegetation.

The Hayswood Nature Preserve is accessible via trail from the reserve's northernmost parking lot. It includes the wooded slopes surrounding Pilot Knob and is bordered to the east by

Indian Creek. The woodland features oak-hickory on the drier sites and beech-maple on the moister sites.

The Hayswood Section of the Indian Creek Trail system, which leads to Corydon, begins at the park's southernmost parking lot and follows the creek for a half mile, crossing it on the Old Rothrock Mill Bridge. A 1915 steel truss structure that was refurbished and reopened in 2011, the bridge used to cross the Blue River. On the creek's other side is a 1.2-mile loop with spurs leading to steep cliffs overlooking woods, farmland, and the city of Corydon. The Indian Creek Trail continues on from the loop toward the state's first capital.

Hayswood's other 181 acres are half-wooded and half-open for recreational uses, including a small lake named Lake Hays.

Activities
Hiking Trails: Four, easy to difficult, 258 feet to 1.2-mile loop.
Other Activities: Basketball court, modern restroom, multiple-use fields, nature study, picnic areas, photography, playgrounds, shelter houses, small lake with handicap-accessible fishing pier, wildlife watching, walking trails.

Directions
GPS coordinates: 38.207957, -86.145220
The preserve trailhead begins at the county park's northernmost parking lot.
From State Road 37
- East on I-64 to State Road 135, 26.8 miles
- South on State Road 135 to the Hayswood Nature Reserve County Park, 2.7 miles

From I-65
- West on I-265 to I-64, 6.4 miles
- West on I-64 to State Road 135, 16.5 miles
- South on State Road 135 to the Hayswood Nature Reserve County Park, 2.7 miles

62. Harrison County Glades
Owned by The Nature Conservancy
The 1,143 acres of wooded bluffs and ridges known as the

Mosquito Creek, Harrison County Glades, Harrison County.

Harrison County Glades are part of a larger complex of protected natural areas in the state's deep south just north of the Ohio River. The preserve includes the noncontiguous Mosquito Creek / Klinstiver Glade, Teeple Glade, and Buena Vista Glade. Situated between Corydon and Louisville, they feature waterfalls, unique plants, and plentiful wildlife.

All told, the "Mosquito Creek Nature Preserve," so-called by the *Corydon Democrat* in 2005, totals sixteen hundred acres and includes property owned or managed by The Nature Conservancy and Department of Natural Resources. Included is the 294-acre Sally Reahard Woods, named after an Indianapolis philanthropist who left $70 million to the nonprofit Nature Conservancy, with $40 million designated for Indiana.

At 1,025 acres, Mosquito Creek Preserve / Klinstiver Glade comprises the bulk of the Harrison County Glades. Its rugged, sandstone-capped hills and limestone bedrock form 150-foot cliffs along Mosquito Creek, which empties into the Ohio River near New Boston. While there is parking at the bridge over Mosquito Creek, there are no signs indicating the property is owned by The Nature Conservancy. The terrain is rugged, and there are no trails.

The glades, or openings, are created by a combination of moisture and soils on limestone bedrock that does not support trees. Yet while the openings won't support trees, the edge where an opening meets the forest supports specimens that, while only a foot thick, are among the state's oldest, having survived more than a century.

Plants usually found in prairies, such as little bluestem grass, big bluestem grass, Indian grass, and hoary puccoon, thrive in these glades. Other noteworthy species include early fen sedge (a.k.a. Crawe sedge), which is on the state threatened list, eastern milk-pea and ginseng, both on the state watch list, and angle pod and grooved yellow flax, both rare.

Other species include the axe-shaped common Saint-John's-wort, ebony spleenwort, false aloe, Carolina buckthorn, narrow-leaved bluet, slender-stalked gaura, golden alexanders, and green milkweed.

Noteworthy animal species that live in the surrounding woodlands include federally endangered Indiana bat, state-endangered Allegheny woodrat (a.k.a. packrat), hooded warbler and rough green snake, both state species of special concern, and eastern spadefoot toad. Copperheads sun on the stone on warm summer afternoons.

Spring wildflowers are few in number, but yellow adder's tongue (a.k.a. yellow trout lily), wild geranium, dwarf larkspur, and blue phlox grow at the tree bases and in the shade of the stone outcrops.

Remnants of two old water mills lie along Mosquito Creek and feature ferns, a small waterfall, and Virginia bluebells.

There is a trail at Teeple Glade, where pale purple coneflowers and yellow crownbeards blanket the site in late spring and early summer.

Activities
Hiking, nature study, photography, wildlife watching.

Directions to Mosquito Creek / Klinstiver Glade

GPS coordinates: 38.025671, -86.037318

From State Road 37

- South on State Road 237 at English to I-64, 9.0 miles
- East on I-64 to State Road 135, 19.6 miles
- South on State Road 135 to State Road 337, 0.9 mile
- South on State Road 337, through Corydon, to State Road 11, 12.7 miles
- South on State Road 11 to Laconia Road at Laconia, 3.7 miles
- East on Laconia to Kintner Bottom Road, 1.6 miles
- South on Kintner Bottom Road to Mosquito Creek Road, 0.5 mile
- East on Mosquito Creek Road to the bridge (park on the bridge's southwest side), 0.9 mile

From I-65

- West on I-265 to I-64, 6.4 miles
- West on I-64 to State Road 135, 16.5 miles
- South on State Road 135 to State Road 337, 0.9 mile
- South on State Road 337, through Corydon, to State Road 11, 12.7 miles
- South on State Road 11 to Laconia Road at Laconia, 3.7 miles
- East on Laconia to Kintner Bottom Road, 1.6 miles
- South on Kintner Bottom Road to Mosquito Creek Road, 0.5 mile
- East on Mosquito Creek Road to the bridge (park on the bridge's southwest side), 0.9 mile

Directions to Teeple Glade

GPS coordinates: 38.033354, -85.960205

From State Road 37

- South on State Road 237 at English to I-64, 9.0 miles
- East on I-64 to State Road 135, 19.6 miles
- South on State Road 135 to State Road 337, 0.9 mile
- South on State Road 337, through Corydon, to State Road 11, 12.7 miles
- East on State Road 11 to Rosewood Road, 5.4 miles

- South on Rosewood Road to Macedonia and Rabbit Hash Road, 2.7 miles
- South on Rabbit Hash Road to Keen Hill Road, 1.5 miles
- Southeast on Keen Hill Road to preserve, 0.25 mile
- Parking is on the right side.

From I-65
- West on I-265 to I-64, 6.4 miles
- West on I-64 to State Road 62, 3.6 miles
- South on State Road 62 to State Road 11, 2.7 miles
- South on State Road 11, through Elizabeth, to Rosewood Road, 13.9 miles
- South on Rosewood Road to Macedonia and Rabbit Hash Road, 2.7 miles
- South on Rabbit Hash Road to Keen Hill Road, 1.5 miles
- Southeast on Keen Hill Road to preserve, 0.25 mile
- Parking is on the right side.

Brown County Hills Section

63. Fred and Dorothy Meyer Nature Preserve
Owned by Central Indiana Land Trust

The Fred and Dorothy Meyer Nature Preserve is sixty-eight acres of unbroken Morgan County forest with forest-interior habitat that is home to native species like cerulean warbler, which is on the state endangered list, hooded warbler, worm-eating warbler, and eastern box turtle, which are state species of special concern.

Tree and plant species that thrive in the acidic, sharply drained, poor soil of the ridges include state-endangered cleft phlox, along with chestnut oak, black oak, pignut hickory, and great chickweed (a.k.a. star chickweed). Species that prefer the protected ravines are American beech, northern red oak, white ash, painted sedge, yellow adder's tongue (a.k.a. yellow trout lily), and bloodroot.

Established in 2013, the preserve was donated by the son and family of Fred Meyer, who was a board member of The Nature Conservancy and was key to establishing the state's

Morgan-Monroe State Forest, Morgan County.

first dedicated nature preserve in 1969—the Pine Hills Nature Preserve in Shades State Park on West-Central Indiana's Sugar Creek.

A well-marked trail traverses the woods.

Activities
Hiking, nature study, photography, wildlife watching.

Directions
GPS coordinates: 39.541558, -86.391545
From State Road 67
- West on Observatory Road (5 miles south of Mooresville, 8.1 miles north of the State Road 39/67 junction at Martinsville) to gravel parking lot on right side, 0.5 mile

64a. Morgan-Monroe State Forest
Owned by Indiana Department of Natural Resources, Division of Forestry
Morgan-Monroe State Forest includes twenty-four thousand acres of steep, forested ridges and valleys in Morgan and Monroe Counties between Martinsville and Bloomington. Indiana's largest state forest abuts the Yellowwood State Forest to the

east, which abuts Brown County State Park and the Hoosier National Forest farther east and south. Together, these public lands comprise one of the largest blocks of predominantly deep-woods ecosystems in Indiana and the Midwest.

Based on Morgan-Monroe's size and significant stands of late- and near-mature forest stands, the National Audubon Society says the forest is one of the most significant sites in Indiana for breeding forest-dependent bird species. This Global Important Bird Area (IBA) and its proximity to Yellowwood State Forest and the Hoosier National Forest's Pleasant Run Unit, also IBAs, constitute the largest block of contiguous forested landscape in Indiana for breeding neotropical migrants.

State-endangered species identified at Morgan-Monroe include cerulean warbler, as well as black-and-white warbler, hooded warbler, worm-eating warbler, broad-winged hawk, and red-shouldered hawk, all state species of special concern. Other noteworthy species that live in or migrate through include Acadian flycatcher, blue-winged warbler, Kentucky warbler, prothonotary warbler, Louisiana waterthrush, ruffed grouse, and wood thrush.

Nineteenth-century settlers cleared and attempted to farm the Morgan-Monroe ridges but found the rocky soils unsuitable for growing anything other than trees. As the landowners abandoned their denuded and rapidly eroding landscape and the Great Depression began, the state began purchasing and reclaiming the land in 1929 to create Indiana's first state forest. Today the forest canopy reaches sixty to eighty feet.

The forty-two-mile Tecumseh Trail, the bulk of which crosses Yellowwood State Forest on its way to southern Brown County near Monroe Lake, begins at the Morgan-Monroe headquarters.

A stone marker in the Stepp Cemetery says it was established in the early 1800s. Like most early nineteenth-century burial grounds in Southern Indiana, Stepp's thirty-two grave markers are dedicated to mostly young women and children. The cemetery is legendary in Haunted Hoosier circles for paranormal activity that includes a "lady in black" who reportedly hovers over a tree stump that resembles a chair to protect her loved ones who are buried there. The cemetery is not identified on maps or by trail to discourage vandalism.

Like all state forests, Morgan-Monroe is managed for "multiple use," meaning it provides a variety of public uses, from resource extraction—primarily logging—to amenities for the public, including hiking, bird watching, fishing, and camping.

Logging in state and federal forests has been a controversial subject since the trees started maturing in the 1960s and 1970s and public expectations for public land management shifted toward preservation over extraction. Increased logging by the Indiana Department of Natural Resources beginning in the mid-2000s has been particularly contentious, with Morgan-Monroe the site of numerous protests.

64b. Scout Ridge Nature Preserve

The fifteen-acre Scout Ridge Nature Preserve in Morgan-Monroe is located on the edge of a glacial formation created 220,000 to 70,000 years ago during the Illinoian Glacial. Indiana is on the far southern end of this formation. The glaciers here extended into the valleys but did not level the surrounding hills. Glacial boulders can be found in the streambed. The bedrock is Mississippian limestone and shale.

The Scout Ridge woods, which was severely damaged by a 1989 tornado, is predominantly beech-maple, with oak-hickory on the western edge.

Hairy spicebush, pawpaw, maple-leaved arrowwood (a.k.a. maple-leaf viburnum), slippery elm (a.k.a. red elm), and sugar maple are common in the understory. Ferns and wildflowers are prevalent in the herbaceous layer.

A self-guiding Tree Identification Trail through the Scout Ridge preserve has forty-three stations, each featuring a particular tree or forest management area.

64c. Morgan-Monroe Back Country Area / Low Gap Nature Preserve

The twenty-seven-hundred-acre Morgan-Monroe Back Country Area was established in 1981 to provide opportunities for rugged outdoor experiences in primitive areas. At the time the agency

Morgan-Monroe State Forest Backcountry Area, Monroe County.

detailed a back-country vision where visitors would disturb the natural woodland ecosystem as little as possible and experience a forest that appears much the same as it may have 150 years ago.

Overnight backpack camping is permitted in the Back Country Area with no fee. Campers must register at the forest office.

Among the unusual and rare plants and animals living in the Back Country Area are state-endangered cerulean warbler, hooded warbler and worm-eating warbler, both state species of special concern, spotted wintergreen, and bobcat.

Located in the Back Country Area, the 320-acre Low Gap Nature Preserve features one of the largest uninterrupted tracts of high-quality forest in Indiana.

Activities
Hiking Trails: Seven, easy to rugged, 0.5 to 10.1 miles.
Camping: Twenty-nine primitive sites, vault toilets, seasonal drinking water, picnic tables, grills, for a fee; youth tent campground: six sites for scouts or other groups, picnic tables, grills.
Backpacking: Back Country Area, no fee, campers must register at the forest office.
Lakes: Bryant Creek Lake, nine acres; Cherry Lake, four acres; and Prather Lake, four acres. Ramps on Bryant Creek and Cherry Lakes (electric trolling motors only). No swimming.

Other Activities: Fishing, hunting, nature study, photography, picnicking, gold panning, shelters, wildlife watching.

Draper Cabin: Primitive, wooden-floored log cabin. Rented on a day-by-day basis. Reservations required.

Cherry Lake Lodge: Comfortable bed, hot and cold running water, indoor restroom and shower, full kitchen.

Directions

GPS coordinates: 39.326825, -86.472108

From State Road 37

- East on Pine Boulevard / County Road 252S, becoming Old State Road 37 (4.3 miles south of the 37/39 junction at Martinsville, 12.1 miles north of the State Road 37/46 junction at Bloomington) to forest entrance, 2.4 miles

From I-65

- West on State Road 44 at Franklin to State Road 37 at Martinsville, 22.1 miles
- South on 37 to Pine Boulevard / County Road 252S (4.3 miles south of the 37/39 junction at Martinsville), 8.0 miles
- East on Pine Boulevard / County Road 252S to forest entrance, 2.4 miles

65. Atterbury Fish & Wildlife Area / Driftwood State Fishing Area

Owned by Indiana Department of Natural Resources, Division of Fish & Wildlife

The ecosystem of the five-thousand-acre Atterbury Fish & Wildlife Area and Driftwood State Fishing Area features upland woods with more than a dozen creeks, marshes, fens, and lakes totaling 270 acres of water. Located in southern Johnson County at its junction with Brown and Bartholomew Counties, this wildlife complex is located in the far northeastern portion of the Brown County Hills.

The Atterbury complex is drained by Nineveh Creek to the west and Sugar Creek and the Big Blue River to the east. It surrounds a Johnson County park and the U.S. Army's Camp Atterbury facility. The Sugar/Blue confluence in the Driftwood fishing area marks the beginning of the Driftwood River, which some have historically argued should be recognized as the East Fork of the White River's upper stream.

As the property signs on School House Road crediting sportsmen for Atterbury's funding make clear, this environment is managed for and dedicated to hunting, trapping, and fishing. The wildlife management unit includes Atterbury, the 263-acre Driftwood State Fishing Area to the southeast, an additional 1,200 acres of adjacent military land, and a separate 2,057-acre unit in Putnam County.

While the Atterbury and Driftwood areas are managed for game, the ecosystem attracts nearly three hundred animal species and provides abundant opportunities for wildlife viewing and photography. The Honker Haven wetland on School House Road features an elevated wildlife-viewing platform. With more than 250 bird species living in the vicinity, Atterbury/Driftwood is known for excellent songbird viewing year-round. Only the tops of sycamore trees emerge from surfaces at Stone Arch Lake and Teal Marsh.

The site of a World War II prisoner of war (POW) camp, Atterbury is also popular with history buffs. Visitors are greeted at the entrance by a marker called the Atterbury Rock, which was created and signed by German and Italian prisoners in 1942, the year the camp opened as a military training site. Also used in the Korean War, the POW camp closed in 1954.

In 1965 the state purchased more than six thousand acres of the military camp and created the Atterbury Fish & Wildlife Area. Land to the south remains a military training ground for National Guard and Army Reserve units.

Channel catfish, bluegill, redear sunfish, and largemouth bass are common in the water bodies, which are created by ten impoundments. The largest are the seventy-five-acre Pisgah Lake and twenty-five-acre Stone Arch Lake.

Boats, kayaks, and canoes are allowed. Boats are limited to 24-volt electric motors. Stone Arch Lake, Beaver Bottom, and Pisgah Lake have concrete ramps, while Teal Marsh and Mallard Marsh have gravel ramps. Beaver Bottom has an accessible fishing pier.

Atterbury Fish & Wildlife Area, Johnson County.

The Atterbury Fish & Wildlife Area is accessible via three north–south roads between State Road 252 and Hospital Road: Airport Road / Stone Arch Road on the west, County Road 325E / School House Road in the center, and Mauxferry Road on the east. While property maps suggest Mauxferry crosses Pisgah Lake, it doesn't.

Hospital Road connects to the Driftwood Fishing Area east of Atterbury.

Activities
Berry picking, boating, fishing, hiking, hunting, nature study, photography, shooting range, mushroom hunting, walnut gathering, wildlife watching.

Directions
GPS coordinates: 39.396826, -86.042482
From State Road 37
- East on State Road 252 at Martinsville to County Road 325E, 22.0 miles
- South on County Road 325E (becoming School House Road) to Atterbury property line, 1.0 mile

From I-65
- West on State Road 252 at Edinburgh to County Road 325E, 8.8 miles
- South on County Road 325E (becoming School House Road) to Atterbury property line, 1.0 mile

66. Lake Lemon Woods
Owned by Sycamore Land Trust

The fifteen-acre Lake Lemon Woods northeast of Bloomington occupies a steep, forested, hundred-foot hillside on the developed north shore of Lake Lemon. A multiloop trail offers a range of hiking routes, from a short, relatively level walk paralleling the road to strenuous ascents to the ridgetop.

The mature forest produces an open, airy feel, even in summer, when colorful fungi dot the trail. The hilltops offer scenic views of Lake Lemon from late fall through early spring when the deciduous hardwoods have shed their leaves.

The privately developed Lake Lemon was built in 1953 as a reservoir to provide drinking water for the city of Bloomington, which it did until the late 1960s.

Parking is limited to the north shoulder of Wildwood Drive. Sycamore also owns a small lot on the south side of Wildwood Drive.

Activities
Hiking, nature study, photography, wildlife watching.

Directions
GPS coordinates: 39.270243, -86.410948
From State Road 37
- East on Sample Road (11 miles south of the State Road 37/39 junction at Martinsville, 5.8 miles north of the 37/46 junction in Bloomington) to Old State Road 37, 1.3 miles
- North on Old State Road 37 to Anderson Road, 0.5 mile
- East on Anderson Road to North Shore Drive, 5.6 miles
- South on North Shore Drive to North Bay Drive, 0.9 mile
- South on North Bay Drive to Wildwood Drive and the preserve, 0.1 mile

Griffy Lake Nature Preserve, Monroe County.

•

From I-65

- West on State Road 46 at Columbus to State Road 135 at Nashville, 16.0 miles
- North on State Road 135 to State Road 45 at Beanblossom, 5.3 miles
- West on State Road 45 to North Shore Drive, 5.5 miles
- West on North Shore Drive to North Bay Drive, 4.5 miles
- South on North Bay Drive to Wildwood Drive and the preserve, 0.1 mile

67. Griffy Lake Nature Preserve
Owned by City of Bloomington

The 1,179-acre Griffy Lake Nature Preserve conserves the forested ridges and ravines that surround the 109-acre Griffy Lake, just north of Bloomington. The verdant hills and valleys drain into the lake and a 14-acre emergent marsh. The nature preserve is almost entirely contained within the 5,160-acre Griffy Lake Watershed.

A 2008 master plan for the City of Bloomington property identified more than 565 plant species, endangered, threatened and rare among them; nearly 160 bird species; and nearly 50 reptile and amphibian species.

Griffy Lake was built in 1924 to provide drinking water to the Bloomington community, which it did until the 1950s. Acquired through land acquisitions between 1922 and 2007, Griffy Lake Nature Preserve was dedicated in 1991.

The lake was drained in late 2012 to facilitate repairs to the dam, which were completed in December 2013. The Indiana Department of Natural Resources restocked the lake with fish in 2014.

Due to ecosystem damage from an overabundance of white-tailed deer in and around the Griffy preserve, city officials in 2014 approved a controversial annual deer kill.

Activities
Hiking Trails: Five, from 0.3 to 1.5 miles.
Other Activities: Canoe, kayak, and rowboat rentals, fishing, nature study, photography, picnicking, wildlife watching.

Directions
GPS coordinates: 39.198637, -86.513297
From State Road 37
- East on State Road 46 to East Matlock Road, 1.9 miles
- North on Matlock Road (turns into Headley Road) to preserve entrance, 1.3 miles

From I-65
- West on State Road 46 to East Matlock Road in Bloomington, 34.6 miles
- North on Matlock Road (turns into Headley Road) to preserve entrance, 1.3 miles

68. Scarlet Oaks Woods
Owned by Sycamore Land Trust
The sixty-six-acre Scarlet Oak Woods east of Bloomington is a mostly mature open forest with a ridge that runs the property's length on the east side and a deep valley with an intermittent stream on the west side. It is named for its scarlet oak trees, with their bristle-tipped leaves that turn a brilliant red in the fall.

Bordering a unit of Morgan-Monroe State Forest, Scarlet Oaks has a 130-plus-foot elevation drop, from 830 feet at the ridgetop to less than 700 feet in the valley bottom. The ridgetop was cleared

Scarlet Oaks Woods, Monroe County.

a few decades ago and now has younger trees than the rest of the preserve. Fungi and wildflowers add color to the forest floor.

A trail begins at the end of Viking Ridge Road and follows the ridge to the property's southeast corner, with a side branch to the right that leads to the creek bottom.

Activities
Hiking, nature study, photography, wildlife watching.

Directions
GPS coordinates: 39.213465, -86.437483

From State Road 37
- East on State Road 45/46 Bypass at Bloomington to State Road 45, 3.4 miles
- East on State Road 45 to Viking Ridge Road, 5.3 miles
- South on Viking Ridge Road to trail access at the end of the road, 0.7 mile

From I-65
- West on State Road 46 at Columbus, through Nashville, to Brummett's Creek Road near Bloomington, 26.0 miles
- North on Brummett's Creek Road to State Road 45 at Unionville, 5.6 miles

Latimer Woods, Bloomington, Monroe County.

- West on State Road 45 to Viking Ridge Road, 1.7 miles
- South on Viking Ridge Road to trail access at the end of the road, 0.7 mile

69. Latimer Woods
Owned by City of Bloomington

Wedged between an apartment complex, an automobile dealership, and the largest indoor shopping mall in Bloomington, the ten-acre Latimer Woods is an impressive piece of old-growth forest as defined by the DNR in a handout called "Stewardship Notes": "A hardwood forest . . . that contains trees 150 to 200 years old and older is often considered an old growth-forest."

As the interpretive signs throughout the property explain, the Latimer family's "hard work, frugality, and love of the land has kept this tract relatively intact for 145 years," and "some of the trees may pre-date the arrival of European settlers."

This preserve is located on the south side of the creek that ran through original settlers Clarence and Lizzie Latimer's farm. They never cleared the woods, using it instead for nuts, fruits, game, and firewood. The land stayed in the family until Hugh Latimer and his family dedicated it to the Bloomington Community Foundation in 1999, which turned its management over to the City of Bloomington Parks & Recreation Department.

The city manages Latimer Woods for low-impact activities such as research, casual visitation, and education.

The forest canopy is primarily beech-maple, with magnificent examples of white ash, black walnut, tulip poplar, sugar maple, and American beech. The open forest floor features native wildflowers such as spring beauty, prairie trillium, mayapple, Dutchman's breeches, rue anemone, and Jack-in-the-pulpit.

Wildlife that frequents this urban forest include deer, rabbits, squirrels, butterflies, and a wide variety of bird species, including yellow-bellied sapsucker, northern flicker, northern cardinal, Carolina wren, Carolina chickadee, brown thrasher, white-breasted nuthatch, and eastern towhee.

Activities
Hiking Trails: One, easy, 0.38 mile.
Other Activities: Nature study, photography, wildlife watching.

Directions
GPS coordinates: 39.157370, -86.492998
From State Road 37
- East on State Road 46 at Bloomington to Clarizz Boulevard (past College Mall), 4.3 miles
- South on Clarizz to the entrance to the Stratum Apartments, 0.5 mile
- West into the apartments, keep right, preserve entrance is on the right, between buildings

From I-65
- West on State Road 46 at Columbus, through Nashville, to Clarizz Boulevard (before College Mall) in Bloomington, 32.1 miles
- South on Clarizz to the entrance to the Stratum Apartments, 0.5 mile
- West into the apartments, keep right, preserve entrance is on the right, between buildings

70. Dan Willard Woods
Owned by Sycamore Land Trust
The fifteen-acre Dan Willard Woods east of Bloomington is a

mature oak woods with a tall ridge that runs the length of the property and a valley with an intermittent stream that borders a unit of the Morgan-Monroe State Forest.

While beautiful, Willard Woods is not user-friendly, starting with a lack of parking. A deer trail leads up a steep hill behind the sign, but there is no trail on the ridgetop, which leads to a unit of Morgan-Monroe.

The preserve is named after the late Indiana University School of Public and Environmental Affairs professor Dan Willard, also a past president of the Sycamore Land Trust. A memorial sign sits at the bottom of the hill near Mount Gilead Road.

Activities
Hiking, nature study, photography, wildlife watching.

Directions
GPS coordinates: 39.197120, -86.435964
From State Road 37
- East on State Road 45/46 Bypass at Bloomington to State Road 45, 3.4 miles
- East on State Road 45 to Mount Gilead Road, 2.3 miles
- South on Mount Gilead Road to the preserve, 2.5 miles
- Parking is limited to the shoulder of Mount Gilead Road.

From I-65
- West on State Road 46 at Columbus to Getty's Creek Road near Bloomington, 27.8 miles
- North on Getty's Creek Road to Mount Gilead Road, 2.8 miles
- North on Mount Gilead Road to the preserve, 0.3 mile
- Parking is limited to the shoulder of Mount Gilead Road.

71. Campbell Preserve
Owned by Sycamore Land Trust
The twenty-seven-acre Campbell Preserve east of Bloomington features a deep wooded ravine and an intermittent stream that runs the length of the property, which borders a unit of the

Morgan-Monroe State Forest located to the south and east. The state forest has a parking area by the southwest corner of the Campbell preserve. There are no trails on the Campbell Preserve.

Activities

Hiking, nature study, photography, wildlife watching.

Directions

GPS coordinates: 39.196826, -86.417062

From State Road 37

- East on State Road 45/46 Bypass at Bloomington to State Road 45, 3.4 miles
- East on State Road 45 to Mount Gilead Road, 2.3 miles
- South on Mount Gilead Road to Birdie Galyan Road, 3.5 miles
- South on Birdie Galyan Road to the preserve, 1.0 mile

From I-65

- West on State Road 46 at Columbus to Getty's Creek Road near Bloomington, 27.8 miles
- North on Getty's Creek Road to Mount Gilead Road, 2.8 miles
- East on Mount Gilead Road to Birdie Galyan Road, 1.3 miles
- South on Birdie Galyan Road to the preserve, 1.0 mile

72. Pizzo Preserve

Owned by Sycamore Land Trust

The twenty-six-acre Pizzo Preserve east of Bloomington consists of steep, two-hundred-foot forested slopes that rise above the North Fork of the Salt Creek, just north of the Northfork Waterfowl Resting Area. A trail begins at a curve on Gross Road and ascends a steep hill to a T. The left branch continues uphill to a field on property owned by the Department of Natural Resources (DNR). The right branch dead-ends at the preserve's west border.

Historically, the property was part of a large farm, much of which became part of the Monroe Lake floodplain and is now managed by the DNR. Dr. Anthony (Tony) and Patricia (Patty) Pizzo purchased the preserve land in the mid-1960s and owned it until 2007, when they donated it to Sycamore Land Trust.

When the trees are free of leaves, the ridgetop offers magnificent views of the Salt Creek Valley below.

Parking is limited. The trail begins 0.1 mile west of Friendship Road.

Activities
Hiking, nature study, photography, wildlife watching.

Directions
GPS coordinates: 39.137972, -86.414758
- Park on Friendship Road. Trail is on Gross Road, just west of Friendship.

From State Road 37
- East on State Road 46 at Bloomington to Friendship Road, 9.3 miles
- South on Friendship Road to Gross Road, 1.1 miles

From I-65
- West on State Road 46 at Columbus, through Nashville, to Friendship Road east of Bloomington, 27.2 miles
- South on Friendship Road to Gross Road, 1.1 miles

73. Stillwater Marsh / Northfork Waterfowl Resting Areas, Monroe Lake

The Stillwater Marsh / Northfork Waterfowl Resting Areas on Monroe Lake together comprise one of three lowland areas along the Salt Creek's upper forks where public access and hunting are limited. The Stillwater and Northfork marshes are situated along the Salt Creek's North Fork in eastern Monroe County and attract both game and nongame species.

Northfork is just east of Bloomington. Two old roadbeds lead to two small parking lots. (See Directions below.) The road to the south leads to the creek. The road to the west leads to the wetlands.

Stillwater, which features a wildlife-viewing platform with benches, adjoins Northfork to the east. The viewing platform is open year-round. Several dirt roads along McGowan Road lead into the marshes.

The marsh areas are closed to the general public from October 1 to April 15.

See no. 81, Middlefork Waterfowl Resting Area, Monroe Lake, and no. 88, Southfork Waterfowl Resting Area, Monroe Lake, for more details on the WRAs. See no. 85, Monroe Lake, for more details on the lake.

Activities
Boating, canoeing, fishing, hiking, hunting, nature study, photography, wildlife watching.

Directions to the Northfork Waterfowl Resting Area
GPS coordinates: 39.129270, -86.396996
From State Road 37
- East on State Road 46 at Bloomington to Friendship Road, 9.3 miles
- South on Friendship Road to the marshes, 2.0 miles
- Friendship Road forks along the area's perimeter, with small parking lots on each path.

From I-65
- West on State Road 46 at Columbus, through Nashville, to Friendship Road east of Bloomington, 27.2 miles
- South on Friendship Road to the marshes, 2.0 miles
- Friendship Road forks along the area's perimeter, with small parking lots on each path.

Directions to Stillwater Marsh
GPS coordinates: 39.143227, -86.392803
From State Road 37
- East on State Road 46 at Bloomington to Kent Road, 9.7 miles
- South on Kent Road to McGowan Road, 0.3 mile
- South on McGowan Road to wildlife-viewing area and marshes, 0.5 mile

From I-65
- West on State Road 46 at Columbus, through Nashville, to Kent Road east of Bloomington, 26.7 miles
- South on Kent Road to McGowan Road, 0.3 mile
- South on McGowan Road to wildlife-viewing area and marshes, 0.5 mile

Trevlac Bluffs Nature Preserve, Brown County.

74. Trevlac Bluffs Nature Preserve
Owned by Sycamore Land Trust

The 233-acre Trevlac Bluffs Nature Preserve in northwestern Brown County features a towering, two-hundred-foot bluff above Beanblossom Creek with a rare stand of native hemlock trees, more than one hundred acres of forested wetlands in the Beanblossom Creek floodplain, and more than a mile of the creek itself.

Trevlac Bluffs adjoins Yellowwood State Forest and, along with other nearby state and national forests and Brown County State Park, is a critical forest block for breeding migratory songbirds.

The hemlock stand, one of roughly twenty in Indiana, is a remnant from a cooler, early postglacial climate that existed thousands of years ago. Hemlocks are now a more northerly species.

The forested uplands, whose forest type is moist–dry, supports a wide diversity of species, including white oak, black oak, northern red oak, shagbark hickory, and sugar maple. Several trees measure close to three feet in diameter.

Beanblossom is the primary feeder creek for Lake Lemon, about a half mile downstream. Lake Lemon is the backup water source for the city of Bloomington.

Trevlac Bluffs is a dedicated State Nature Preserve in recognition of the statewide significance of its natural communities.

Sycamore Land Trust assumed ownership of Trevlac Bluffs in 2011 and is developing trails. The preserve borders private property. Care should be taken to avoid trespassing.

Activities

Hiking, nature study, photography, wildlife watching.

Directions

GPS coordinates: 39.266201, -86.330529

From State Road 37

- East on State Road 45/46 at Bloomington to State Road 45, 3.4 miles
- East on State Road 45, through Trevlac, to the preserve, 14.7 miles

From I-65

- West on State Road 46 at Columbus to State Road 135 at Nashville, 15.9 miles
- North on State Road 135 to State Road 45 at Beanblossom, 5.3 miles
- West on State Road 45 to the preserve, 4.9 miles

75. Yellowwood State Forest

Owned by Indiana Department of Natural Resources,
Division of Forestry

Situated between Morgan-Monroe State Forest, Brown County State Park, Monroe Lake, and the Hoosier National Forest, Yellowwood State Forest's 23,326 acres are some of the most pristine and rugged in Southern Indiana. And like most public lands in the state, Yellowwood's unique upland forest ecosystems survive in part due to the inhospitable terrain—steep ridges and valleys from one hundred to three hundred feet deep—and decades of public stewardship.

Many of the amenities available today—three lakes, a shelter house, and a residence, for example—were built by the New Deal–era Civilian Conservation Corps (CCC). The 133-acre, 30-foot-deep Yellowwood Lake was completed in 1939. The

Yellowwood State Forest, Brown County.

forest itself owes its resurgence to CCC workers who planted fast-growing jack pine, shortleaf pine, white pine, and scotch pine to reverse the erosion, as well as black locust, black walnut, white oak, and northern red oak to rejuvenate the native hardwoods. Jack pine and white pine are still rare.

As the government workers completed their missions and the forest began recovering, the federal government leased the Yellowwood acreage to the state to create the state forest in 1940, deeding it permanently in 1956. Yellowwood today is composed of separate parcels scattered throughout the area.

This state forest draws its name from the state threatened yellowwood tree, which lives in scattered locations in the Mid-South and is more typical of the Ozark and Southern Appalachian Mountains. The name reflects its hard, dense, bright-yellow heartwood. Rare as far north as Indiana, this understory tree grows only on moist, sheltered, steep, northeast-facing slopes on fewer than two hundred acres near Crooked Creek Lake. A specimen is planted at the Forest Office.

Yellowwood's trail system includes the bulk of the forty-two-mile Tecumseh Trail, which starts at the Morgan-Monroe State Forest office and ends near Monroe Lake where Panther Creek meets Crooked Creek. The trail, built between 1998 and

2002 by the Hoosier Hikers Council, is named after the Shawnee Indian chief Tecumseh, who organized eastern tribes in a last stand against the Europeans in the early 1800s.

Yellowwood Lake is known as an excellent fishing spot, with boat launches at the north and south ends. Motors are limited to electric trolling only, and rowboat rental is available seasonally.

The National Audubon Society has designated the Yellowwood–Brown County State Park area a Global Important Bird Area for supporting "one of the largest populations of forest-dependent neotropical migratory birds in the state of Indiana" and a diversity of species that "may be unparalleled when compared to the mature forests located within the Highland Rim Natural Region," according to its website.

State-endangered cerulean warbler, as well as black-and-white warbler, hooded warbler, and worm-eating warbler, all state species of special concern, have been identified at Morgan-Monroe. Other noteworthy species that live in or migrate through include Acadian flycatcher, eastern wood-pewee, yellow-throated warbler, blue-winged warbler, prairie warbler, Kentucky warbler, yellow-billed cuckoo, red-eyed vireo, scarlet tanager, yellow-breasted chat, wood thrush, and yellow-throated vireo.

Other wildlife include deer, grouse, turkey, squirrel, fox, raccoon, and snake, including state-endangered timber rattlesnake and northern copperhead, both of which are venomous.

Activities
Hiking Trails: Six, from 0.5 to 4.5 miles, one wheelchair accessible. The bulk of the forty-two-mile Tecumseh Trail passes through Yellowwood and follows some of the other trails in places.

Bridle Trails: Five, ranging from 2.0 to 8.6 miles. Annual horse use tag is required.

Camping: Eighty primitive sites, one carry-in tent site, vault toilets, drinking water, ten horse sites.

Other Activities: Fishing, hunting, gold panning (permit required), nature study, photography, picnicking, playground, wildlife watching.

Directions
GPS coordinates: 39.182621, -86.337040
From State Road 37
- East on State Road 46 at Bloomington to Yellowwood Road, 14.6 miles
- North on Yellowwood Road (turn left after the bridge) to Yellowwood Lake Road, 2.1 miles

From I-65
- West on State Road 46 at Columbus, through Nashville, to Yellowwood Road, 21.8 miles
- North on Yellowwood Road (turn left after the bridge) to Yellowwood Lake Road, 2.1 miles

76. Hitz-Rhodehamel Woods

Owned by The Nature Conservancy

The 484-acre Hitz-Rhodehamel Woods north of Nashville is a mature, high-quality oak forest that spans sharp ridgetops and steep ravines with two-hundred-foot descents along a narrow, twisty, scenic road that passes artist studios and other curious dwellings.

A well-marked, rugged-plus trail with switchbacks winds through the steep terrain, offering magnificent views. The trail is narrow, with two two-hundred-foot climbs along some sharp relief, and is crisscrossed by a variety of former trails.

The dry ridges support chestnut-oak forests, while the ravines support white oak forests. Migrating warblers perform high-pitched serenades in spring. Wildflowers color the forest floor in spring and line the trail in summer. Autumn colors electrify the canopy.

The chestnut-oak woods features an open understory with large whorled pogonia, on the state watch list, painted sedge, early low blueberry, and huckleberry, along with diverse mosses and lichens.

Hitz-Rhodehamel management efforts emphasize forest-interior birds like the state-endangered cerulean warbler and worm-eating warbler, a state species of special concern, along with yellow-billed cuckoo, whip-poor-will, eastern wood-pewee, wood thrush, Louisiana waterthrush, and Kentucky warbler. Other forest wildlife includes deer, turkey, coyote, and woodpecker.

Hitz-Rhodehamel Woods, Brown County.

Activities

Hiking Trails: One, rugged, three-mile loop.

Other Activities: Nature study, photography, wildlife watching.

Directions

The preserve is on both sides of the road. A small parking area is located on the north side of the road. Look for a wooden preserve sign. The trailhead is located at the east end of the parking area.

GPS coordinates: 39.254945, -86.229053

From State Road 37

- East on State Road 46 at Bloomington to State Road 135 at Nashville, 20.5 miles
- North on State Road 135 to Greasy Creek Road, 4.4 miles
- South on Greasy Creek Road to Freeman Ridge Road, 150 feet
- East on Freeman Ridge Road to trailhead on the right side of the road, 1.2 miles

From I-65

- West on State Road 46 at Columbus to State Road 135 at Nashville, 16.0 miles
- North on State Road 135 to Greasy Creek Road, 4.4 miles
- South on Greasy Creek Road to Freeman Ridge Road, 150 feet
- East on Freeman Ridge Road to trailhead on the right side of the road, 1.2 miles

77. Selma Steele State Nature Preserve

Owned by Indiana State Museums and Historic Sites

The ninety-two-acre Selma Steele State Nature Preserve between Bloomington and Nashville protects a high-quality, moist and dry–moist upland forest community with two deep ravines, formed by two seasonally flowing streams that cut through Brown County Hills' soft bedrock. Selma, whose husband was legendary artist T. C. Steele, donated the preserve and entire tract—now the T. C. Steele State Historic Site—to the state in 1945 with the proviso: "I trust that the whole surrounding forest will be preserved."

Selma's own Whippoorwill Haunt Trail begins on the preserve's south end across from the Steele site's upper parking lot and traverses a narrow path through its wooded hillsides. The Whippoorwill ends in the valley, where it meets the Peckerwood Trail, which emerges at the preserve's north end by the historic site's stone entry arches. Rich undergrowth provides a colorful wildflower display in the spring.

While Chicago painter Adolph Schulz, who first encountered the Brown County hills in 1900, is considered the Nashville Art Colony's founder, Hoosier Group impressionist T. C. Steele was the first major artist to settle in the county. He and Selma purchased the ridgetop property in 1907 for their residence and studio. They chose the site in part because of its scenic beauty.

The original 211-acre Steele property, including the state-dedicated nature preserve, is part of the state historic site, which also includes a studio with more than fifty paintings on display; the couple's home, the House of the Singing Winds, with original furnishings; the historic Dewar Log Cabin; and five hiking trails. Selma's world-famous gardens have been restored.

The Selma Steele State Nature Preserve and T. C. Steele State Historic Site are open to the public. There are admission fees for building tours, including the home and studio.

Activities

Hiking Trails: Two, 0.5 to 0.75 mile, moderate to difficult.

Brown County State Park, Brown County.

Other Activities: Nature study, hiking, photography, wildlife watching.

Directions
GPS coordinates: 39.129460, -86.349084
From State Road 37
- East on State Road 46 at Bloomington to T. C. Steele Road, 12.7 miles
- South on T. C. Steele Road to T. C. Steele Historic Site, 1.7 miles

From I-65
- West on State Road 46 at Columbus, through Nashville, to T. C. Steele Road, 23.7 miles
- South on T. C. Steele Road to T. C. Steele Historic Site, 1.7 miles

78. Brown County State Park
Owned by Indiana Department of Natural Resources,
Division of State Parks & Reservoirs
The view from the West Lookout Tower just inside the 15,776-acre Brown County State Park's West Gate speaks volumes about the near seamless connections between the park's present and past. The 360-degree vista across one of the Midwest's largest

expanses of contiguous forestland showcases the scenic wonder that has attracted the creative, curious, and adventurous since before the early twentieth century, when artists like Adolph Schulz and T. C. Steele arrived.

Brown County is not only Indiana's biggest state park but also the most popular. High among the reasons for its acclaim are the scenic views from the two lookout towers and various overlooks throughout the park, especially in the fall, when visitors from around the world flock to the park for the annual changing of the leaves. The fire tower by the park office on Weed Patch Hill sits 1,058 feet above sea level and is one of the state's highest elevations.

These vistas, along with two lakes, shelter houses, trails, and other improvements, were built by crews from the New Deal–era Civilian Conservation Corps (CCC) after the park was established in 1929. The CCC crews also planted black locust, black walnut, and various pine and spruce trees to reclaim the land.

The park has been nicknamed the Little Smokies for its foggy ravines' resemblance to the Great Smoky Mountains.

Historical records from the late 1880s say bears, wolves, and cougars still roamed the Brown County Hills in the mid-nineteenth century. Local legend says a couple bears called Weed Patch Hill home.

The park's wildlife today are forest species, including white-tailed deer, raccoon, and gray squirrel, and a wide variety of bird species—American robin, white-breasted nuthatch, blue jay, northern cardinal, dark-eyed junco, American crow, wild turkey, and many nesting neotropicals, including warblers, vireos, and tanagers.

Snakes, including the northern copperhead and state-endangered timber rattlesnake, both venomous, also inhabit Brown County State Park.

The nature center includes a snake exhibit, bird-watching room, and other displays, with naturalist services available year-round.

The horse camp entrance is off State Road 135 South. RVs use the West Gate.

Activities

Hiking Trails: Twelve, easy to rugged, 0.75 to 3.5 miles.

Mountain Bike Trails: Twenty miles.

Bridle Trails: Seventy miles, saddle barn, escorted rides.

Camping: 401 electric sites, 28 nonelectric sites, 60 rally sites, 118 electric horse sites, 86 nonelectric horse sites, youth tent areas, camp store, dumping station.

Lodging: Abe Martin Lodge, eighty-four rooms, dining room, indoor water park.

Cabins: Twenty family housekeeping cabins, two wheelchair accessible, available year-round with electric or wood heating and air-conditioning, furnished with dishes, kitchen utensils, pots and pans, and linens, blankets, and pillows. Twenty-four sleeping cabins with a total of 56 bedrooms.

Other Activities: Country store, fishing lakes with fishing and ice fishing, nature center / interpretive naturalist services, nature study, open fields, photography, picnicking, playground equipment, shelter houses (reservations), swimming pool, tennis courts, wildlife watching.

Directions

GPS coordinates: 39.169024, -86.221667

From State Road 37

- East on State Road 46 at Bloomington to park's West Gatehouse, 18.5 miles

From I-65

- West on State Road 46 at Columbus to the park's North Gatehouse, 14.5 miles

79. Laura Hare Nature Preserve at Downey Hill

Owned by Sycamore Land Trust

The six-hundred-acre Laura Hare Nature Preserve at Downey Hill east of Brown County State Park offers moderate to rugged hikes through precipitous, V-shaped Brown County hills and valleys that drop one hundred to two hundred feet.

Nearly a square mile in size, the preserve east of Nashville, just past Gnawbone, is crossed by other old roads that lead past

Laura Hare Nature Preserve at Downey Hill, Brown County.

old homesite plots along side ridges. It also has several seasonal ponds and intermittent streams deep in the valleys.

The Laura Hare preserve is part of a contiguous, eighteen-thousand-acre block of protected forest that includes Brown County State Park and Gnawbone Camp, which the state protects under a permanent conservation easement.

The old county roads that cross Laura Hare are wide and easy to follow. The main roadbed from the parking lot that traverses the property from west to east is a moderate, four-fifths-mile hike along a nine-hundred-foot-high ridgetop.

The Hoosier Hikers Council built a two-mile loop trail (projected for opening in mid-2016) that leads from the parking area to an old county road on the property's east side and back.

Access to private property within the preserve's boundaries is blocked by a chain.

The site is named after the Laura Hare Charitable Trust, which contributed a grant for its purchase.

Activities
Hiking, nature study, photography, wildlife watching.

Austin and Mary Ann Gardner Memorial Woods, Brown County.

Directions
GPS coordinates: 39.173080, -86.146056
From State Road 37
- East on State Road 46 at Bloomington, through Nashville, to Valley Branch Road, 26.2 miles
- South on Valley Branch Road to the preserve, 1.5 miles

From I-65
- West on State Road 46 at Columbus to Valley Branch Road east of Nashville, 10.9 miles
- South on Valley Branch Road to the preserve, 1.5 miles

80. Austin and Mary Ann Gardner Memorial Woods
Owned by Sycamore Land Trust

The sixty-two-acre Austin and Mary Ann Gardner Memorial Woods features a rugged, forested landscape with a terraced slope face that overlooks a deep valley on the edge of Monroe Lake in southwestern Brown County. Its steep slopes and mature woods border the Hoosier National Forest to the north and east. A lake inlet separates five acres that are only accessible by boat or hiking trail through the Hoosier.

This natural area preserves the memory of its former

owners, Austin "Bud" and Mary Ann Gardner. The family placed a stone bench on the remote, five-acre parcel to provide a place of contemplation.

Gardner Woods has no parking area or trail system. Parking is along the side of Elkins Road. The hike from ridge to valley is scenic and steep. The surrounding area is private family residences, with boundary lines marked with No Trespassing signs. Sycamore Land Trust signs clearly mark the property boundaries.

Activities
Hiking, nature study, photography, wildlife watching.

Directions
GPS coordinates: 39.083228, -86.369143
From State Road 37
- East on State Road 46 at Bloomington to T. C. Steele Road, 12.7 miles
- South on T. C. Steele Road to Gilmore Ridge Road, 1.9 miles
- South on Gilmore Ridge Road to Elkins Road, 3.0 miles
- South on Elkins Road (becoming County Line Road), bear left twice, to the preserve, 1.5 miles

From I-65
- West on State Road 46 at Columbus, through Nashville, to T. C. Steele Road, 23.7 miles
- South on T. C. Steele Road to Gilmore Ridge Road, 1.9 miles
- South on Gilmore Ridge Road to Elkins Road, 3.0 miles
- South on Elkins Road (becoming County Line Road), bear left twice, to the preserve, 1.5 miles

81. Middlefork Waterfowl Resting Area, Monroe Lake
The Middlefork Waterfowl Resting Area is one of three lowland areas along the Salt Creek's upper forks where public access and hunting are limited. Middlefork is located in southwestern Brown County and has limited parking. (See Directions below.)

The marsh area is closed to the general public from October 1 to April 15.

See no. 73, Stillwater Marsh / Northfork Waterfowl Resting Areas, and no. 88, Southfork Waterfowl Resting Area, Monroe

Lake, for more details on the WRAs. See no. 85, Monroe Lake, for more details on the lake.

Activities
Boating, canoeing, fishing, hiking, hunting, nature study, photography, wildlife watching.

Directions to Middlefork Waterfowl Resting Area
GPS coordinates: 39.077794, -86.346434
- Parking is limited to one car at each access point.

From State Road 37
- East on State Road 46 at Bloomington to T. C. Steele Road, 12.7 miles
- South on T. C. Steele Road to Gilmore Ridge Road, 1.9 miles
- South on Gilmore Ridge Road to Deckard Ridge Road, 1.4 miles
- Southeast on Deckard Ridge Road, just past the intersection with Axsom Branch Road, to the dead end and the waterfowl area boundary, 3.7 miles
- Or go south on Axsom Branch Road to the dead end, 1.2 miles

From I-65
- West on State Road 46 at Columbus, through Nashville, to T. C. Steele Road, 23.7 miles
- South on T. C. Steele Road to Gilmore Ridge Road, 1.9 miles
- South on Gilmore Ridge Road to Deckard Ridge Road, 1.4 miles
- Southeast on Deckard Ridge Road, just past the intersection with Axsom Branch Road, to the dead end and the waterfowl area boundary, 3.7 miles
- Or go south on Axsom Branch Road to the dead end, 1.2 miles
- Parking is limited to one car at each access point.

82. Crooked Creek Marsh, Monroe Lake
The Crooked Creek Marsh in southwestern Brown County is accessible by foot and by boat from the Crooked Creek State Recreation Area (SRA) on the Salt Creek's Middle Fork on Monroe Lake. A boat ramp is located at the Crooked Creek SRA

Crooked Creek Marsh, Monroe Lake, Brown County.

parking lot. An old roadbed located just east of the lot serves as a footpath to the marsh area. The road is closed to vehicles.

The marsh area is open year-round. It is located between Stillwater Marsh / Northfork and Middlefork Waterfowl Resting Areas (WRAs). Care should be taken to avoid crossing the WRA boundaries when those areas are closed.

See no. 73, Stillwater Marsh / Northfork Waterfowl Resting Areas, no. 81, Middlefork Waterfowl Resting Area, Monroe Lake, and no. 88, Southfork Waterfowl Resting Area, Monroe Lake, for more details on Monroe marshes. See no. 85, Monroe Lake, for more details on the lake.

Activities
Boat launch ramp, canoeing, fishing, hiking, hunting, nature study, photography, wildlife watching.

Directions to Crooked Creek Marsh
GPS coordinates: 39.094259, -86.329758

From State Road 37

- East on State Road 46 at Bloomington to T. C. Steele Road, 12.7 miles
- South on T. C. Steele Road to Crooked Creek SRA, 4.7 miles

From I-65

- West on State Road 46 at Columbus, through Nashville, to T. C. Steele Road, 23.7 miles
- South on T. C. Steele Road to Crooked Creek SRA, 4.7 miles

83. Maines Pond Watchable Wildlife Site, Hoosier National Forest, Pleasant Run Unit

Owned by U.S. Forest Service

The five-acre Maines Pond Watchable Wildlife Site is located in southeastern Brown County on the Jackson county line. Natural features include a small pond, open grasslands with prairie grasses, wildflowers, brush and cedar thickets, and patches of small trees.

Watchable Wildlife Sites are areas where the odds of seeing wildlife are high.

A mowed pipeline corridor behind the pond attracts a variety of small mammals and songbirds. Meadowlarks, bluebirds, sparrows, quail, and other birds are also present.

Fishing and hunting are permitted at Maines Pond.

See no. 86, Hoosier National Forest, for more details on the national forest.

Activities

Fishing, hunting, nature study, photography, wildlife watching.

Directions

GPS coordinates: 39.054187, -86.164230

From State Road 37

- East on State Road 46 at Bloomington, through Nashville, to State Road 135 at Gnaw Bone, 24.5 miles
- South on State Road 135 to Houston Road, 13.7 miles
- South on Houston Road to Maines Pond, 2.0 miles

From I-65

- West on State Road 46 at Columbus to State Road 135 at Gnaw Bone, 12.9 miles

- South on State Road 135 to Houston Road, 13.7 miles
- South on Houston Road to Maines Pond, 2.0 miles

84. Sundance Lake, Hoosier National Forest, Pleasant Run Unit

Owned by U.S. Forest Service

The Forest Service chose one of the most scenic locations on the forest when it built the 5.3-acre Sundance Lake in 1992 to expand fishing options in southeastern Brown County. Located near Spurgeons Corner and Becks Grove, the site is named for a Native American spiritual dance that is held nearby each year. Sundance Lake has accessible fishing piers. Swimming is not permitted.

See no. 86, Hoosier National Forest, for more details on the national forest.

Activities
Fishing, hunting, nature study, photography, wildlife watching.

Directions
GPS coordinates: 39.060472, -86.109912
From State Road 37
- East on State Road 46 at Bloomington to State Road 135 at Gnaw Bone, 20.5 miles
- South on State Road 135 to County Road 1190N, 16.0 miles
- East on County Road 1190N to gravel road on left, 3.0 miles (County Road 1190N bears east [left] at intersection with County Road 450W at 0.7 mile and east again [left] at intersection with County Road 400W at another 0.9 mile)
- North (left) on gravel road, bear right to lake, 0.2 mile

From I-65
- West on State Road 46 at Columbus to State Road 135 at Gnaw Bone, 12.9 miles
- South on State Road 135 to County Road 1190N, 16.0 miles
- East on County Road 1190N to ninety-degree intersection with County Road 450W, 0.7 mile
- East (left) on County Road 1190N to intersection with County Road 400W, 0.9 mile

Monroe Lake, Monroe County.

- East (left) County Road 1190N to gravel road on left, 1.4 miles
- North (left) on gravel road, bear right to lake, 0.2 mile

85. Monroe Lake

Owned by U.S. Army Corps of Engineers, managed by
Indiana Department of Natural Resources,
Division of State Parks & Reservoirs

As Indiana's largest water body, the 10,750-acre Monroe Lake has the reputation as the state's premier outdoor getaway. With nine boat ramps, nine State Recreation Areas, one Federal Recreation Area (with one of the nine ramps), three Waterfowl Resting Areas, three marinas, and a resort, all surrounded by thousands of acres of pristine upland woods, deep ravines, and feeder creeks, Monroe offers just about any activity a nature lover might desire.

Monroe Lake, more commonly known as Lake Monroe, snakes west from the Middle Fork of the Salt Creek in southeastern Brown County to the Monroe Dam on Salt Creek in southern Monroe County. Salt Creek has three forks—North, Middle, and South—that meet to create the large pool just east of the State Road 446 Causeway. Under a cooperative arrangement, the lake is managed by the state DNR.

Monroe Lake's 441-square-mile watershed extends beyond Monroe and Brown into Bartholomew, Jackson, and Lawrence Counties. According to a 1996 study by the Indiana University School of Public and Environmental Affairs, 90 percent of it is forested. That includes acreage in Yellowwood State Forest and the Hoosier National Forest.

Monroe Lake is recognized as one of the state's premier bird-watching sites, with more than three hundred species documented in its environs. Common birds that live in or migrate through the lake's ecosystems include ducks, geese, herons, turkeys, grouse, woodpeckers, doves, vultures, hawks, grebes, loons, pelicans, gulls, and terns. Bald eagles, a state species of special concern, nest at several sites around the lake. The Indiana Department of Natural Resources manages three up-creek marshes as Waterfowl Resting Areas for migrating waterfowl. (See no. 73, Stillwater Marsh / Northfork Waterfowl Resting Areas, no. 81, Middlefork Waterfowl Resting Area, Monroe Lake, and no. 88, Southfork Waterfowl Resting Area, Monroe Lake, for more details.)

For management purposes, Monroe is divided into two sections, bisected by the State Road 446 Causeway.

East of the causeway from the Paynetown State Recreation Area, the lake is managed for wildlife and low-impact human activity. Motorboats are allowed, but they are limited to idle speed only. The 12,953-acre Charles C. Deam Wilderness Area, the only federally designated wilderness in the state, sits on the lake's south side just past the Cutright State Recreation Area. (See no. 87a, Charles C. Deam Wilderness Area, for details.) The waterfowl preserves are located upstream along the Salt Creek's North, Middle, and South Forks.

West, from the causeway past the developed Fairfax State Recreation Area to the Monroe Dam, the lake has plenty of wild and natural areas. But it is more developed and managed for human recreation. Speedboats and waterskiing are allowed on the lake surface. The Fairfax State Recreation Area includes a swimming beach and full-amenity resort. Swimming beaches are also located at Paynetown State Recreation Area and Hardin Ridge Recreation Area in the Hoosier National Forest.

The National Audubon Society has designated Monroe Lake as a Global Important Bird Area, citing state-endangered cerulean warbler, along with hooded warbler, worm-eating warbler, bald eagle, and red-shouldered hawk, all state species of special concern. Other noteworthy species that live in or migrate through include Acadian flycatcher, American black duck, blue-winged warbler, chuck-will's-widow, Kentucky warbler, prothonotary warbler, Louisiana waterthrush, northern pintail, red-headed woodpecker, ring-necked duck, rusty blackbird, whip-poor-will, and wood thrush.

The upland forests and fields surrounding the lake feature abundant wildlife, including deer, turkeys, squirrels, butterflies, snakes, coyotes, rabbits, raccoons, and foxes.

The lake waters support thirty game and nongame fish species, including bluegill, largemouth bass, striped bass, channel catfish, black crappie, white crappie, and walleye.

The Army Corps dammed Salt Creek between 1960 and 1965 to create Monroe Lake and control downstream flooding. Providing drinking water, recreational opportunities, and wildlife management were also priorities.

The lake has nine State Recreation Areas (SRA) and one Federal Recreation Area that offer a variety of outdoor opportunities. They are listed here in alphabetical order.

Allen's Creek SRA, State Road 446: Boat launch, pit toilets, hiking trail.

Cartop SRA, Stipp Road: Cartop boat launching.

Crooked Creek SRA, far south end of T. C. Steele Road in eastern Monroe County: Boat launch, pit toilets.

Cutright SRA, State Road 446: Boat launch, boat rental, marina, picnicking, pit toilets, shelter.

Fairfax SRA, Pointe Road or Fairfax Road: Beach, boat launch, boat rental, lodging, marina, picnicking, playground, restrooms, shelters, hiking trail, showers.

Hardin Ridge Recreation Area, Hoosier National Forest,

Hardin Ridge Recreation Area, Hoosier National Forest, Monroe County.

Chapel Hill Road: Camping, beach, boat launch, restrooms, shelter, summer activities director.

Moore's Creek SRA, South Shields Ridge Road: Boat launch, shelter, pit toilets.

Paynetown SRA, State Road 446, accessible: Beach, boat launch, boat rentals, camping, hiking, activity center and interpretive naturalist service, marina, picnicking, playground, restrooms, showers, store, visitors' center (office), shelters, hiking trails, fishing pier.

Pine Grove SRA, State Road 446: Boat launch, pit toilets.

Salt Creek SRA, Monroe Dam Road: Boat launch, pit toilets.

The dam and tailwater area on Monroe Dam Road is not classified as an SRA, as it is operated by the U.S. Army Corps of Engineers. But it offers picnicking, a playground, restrooms, shelters, an overlook, and a visitors' center (office).

DNR manages most of the shallow eastern reaches of Monroe Lake as wetland habitat for migrating waterfowl.

See no. 73, Stillwater Marsh / Northfork Waterfowl Resting

Areas, no. 81, Middlefork Waterfowl Resting Area, Monroe Lake, and no. 88, Southfork Waterfowl Resting Area, Monroe Lake, for more details on the WRAs.

Activities
Hiking Trails: Five, easy to moderate, 0.5 to 1.75 miles.
Camping: 226 nonelectric sites, 94 electric sites, camp store, dumping station.
Other Activities: Three beaches, nine boat launch ramps, canoeing, marinas, fishing boat and pontoon rentals; berry, nut, and mushroom collecting; fishing, ice fishing, fishing piers; hunting and trapping; lodging; activity center / interpretive naturalist services; nature study; photography; picnicking / shelter house (reservations); playgrounds; resort; swimming; waterskiing; wildlife watching.

Directions to Monroe Lake Dam, U.S. Army Corps of Engineers Office
GPS coordinates: 39.006907, -86.512829
From State Road 37
- East at the Harrodsburg Exit on Monroe Dam Road, between Bloomington and Bedford, to the dam and office, 1.8 miles

From State Road 65
- West on State Road 46 at Columbus to State Road 37 in Bloomington, 37.6 miles
- South on State Road 37 to Harrodsburg Exit, 12.7 miles
- East on Monroe Dam Road to the dam and office, 1.8 miles

Directions to Fairfax State Recreation Area
GPS coordinates: 39.030713, -86.489921
From State Road 37
- East on Smithville Road (south of Bloomington) to Fairfax Road, 1.8 miles
- South on Fairfax to the lake, 2.9 miles

From I-65
- West on State Road 46 at Columbus, through Nashville, to State Road 446 at Bloomington, 31.1 miles

- South on State Road 446 to Moore's Pike, 1.0 mile
- West on Moore's Pike to South Henderson Street (Walnut Street Pike), 3.0 miles
- South on South Henderson Street to Fairfax Road, 3.0 miles
- East on Fairfax Road to the lake, 6.0 miles

Directions to Paynetown State Recreation Area, Monroe Lake Office
GPS coordinates: 39.092226, -86.423335
From State Road 37
- East on State Road 46 at Bloomington to State Road 446, 5.3 miles
- South on State Road 446 to the recreation area, 6.2 miles

From I-65
- West on State Road 46 at Columbus, through Nashville, to State Road 446 at Bloomington, 31.1 miles
- South on State Road 446 to the recreation area, 6.2 miles

86. Hoosier National Forest
Owned by U.S. Forest Service

With 202,000 acres stretching from the shores of Monroe Lake to the Ohio River, the Hoosier National Forest (HNF) is Indiana's largest public landholding by far, occupying landscape in all five sections of the Shawnee Hills and Highland Rim Natural Regions. Its forest ecosystems comprise about half of the public forest land in Indiana and therefore play key roles in regional biodiversity.

The Hoosier is one of 153 federally owned forests and grasslands nationwide that constitute the National Forest System. They are managed by the U.S. Forest Service, whose mission is "to sustain the health, diversity, and productivity of the nation's forests and grasslands to meet the needs of present and future generations."

Among the Forest Service goals for the Hoosier are conserving threatened and endangered species habitat, maintaining and restoring sustainable ecosystems and watershed health, protecting cultural heritage, and providing recreation that is harmonious with natural communities.

Hoosier National Forest, Orange County.

As with many public lands in Southern Indiana, much of the acreage that would become the Hoosier had been heavily settled, farmed, logged, and abandoned between the late 1800s and early 1900s and was rejuvenated by New Deal–era Civilian Conservation Corps workers. Fast-growing pines, for example, were planted to stabilize the eroding landscape.

But the HNF is not, as maps suggest, a single land mass stretching from Monroe Lake near Bloomington to the Ohio River at Tell City. The solid green area identified by mapmakers as the Hoosier represents the "purchase area" within which the U.S. Forest Service is authorized to buy land for the national forest.

The Hoosier is one of the most fragmented in the nation and is composed of thousands of scattered parcels of woodlands in nine counties, from Monroe to Perry. They are organized geographically around four distinct "units," in Forest Service terms, from north to south: Pleasant Run, Lost River, Patoka, and Tell City. (Sections on individual HNF natural areas are listed in this book by their Natural Regions.)

South-central Indiana is central-hardwood territory, with

deciduous hardwood trees—primarily oak and hickory—dominating the range of forest communities that thrive in the Hoosier's unglaciated landforms. The Forest Service has identified thirty-eight different forest types growing on the national forest.

Karst topography—soluble bedrock with fractures that lead to the development of underground streams and rivers, caves, limestone bluffs, fossils, and geodes—underlies much of the Hoosier. Sandstone and shale underlie many other areas. Gold and gems, carried by glacial meltwaters, may also be present.

From the wooded ridges and ravines on the north to the barrens on the south, each HNF unit is unique and features high-quality, resilient, and rare native ecosystems. Four federally endangered species include the Hoosier in their ranges: Indiana bat, gray bat, rough pigtoe mussel, and fanshell mussel.

The National Audubon Society has designated the Pleasant Run Unit and Tell City Units as Global and State Important Areas, respectively, in part due to the presence of state-endangered cerulean warbler and black-and-white warbler, worm-eating warbler, hooded warbler, broad-winged hawk, and red-shouldered hawk, all state species of special concern. Other noteworthy species that live in or migrate through include Acadian flycatcher, black-throated green warbler, Kentucky warbler, yellow-throated warbler, prairie warbler, eastern wood-pewee, Louisiana waterthrush, ovenbird, red-eyed vireo, scarlet tanager, summer tanager, wood thrush, yellow-billed cuckoo, and yellow-breasted chat.

The Hoosier's mix of open land, deep forest, riparian, and karst features produces habitat for deer, foxes, woodchucks (a.k.a. groundhogs), opossums, squirrels, turkeys, woodpeckers, neotropical migrant songbirds, migratory waterfowl, and unusual cave species.

The Perry County barrens communities, where bedrock near the surface does not support trees, are burned periodically to support the rare, fire-dependent species that inhabit them.

The Hoosier National Forest offers just about any type of outdoor recreational opportunity imaginable on land, water,

Hoosier National Forest, Orange County.

and road, from 250-plus miles of hiking, horseback riding, and mountain bike trails, to a boat launch on the state's largest lake, to scenic drives with views of the Ohio River and Kentucky farmland on the opposite shore.

With few restrictions—groups in the Charles C. Deam Wilderness Area are limited to 10, for example—the entire forest is open to the public for hiking, backpacking, and other activities.

From north to south, the Hoosier features more than two dozen trails, Recreation Areas, Watchable Wildlife Sites, and other Special Places, including the Hardin Ridge Recreation Area on Monroe Lake in the Pleasant Run Unit, Springs Valley Recreation Area in the Lost River Unit, and Indian-Celina Lake Recreation Area, Tipsaw Recreation Area, and German Ridge Recreation Area in the Tell City Unit.

The Hoosier features several Watchable Wildlife Sites where the landscape, usually brushy areas or wetlands, offers unique or exceptional chances to view wildlife in their natural environments. Five of the *Indiana Wildlife Viewing Guide*'s eighty-nine best locations to watch wildlife in their natural habitats are on the Hoosier: Maines Pond, Paw Paw Marsh, Indian-Celina Lake, Buzzard Roost, and the Little Blue River.

The South and Middle Forks of Salt Creek, Patoka River, and Little Blue River offer opportunities for seasonal float trips through the forest.

Two scenic byways pass through the Hoosier. The Ohio River Scenic Byway offers panoramic views of the forested countryside as it winds its way along the Ohio River. The Historic Pathways National Byway largely follows the old Buffalo Trace, a path blazed first by buffalo migrating from the Falls of the Ohio River near Louisville to the Wabash River at Vincennes and prairies before and beyond. Stagecoaches, railroads, and now automobiles have followed the bison's lead along a route that today parallels or includes portions of U.S. 150 and State Road 56.

The forest abounds in archaeological sites, cemeteries, and historic buildings, remnants of human use from hundreds and thousands of years ago. Many, like the Buffalo Trace, Brooks Cabin, Hickory Ridge Lookout Tower, Mano Point, and Rickenbaugh House, feature interpretive signs.

Activities

Hiking/Bike/Bridle Trails: More than 260 miles throughout the forest's four units.

Camping: Camping is allowed on most areas of the forest, with a few exceptions. Camps are not allowed at trailheads or within three hundred feet of trailheads. At recreation area campgrounds, the designated campsites must be used. Campers may stay up to fourteen consecutive days within a twenty-one-day period, but they may not stay on the forest for more than thirty days total in a calendar year. At least one person must occupy a camping area during the first night after camp has been set up. Campsites cannot be left unattended for more than twenty-four hours.

Other Activities: Backpacking, boating, canoeing, caving, fishing, hunting, nature study, photography, picnicking, rock climbing, scenic drives, swimming, wildflowers, wildlife watching. (Please see individual Hoosier Forest sites for more details.)

Directions to Forest Service Supervisor Office, Brownstown Ranger District in Bedford
GPS coordinates: 38.870284, -86.518963
From State Road 37
- East on John Williams Drive at Bedford to Constitution Avenue, 0.1 mile
- North on Constitution Avenue to office, 0.1 mile

Directions to Tell City Ranger District Office
GPS coordinates: 37.944644, -86.760190
From State Road 37
- South on State Road 37 at I-64 junction to State Road 66 in Tell City, 22.1 miles
- South on State Road 66 to Washington Street, 1.1 miles
- East on Washington Street to 15th Street, 0.2 mile
- South on 15th Street to the office, one-half block

87a. Charles C. Deam Wilderness Area, Hoosier National Forest, Pleasant Run Unit

Owned by U.S. Forest Service

Located on the south shore of Monroe Lake east of the State Road 446 Causeway, the 12,953-acre Charles C. Deam Wilderness Area is Indiana's only congressionally designated wilderness. As such, it is protected in perpetuity from extractive forest uses, such as road building and logging, and provides for solitude and remote backcountry experiences unmatched anywhere else in the state.

The Deam was designated by Congress as a wilderness area in 1982, giving it a special legal status under the 1975 Eastern Wilderness Act. It is managed to preserve natural conditions and provide opportunities for solitude. It's named after Charles C. Deam, Indiana's first state forester. (See no. 95, Deam Lake State Recreation Area, for more on Charles Deam.)

More than thirty-seven miles of trails are provided for hiking, backpacking, and horse riding. Wheeled vehicles are prohibited.

Charles C. Deam Wilderness, Hoosier National Forest, Monroe County.

Walk-in camping is allowed, but not within three hundred feet of designated trailheads, wilderness access points, and horse camps. Camping within one hundred feet of ponds, streams, Monroe Lake, and designated trails is permitted only on designated sites.

Horse riders are required to have permits and must stay on designated trails. Permits are available from Forest Service offices and local vendors.

Archaeological remnants of once-heavy, late nineteenth- and early twentieth-century settlement in the Deam include house foundations, domestic plants, old fences, and five cemeteries.

Parking is allowed on Tower Ridge Road at the Blackwell Horse Camp, Grubb Ridge Trailhead, and Hickory Ridge Lookout Tower. Parking is not allowed on Tower Ridge Road.

Campsites must be occupied the first night and may not be left unattended for more than twenty-four hours without permission. Camping is limited to fourteen days.

Hunting is permitted in the Deam Wilderness. Target practice is not.

To limit impacts on the wilderness area, groups entering the Deam are limited to ten individuals.

The Brooks Cabin, across from the Blackwell Horse Camp,

serves as a visitors' contact station and information center, with maps and other resources. It is rarely staffed, but information kiosks are regularly stocked. Behind the relocated log cabin is Blackwell Lake.

Activities
Archaeological study, backpacking, fishing, hiking, horseback riding, hunting, nature study, photography, wildlife watching.

Directions
GPS coordinates: 39.014891, -86.400584
From State Road 37
- East on State Road 46 at Bloomington to State Road 446, 5.3 miles
- South on State Road 446 to Tower Ridge Road, 12.3 miles
- East on Tower Ridge Road: Deam Wilderness is on both sides for 6 miles (to Hickory Ridge Lookout Tower), on north side only for 2 miles past the tower

From I-65
- West on State Road 46 at Columbus, through Nashville,
- to State Road 446 at Bloomington, 31.1 miles
- South on State Road 446 to Tower Ridge Road, 12.3 miles
- East on Tower Ridge Road: Deam Wilderness is on both sides for 6 miles (to Hickory Ridge Lookout Tower), on north side only for 2 miles past the tower

87b. Hickory Ridge Lookout Tower
Owned by U.S. Forest Service
The Hickory Ridge Lookout Tower was built in 1939 by the New Deal–era Civilian Conservation Corps to help protect the early successional forest from wildfire. The last lookout tower remaining on the Hoosier today, Hickory Ridge was used until the 1970s. The steel tower is one hundred feet tall and has 123 metal steps.

Most lookout towers on national forests were built between the 1930s and 1950s. The number peaked in 1953 at 5,060, 9 of them on the Hoosier National Forest. The Hickory Ridge tower site initially included a cabin or guard station, a latrine, and a garage.

The tower is located on Terrill Ridge on the edge of the Charles C. Deam Wilderness Area but is not part of the wilderness. The

Hickory Ridge Fire Tower, Monroe County.

cab at the top is open to the public and offers a spectacular, 360-degree view of the wooded hillsides in four counties.

Directions

GPS coordinates: 39.034441, -86.321002

From State Road 37

- East on State Road 46 at Bloomington to State Road 446, 5.3 miles
- South on State Road 446 to Tower Ridge Road, 12.3 miles
- East on Tower Ridge Road to tower, 6.0 miles

From I-65

- West on State Road 46 at Columbus, through Nashville, to State Road 446 at Bloomington, 31.1 miles
- South on State Road 446 to Tower Ridge Road, 12.3 miles
- East on Tower Ridge Road to tower, 6.0 miles

88. Southfork Waterfowl Resting Area, Monroe Lake

The Southfork Waterfowl Resting Area is one of three lowland areas along the Salt Creek's upper forks where public access and hunting are limited. Southfork is located in southern Brown and northeastern Jackson Counties and is due east of the Charles C. Deam Wilderness Area in the Hoosier National Forest.

The marsh area is closed to the general public from October 1 to April 15.

See no. 73, Stillwater Marsh / Northfork Waterfowl Resting Areas, and no. 81, Middlefork Waterfowl Resting Area, Monroe Lake, for more details on the WRAs. See no. 85, Monroe Lake, for more details on the lake.

Activities
Boating, canoeing, fishing, hiking, hunting, nature study, photography, wildlife watching.

Directions to the Southfork Waterfowl Resting Area
GPS coordinates: 39.049969, -86.289405
From State Road 37
- East on State Road 46 at Bloomington to State Road 446, 5.3 miles
- South on State Road 446 to Tower Ridge Road, 12.3 miles
- East on Tower Ridge Road, past Hickory Ridge Fire Tower, to County Road 1100N, 8.4 miles
- Northeast on County Road 1100N to County Road 1250W at the Robertson Cemetery, 0.7 mile
- North on County Road 1250W to resting area

From I-65
- West on State Road 46 at Columbus, through Nashville, to State Road 446 at Bloomington, 31.1 miles
- South on State Road 446 to Tower Ridge Road, 12.3 miles
- East on Tower Ridge Road, past Hickory Ridge Fire Tower, to County Road 1100N, 8.4 miles
- Northeast on County Road 1100N to County Road 1250W at the Robertson Cemetery, 0.7 mile
- North on County Road 1250W to resting area

89. Hardin Ridge Recreation Area, Hoosier National Forest, Pleasant Run Unit
Owned by U.S. Forest Service
The twelve-hundred-acre Hardin Ridge Recreation Area is located on the shores of Monroe Lake southeast of Bloomington

across the water from the Fairfax State Recreation Area. It offers camping, picnicking, boat launching, swimming, nature walks, scenic views, and interpretive programs.

The two-mile hike-and-bike trail paralleling the road between the camping areas and the beach is the only trail on the Hoosier National Forest where bicycles can be ridden without a trail permit.

The campground is operated by a concessionaire and is open twenty-four hours a day, with at least one camp loop open year-round. Some loops are closed seasonally. Water is shut off in winter months.

Fees are charged for day use and camping between April 15 and October 31. Annual permits are available and can also be used at Tipsaw Lake Recreation Area and Indian-Celina Lake Recreation Area.

Drinking water and restrooms with showers are available. Some sites have electricity.

Activities

Camping: 203 sites total, 36 walk-ins. Electric hookups at about half the non-walk-in sites. Centralized water, flush toilets, and showers. Some campsites may be reserved. Others have available on a first-come basis.

Other activities: Biking, boat launching, hiking, interpretive programs, nature study, photography, picnicking, shelter houses, swimming beach (no life guards), wildlife watching.

Directions

GPS coordinates: 39.010069, -86.428529
From State Road 37

- East on State Road 46 at Bloomington to State Road 446, 5.3 miles
- South on State Road 446 to Chapel Hill Road, 11.5 miles
- West on Chapel Hill Road to campground entrance, 1.9 miles
From I-65
- West on State Road 46 at Columbus, through Nashville, to State Road 446 at Bloomington, 31.2 miles

- South on State Road 446 to Chapel Hill Road, 11.5 miles
- West on Chapel Hill Road to campground entrance, 1.9 miles

90. Jeremy K. Oakley Preserve
Owned by Sycamore Land Trust

The fifteen-acre Jeremy K. Oakley Preserve in eastern Lawrence County on the Jackson County line features a forested creek ravine with an open field northeast of Bedford. It is a living memorial to Jeremy Keith Oakley from his mother, Kathy Oakley, to provide a place for people—especially children—to understand the fragility and value of nature "as a haven to all spirits [to] enrich the human soul," Kathy said during a 2002 dedication ceremony recorded on the Sycamore website. The property would have been a gift to Jeremy, on his twenty-fifth birthday, had he lived to see it.

Parking and a gate are situated on the road at the edge of the field. A mowed trail with butterfly weed, rose gentian (a.k.a. rose pink), tall ironweed, and other species passes a memorial sign dedicated to Oakley and other family and friends: Kenny Long, Josh Mooney, and Justin Mund. The trail leads into the woods and down to a creek in a ravine.

The Oakley woods is relatively young in front and gets progressively older as it approaches the back of the property and the ravine, which features a rock exposure along a creek.

Activities
Hiking, nature study, photography, wildlife watching.

Directions
GPS coordinates: 38.856887, -86.283958
From State Road 37
- East on U.S. 50 at Bedford (16th Street) to Leesville Road, 13.4 miles
- South on Leesville Road to the preserve gate on the east side of the road, 1.3 miles

From I-65
- West on U.S. 50 at Seymour to Leesville Road east of Bedford, 26.3 miles

Hemlock Bluff Nature Preserve, Jackson County.

- South on Leesville Road to the preserve gate on the east side of the road, 1.3 miles

91. Hemlock Bluff Nature Preserve

Owned by Indiana Department of Natural Resources,
Division of Nature Preserves

The forty-four-acre Hemlock Bluff Nature Preserve in southwestern Jackson County is home to an impressive stand of hemlock trees, one of the state's largest among them—a giant measuring 33 inches in diameter at 4.5 feet above ground level. The evergreen hemlocks are remnants of the Wisconsin Glacial period, which retreated from Indiana some 13,600 years ago, and persist this far south only on cool, north-facing slopes.

Hemlock Bluff is located on a scenic, precipitous slope on the south bank of Guthrie Creek, where Jackson and Lawrence Counties meet. Its rugged environment supports mixed stands of hemlock and hardwood tree species, including American beech, sugar maple, northern red oak, basswood, and red elm.

Guthrie Creek, which follows a torturous, southwesterly course before meeting the East Fork of the White River south and east of Bedford, runs most of the year. At one location, it cuts into the bluff to expose a steep bank of Mississippian shale.

Hemlock Bluff also features varieties of wildflowers and wildlife, including long-tailed weasel, mink, and fox squirrel.

Hemlock Bluff Nature Preserve should not be confused with Hemlock Cliffs in the Hoosier National Forest in Crawford County.

Activities
Hiking Trails: One loop, with breathtaking views, narrow, windy, hilly.
Other Activities: Nature study, photography, wildlife watching.

Directions
GPS coordinates: 38.845833, -86.261126
From State Road 37
- East on U.S. 50 at Bedford (16th Street) to Leesville Road, 13.5 miles
- South on Leesville Road through Leesville to the Y with signs to Fort Ritner and Sparksville Road, 2.3 miles
- East on Sparksville Road to preserve parking lot, 1.3 miles

From I-65
- West on U.S. 50 at Seymour to Leesville Road, before Bedford, 26.3 miles
- South on Leesville Road through Leesville to the Y with signs to Fort Ritner and Sparksville Road, 2.3 miles
- East on Sparksville Road to preserve parking lot, 1.3 miles

92a. Jackson-Washington State Forest, North Unit
Owned by Indiana Department of Natural Resources,
Division of Forestry

Jackson-Washington State Forest may indeed be Southern Indiana's "best-kept secret," as one DNR employee in the office put it. But with two geographically distinct state forest units and the nearby Starve Hollow State Recreation Area, the roughly eighteen thousand acres of state land are rich with outdoor recreational offerings, from backcountry hiking and backpack camping to developed swimming beaches.

Situated on the northern end of the state's knobs region between the East Fork of the White River and the Muscatatuck River, the Jackson-Washington / Starve Hollow natural complex includes scattered parcels of land across two sections of the Highland Rim Natural Region. Its landscape traverses a variety

Jackson-Washington State Forest, Jackson County.

of landforms, from deep, forested, knobby hills to old field sites, fishing lakes, pine plantations, semipermanent wildlife openings and ponds, and bottomlands.

The National Audubon Society has designated Jackson-Washington and the nearby Clark State Forest as a State Important Bird Area in part due to the presence of state-endangered cerulean warbler, along with black-and-white warbler, hooded warbler, worm-eating warbler, broad-winged hawk, and red-shouldered hawk, all state species of special concern. Other noteworthy species that live in or migrate through include Kentucky warbler, pine warbler, Louisiana waterthrush, ruffed grouse, scarlet tanager, summer tanager, and wood thrush.

Jackson-Washington tree species include northern red oak, scarlet oak, white oak, black oak, chestnut oak, shagbark hickory, pignut hickory, white ash, sugar maple, sycamore, American beech, sweet gum, and tulip poplar.

Among the wildlife living there are deer, grouse, turkey, rabbit, quail, dove, squirrel, fox, coyote, and raccoon.

Jackson-Washington's North Unit in Jackson County, where the forest headquarters is located, and the Starve Hollow Recreation Area lie in the Brownstown Hills, an island of the Brown County Hills Section separated by the East Fork of the

White River and surrounded by the Scottsburg Lowland Section of the Bluegrass Natural Region.

While the North Unit does include a nature preserve, it is more developed than the South Unit and features magnificent vistas—from both trails and roads—of the surrounding knobs, farm fields, and nearby community of Brownstown. On a clear day, the stacks from the Clifty Creek Power Plant on the Ohio River some forty miles to the east are visible from the forest's Skyline Drive, which also features a 360-degree view from a fire tower.

The North Unit features two water bodies, all stocked with largemouth bass, bluegill, redear sunfish, and channel catfish: Knob Lake, seven acres, and Cypress Pond, one acre. Knob allows boats limited to electric trolling motors and wheelchair-accessible docks.

The South Unit lies in the Highland Rim Natural Region's Escarpment Section.

See no. 93, Jackson-Washington State Forest / South Unit, for more details.

92b. Knobstone Glade Nature Preserve

The sixty-acre Knobstone Glade Nature Preserve is located in the North Unit of the Jackson-Washington State Forest, east of the Starve Hollow State Recreation Area. It is composed of three separate tracts of land, each featuring glades, or forest openings, with sparse vegetation growing on and around bedrock outcrops.

Tree species include stunted, gnarly chestnut oak and blackjack oak sharing the ecosystem with early low blueberry, one of the few shrubby species that are found in glades. Some prairie plants also live in the preserve's dry, open conditions.

Knobstone Glade preserve is accessible via trail from the Vallonia Nursery or Starve Hollow State Recreation Area.

Activities
Hiking Trails: Eleven, easy to rugged, one wheelchair accessible, 0.25 to 8 miles, Tree Identification and Sawmill Hollow interpretive trails. The fifty-nine-mile Knobstone Trail passes through and has a trailhead at Spurgeon Hollow Lake.
Bridle Trails: Two, 13.9 total miles.

Mountain Bike Trails: Two, 12.2 total miles.

Camping: Fifty-six primitive sites, two wheelchair accessible, some waterfront sites on Knob Lake, others situated among hardwoods or rare, towering white pines; backcountry camping available along the backcountry hiking trail in Washington County. Youth Tent Campground: For scouts and other groups.

Other Activities: Archery range, fishing, hunting, picnicking, nature study, photography, playgrounds, shelters, scenic drive, wildlife watching.

Directions to North Unit

GPS coordinates: 38.856021, -86.014089

From State Road 37 to Jackson-Washington Office

- East on U.S. 50 at Bedford to State Road 250 at Brownstown, 27.2 miles
- Southeast on State Road 250 to forest entrance, 2.2 miles

From I-65 to Jackson-Washington Office

- West on U.S. 50 at Seymour to State Road 250 at Brownstown, 12.7 miles
- Southeast on State Road 250 to forest entrance, 2.2 miles

92c. Starve Hollow State Recreation Area

Owned by Indiana Department of Natural Resources,
Division of Forestry

When the now-145-acre Starve Hollow Lake was built in 1938, it was the largest man-made lake in Indiana. Today, the water is the centerpiece around which the 280-acre Starve Hollow State Recreation Area revolves. It is located south of the Jackson-Washington State Forest's North Unit, to which it is connected by road and trail. It lies in the Brownstown Hills, a separate tract in the Brown County Hills Section, in between the forest's north and south units.

Dedicated to camping and an array of recreational opportunities, from rugged hiking trails to a developed swimming beach with bathhouse, the recreation area's terrain ranges from lowlands to dry ridgetops. Interpretive naturalist services are available at the nature center.

Starve Hollow State Recreation Area, Jackson County.

Activities

Hiking Trails: Six, from 0.6 to 5.6 miles, easy to rugged.

Mountain Bike Trails: A trail from Starve Hollow connects to the mountain bike trails in Jackson-Washington State Forest.

Camping: Fifty-three full hookup electric sites with sewer, water, fire ring, picnic table, and parking spur, modern restrooms/ showers (wheelchair accessible) available nearby, three are wheelchair accessible; eighty-seven electric hookup sites with fire ring, picnic table, and parking spur, drinking water, modern restrooms/showers (wheelchair accessible), dumping station, four sites are wheelchair accessible; ten nonelectric sites with drinking water supply, modern restrooms/showers (wheelchair accessible), one site is wheelchair accessible.

Cabins: Thirteen Rent-a-Camp Program cabins available year-round.

Other Activities: Basketball courts; boating (trolling only) and ramps (two wheelchair accessible); canoe and rowboat rentals; fishing/fish-cleaning station for campers; horseshoe pits; nature center with education center and full-time interpretive naturalist; nature study; photography; picnicking; shelters;

playground; softball fields; sand volleyball court; swimming beach with restrooms, dressing facilities, showers, food concessions, and wheelchair ramps; wildlife watching.

Directions
GPS coordinates: 38.816060, -86.084760
From State Road 37
- East on U.S. 50 at Bedford to State Road 135 at Brownstown, 27.2 miles
- South on State Road 135 to Starve Hollow sign, 3.8 miles

From I-65
- West on U.S. 50 at Seymour to State Road 135 at Brownstown, 13.6
- South on State Road 135 to Starve Hollow sign, 3.8 miles

93. Jackson-Washington State Forest, South Unit

The Jackson-Washington State Forest's South Unit, which lies in Washington County and the Knobstone Escarpment Section south of the Muscatatuck River, is more isolated and less developed than the North Unit. It offers outdoor experiences that are more rugged, including backcountry hiking and camping.

The South Unit includes a 2,500-acre Back Country Area, one of three such sites established on state forests in 1981 to provide opportunities for isolated outdoor experiences in primitive areas. (See no. 64c, Morgan-Monroe State Forest Back Country Area, for more details.)

The South Unit's scenic vistas are limited to the trails, which include the Spurgeon Hollow Trail, which passes through the Back Country Area. The Spurgeon Hollow Trailhead is also trailhead for the fifty-nine-mile Knobstone Trail, the state's longest hiking trail.

The South Unit features three water bodies, also stocked with largemouth bass, bluegill, redear sunfish, and channel catfish: Spurgeon Hollow, twelve acres; Potter Lake, ten acres; and Plattsburg Pond, eight acres. Spurgeon Hollow has a ramp, with boats limited to trolling motors only. Potter and Plattsburg are walk-ins.

Directions to South Unit

GPS coordinates: 38.719928, -86.087774

From State Road 37 to Rooster Hill Road

- East on State Road 60 south of Mitchell to State Road 135 at Salem, 23.3 miles
- North on State Road 135 to Rooster Hill Road, 8.1 miles

From I-65 to Rooster Hill Road

- West on State Road 256 at Austin to State Road 39, 6.4 miles
- North on State Road 39 to East County Road 700S, 2.5 miles
- West on County Road 700W / W County Road 650S to State Road 135, 8.7 miles
- South on State Road 135 to Rooster Hill Road, 5.7 miles

Knobstone Escarpment Section

94a. Clark State Forest

Owned by Indiana Department of Natural Resources,
Division of Forestry

The twenty-four-thousand-acre Clark State Forest, which is bisected on the far east end by I-65 about ten miles south of Scottsburg, was home to some of the nation's earliest developments in the field of forestry. Two years after two thousand of its acres were established as Indiana's first state forest in 1903—perhaps the nation's first, according to the DNR—Clark became a forest research facility and nursery.

Between 1905 and 1935 more than 150 experimental tree plantings were established on Clark State Forest to allow foresters to learn how to reforest cultivated and denuded lands. Much of Southern Indiana, including most of the public lands that today are managed as state and federal forests and parks, had been cleared for logging or agriculture in the late nineteenth and early twentieth centuries.

The vast majority of these trial-and-error efforts were overseen by botanist Charles C. Deam, who was appointed Indiana's first state forester in 1909 and served fifteen years over two terms between then and 1928. (See no. 95, Deam Lake State Recreation Area, for more on Charles Deam.)

During the Great Depression, Clark became a Civilian Conservation Corps (CCC) training center and the federal make-work project's largest camp. CCC workers, paid by President Franklin D. Roosevelt's Works Progress Administration, built the forest's seven lakes, bridges, and scenic spots.

Clark includes a 2,000-acre Back Country Area, one of three such sites established on state forests in 1981 to provide opportunities for rugged outdoor experiences in primitive areas. (See no. 64c, Morgan-Monroe State Forest Back Country Area, for more details.)

Along with two nature preserves dedicated to specific tree species, Clark State Forest's mature oak-hickory canopy features white oak, northern red oak, black oak, scarlet oak, post oak, chestnut oak, pignut hickory, shagbark hickory, bitternut hickory, American beech, and various maples and gums. Scrub pine (a.k.a. Virginia pine), on the state watch list, is scattered throughout its knobby uplands.

The National Audubon Society has designated Clark and the nearby Jackson-Washington State Forest as a State Important Bird Area in part due to the presence of state-endangered cerulean warbler and black-and-white warbler, hooded warbler, worm-eating warbler, broad-winged hawk, and red-shouldered hawk, all state species of special concern. Other noteworthy species that live in or migrate through include Kentucky warbler, pine warbler, Louisiana waterthrush, ruffed grouse, scarlet tanager, summer tanager, and wood thrush.

Other wildlife includes deer, turkey, squirrel, fox, woodcock, and raccoon.

The forest floor sports spring beauty, shooting star, devil's paintbrush (a.k.a. orange hawkweed), blue phlox, fire pink, bluets, goat's rue, Indian turnip (a.k.a. Jack-in-the-pulpit), wild ginger, wild geranium, and mayapple, along with a variety of ferns in the moist areas.

Clark has seven lakes: Schlamm Lake, 18 acres; Shaw Lake, 13 acres; Franke Lake, 12 acres; Bowen Lake, 7 acres; Wilcox Lake, 5 acres; Oak Lake, 2.5 acres; and Pine Lake, 2 acres.

White Oak Nature Preserve, Clark State Forest, Clark County.

Information should be available at the information booth outside the office.

94b. Virginia Pine–Chestnut Oak Nature Preserve
The twenty-four acre Virginia Pine–Chestnut Oak Nature Preserve encompasses a ridgetop and surrounding slopes in an exceptionally hilly area of Clark State Forest atop Lower Mississippian sandstones and shale.

The upper slopes are mostly naturally occurring scrub pine (a.k.a. Virginia pine), a state watch list species that is confined to the Knobstone Region in Floyd, Clark, and Scott Counties. Scrub pine has been planted elsewhere. White oak and scarlet oak intermix, with the two dominant species in a transition zone to the lower slopes, which are predominantly chestnut oak.

The fifty-nine-mile Knobstone Trail, the state's longest hiking trail, runs southwest through the preserve.

94c. White Oak Nature Preserve
Named after its dominant tree, the 143-acre White Oak Nature Preserve provides an outstanding example of an oak-hickory forest, with a 0.9-mile self-guiding loop trail with twenty-five identification stops. Stop no. 1 is a gray-barked white oak.

Information available at the forest office kiosk explains that White Oak's ecosystem includes a "dry upland slope and moist cover with contrasting varieties of trees, shrubs, and wildflowers."

In addition to scrub pine, white oak, scarlet oak, northern red oak, black oak, chestnut oak, post oak, shagbark hickory, pignut hickory, and bitternut hickory, the White Oak Nature Preserve supports American beech, black maple, sugar maple, white ash, and black gum.

Understory tree and shrub species include flowering dogwood, juneberry, maple-leaved arrowwood (a.k.a. mapleleaf viburnum), blue beech (a.k.a. hornbeam), serviceberry, Virginia creeper, pasture rose, and late low blueberry clumps.

The preserve is located just west of the I-65 overpass. Highway sounds are audible at the trailhead.

Activities

Hiking Trails: Hiking is permitted on the entire forest property, including fire and bridle trails. Two self-guiding trails, 0.9 and 1.0 mile. Thirty of the Knobstone Trail's fifty-nine miles pass through Clark State Forest.

Bridle Trails: Eighty miles.

Mountain Bike Trails: Five miles of designated trails.

Camping: Thirty-eight primitive sites with pit toilets and seasonal drinking water, picnic table and grill; twenty-six primitive sites at the horse campground, dump station.

Other Activities: Baseball fields, basketball court, boat ramps (electric trolling motors only), fire tower, fishing, hunting, nature study, photography, picnicking, playgrounds, tennis court, shooting range, shelters, wildlife watching.

Directions

GPS coordinates: 38.552943, -85.766599
From I-65

- East on State Road 160 to U.S. 31 at Henryville, 0.4 mile
- North on U.S. 31 to state forest, 1.0 mile

95. Deam Lake State Recreation Area

Owned by Indiana Department of Natural Resources,
Division of Forestry

The thirteen-hundred-acre Deam Lake State Recreation Area is situated amid Southern Indiana knob country north of New

Deam Lake State Recreation Area, Clark County.

Albany, adjacent to remote sections of the Clark State Forest to the north. Its wooded hillsides surround a peaceful, 194-acre lake named after Indiana's first state forester, Charles C. Deam. The lake was built in 1964 to honor the Bluffton native, who served as state forester from 1909 to 1913 and 1917 to 1928.

An entrance fee is charged.

The Deam Lake area's bottomlands are often muddy and sometimes underwater during wet seasons. Its wooded hillsides include uncommon stands of scrub pine (a.k.a. Virginia pine), on the state watch list, some of which suffered storm damage in 2008 and 2009. A rock cutout on the property's longest and most rugged trail offers a scenic view of the lake.

Wildlife species that inhabit the area include white-tailed deer, ruffed grouse, wild turkey, red fox, and raccoon.

A Forest Education Center is managed by a full-time naturalist, with displays and hands-on activities for children and adults.

The southernmost trailhead for the fifty-nine-mile Knobstone Trail, the state's longest footpath, lies just outside the Deam Lake Recreation Area. The Lake Vista Trail offers a scenic view of the lake and surrounding knobs.

Charles C. Deam, who was stationed at the adjacent Clark State Forest, also worked as the state's research forester and collected and wrote about state plants. His books, *Trees of Indiana* (1911), *Shrubs of Indiana* (1924), *Grasses of Indiana* (1929), and *Flora of Indiana* (1940), are still used as references today. He also authored the Indiana Forest Classification Act of 1921, which exempted farmers from paying taxes on forestland they leave relatively undisturbed and has conserved hundreds of thousands of acres of Indiana woods.

Two other Indiana properties are named after him: the Charles C. Deam Wilderness Area in Monroe, Brown, and Jackson Counties, the state's only federally protected wilderness area; and the Charles C. Deam Nature Preserve on the Ohio River in Harrison-Crawford State Forest.

Activities

Hiking Trails: Five, easy to rugged, 0.2 to 3.2 miles; a trailhead to the Knobstone Trail is also located on the property.

Mountain Bike Trails: Five miles.

Camping: 116 electric campsites, with electrical hookup, modern restrooms/showers, picnic tables, fire rings, parking spurs, drinking water, dump station; 68 electric horse camp stall sites with lead-outs connecting to the Clark State Forest bridle trails.

Cabins: Twelve Rent-a-Camp Program cabins available year-round, including three in the horse campground. Reservations available. No pets, smoking, or cooking permitted in cabins.

Other Activities: Boat launch ramp (electric trolling motors only), fishing, forest education center with full-time naturalist, hunting, nature study, photography, picnicking, playground, rowboat rental, swimming beach with restrooms, dressing facilities, showers, and food concessions, wheelchair ramp to beach area, shelter, wildlife watching.

Directions

GPS coordinates: 38.461572, -85.865455

From State Road 37

- East on State Road 60 at Mitchell, through Salem, to Deam Lake Road, 42.6 miles
- North on Deam Lake Road to gatehouse

From I-65

- West on State Road 60 to Deam Lake Road, 8.6 miles
- North on Deam Lake Road to gatehouse.

Minton Nature Preserve, Clark County.

96. Minton Nature Preserve

Owned by Indiana Department of Natural Resources,
Division of Nature Preserves

The Minton Nature Preserve encompasses 1,301 acres of the Southern Indiana Knobstone Hills just west of the Ohio River and south of New Albany. The landscape features steep, dissected, forested hills with moist ravines. Among the natural communities that thrive there are dry, dry–moist, and moist-upland forests and a few siltstone glades, which are exceedingly rare worldwide.

The Minton preserve is one of the less-accessible refuges in the state. There are no signs indicating its existence, and it has no trails, aside from an old county roadbed that bisects the site. And while off-road parking exists, the road leading in is chained with a No Parking sign and may be blocked by construction equipment. The road initially parallels a utility cut and is lined with large rocks that are awkward to traverse. The preserve has no trails and is open to hunting in season. A nearby police shooting range frequently shatters the silence.

This preserve is named after the late Dr. Sherman A. Minton, who wrote *Amphibians and Reptiles of Indiana*. He is the son of former U.S. senator and Supreme Court justice Sherman Minton.

Activities
Hiking, nature study, photography, wildlife watching.

Directions
GPS coordinates: 38.220173, -85.900485

From State Road 37

- East on I-64 to I-265 at New Albany, 43.0 miles
- Northeast on I-265 to State Road 111 / Grant Line Road, 3.1 miles
- South on State Road 111 to Budd Road, 6.5 miles
- West on Budd Road to Minton Nature Preserve (just past fenced pumping station), 5.6 miles

From I-65

- West on I-265 to State Road 111 / Grant Line Road, 4.0 miles
- South on State Road 111 to Budd Road, 6.5 miles
- West on Budd Road to Minton Nature Preserve (just past fenced pumping station), 5.6 miles
- Park on the right side of the road. Follow the gravel lane into the preserve on foot.

(*Facing*) Falls of the Ohio State Park, Floyd County.

BIG RIVERS
NATURAL REGION

BIG RIVERS NATURAL REGION

97. Falls of the Ohio State Park

Owned/leased by Indiana Department of Natural Resources,
Division of State Parks & Reservoirs

Located on the banks of the Ohio River at Clarksville, the 165-acre Falls of the Ohio State Park features one of the world's largest displays of exposed, four-hundred-million-year-old fossil beds. Indiana's smallest state park lies within the Falls of the Ohio National Wildlife Conservation Area, which is composed of 1,404 acres of federally protected land and water.

The fossil beds were designated a National Natural Landmark in 1966 by the National Park Service. A sixteen-thousand-square-foot interpretive center overlooks the fossil beds and features a fourteen-minute movie, exhibit gallery, and river and marine aquariums.

Fossil collecting is prohibited at the Falls of the Ohio, but visitors may access and explore the beds via walkways that lead down from the visitors' center. August through October, when the river is at its lowest level, is the optimum time for fossil viewing.

The fossils formed some 387 million years ago, during the geologic period known as the Devonian, when a shallow tropical sea covered much of the Eastern United States. Included was all of Michigan, nearly all of Kentucky, most of Ohio, and the southern part of Indiana, with a shoreline that extended from just north of New Albany and the Falls of the Ohio to Terre Haute.

As the sponges, brachiopods, mollusks, echinoderms, fish, and other life forms that thrived in the marine environment died, they fossilized beneath layers of limey sediment. The fossils remained buried beneath successive layers of rock until seven hundred thousand years ago, when rushing meltwaters from retreating Kansan glaciers began carving the Ohio River Basin and exposing the Falls of the Ohio fossil beds.

More than 600 fossil species, including 250 coral species from the period, have been identified at the Falls of the Ohio.

The fossil beds are divided into lower and upper layers.

The lower beds are the acres of flat rocks that can be walked upon, similar to walking on a dry ocean floor. Corals and sponges thrived on these now smooth limestone layers, which are underwater much of the year.

The upper beds have a wider variety of fossils, albeit mostly smaller, and are exposed most of the year. Fossils here include corals, brachiopods, and bryozoans, as well as crinoids, snails, and trilobites.

In addition to the fossil beds, the Falls of the Ohio includes the seventy-six-acre Buttonbush Woods and eight-acre George Rogers Clark Homesite. The habitat includes open water, marsh, mud bank, prairie, sand bar, and woodland. More than 270 bird species and roughly 125 fish species, including the primitive paddlefish, have been identified there.

Bird species include osprey and black-crowned night heron, both state endangered, along with bald eagle, peregrine falcon, and great egret, all state species of special concern. Osprey and bald eagles nest in the area. Other species that live in or migrate through include great blue heron, black vulture, double-crested cormorant, and ring-billed gull.

Among the National Audubon Society's noteworthy records at the Falls are ruddy turnstone, a state species of special concern, American golden plover, American avocet, American white pelican, black-bellied plover, black scoter, surf scoter, white-winged scoter, Baird's sandpiper, stilt sandpiper, buff-breasted sandpiper, eared grebe, Franklin's gull, great black-backed gull, laughing gull, lesser black-backed gull, little blue heron, marbled godwit, red-necked phalarope, snowy egret, American white ibis, and willet.

The woods feature stands of giant cane (a.k.a. canebrake), a southern plant at its northernmost limits here, century-old cottonwood trees, snag trees, and shelf fungi, known as "conks," on black locust trees. A variety of understory plant species thrive in this riparian environment, including wildflowers such as Virginia bluebells, Canada wild ginger, and celandine poppy (a.k.a. wood poppy); vines such as trumpet creeper, poison ivy, and cross vine; and pawpaw and other tree species.

Clark established the first permanent English-speaking settlement in the Northwest Territory on nearby Corn Island in 1778 and played a primary role in the United States defeating the British and securing the region during the Revolutionary War. As compensation for his service, the federal government in 1783 granted Clark a homestead on the Ohio shore, where he founded Clarksville. Clark's Grant stretched north to include a significant chunk of what is now Clark State Forest.

The Falls of the Ohio were actually a series of rapids, falls, and chutes flowing over ledges of hard limestone that began at what is now downtown Louisville and extended 2.5 miles west to Sand Island, dropping twenty-six feet along the way. John James Audubon lived in the area from 1808 to 1810 and said of the falls: "The rumbling sound of the waters as they tumble over the rock-paved rapids is at all times soothing to the ear," Audubon wrote in his journal. Walt Whitman and Mark Twain also wrote about them.

Since before the European settlers arrived, bison and other animals used the Falls of the Ohio as a crossing point over the river on their regular journeys from the salt licks in Northern Kentucky to the Western Indiana and Illinois prairies. Boats could pass safely only during high water. Many crashed attempting to navigate the falls' natural chutes when the river level dropped. This stretch of rapids is the only point on the Ohio where the riverbed is rock from one side to the other and was the only point between Pittsburgh and New Orleans where riverboats faced such obstacles.

Early nineteenth-century attempts to circumvent the falls with a canal on the Indiana side failed due to the solid limestone walls that bordered the riverbank. A similar effort on the Kentucky side proved more fruitful. The Louisville & Portland Canal began operations on the Kentucky side in 1830.

Ninety years later, the U.S. Army Corps of Engineers built a series of locks and dams that constricted the river's flow and drowned the falls, only remnants of which remain today. The Falls of the Ohio fossils were uncovered when the corps redirected the channel.

Activities

Hiking Trails: One easy to moderate woodland loop; 175 acres of fossil beds are available for walking when the water level is low, easy to rugged.

Other Activities: Boat launch ramp on the Ohio River, fishing, fossil viewing, interpretive naturalist services, nature study, photography, picnicking, wildlife watching.

Directions

GPS coordinates: 38.276415, -85.763372

From State Road 37

- East on I-64 to I-265, 43 miles
- Northeast on I-265 to I-65, 6.4 miles
- South on I-65 to Exit 0, 5.3 miles
- West Market Street / Riverside Drive to park, 1.1 miles

From I-65

- Exit 0 to West Market Street / Riverside Drive to park, 1.1 miles

Section 4

BLUEGRASS NATURAL REGION

Scottsburg Lowland Section

Muscatatuck Flats and Canyon Section

Switzerland Hills Section

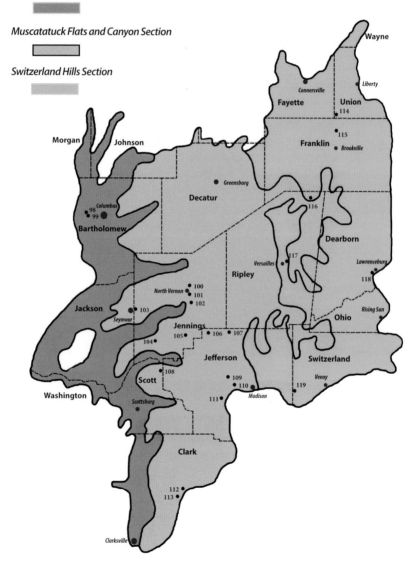

Section 4

BLUEGRASS NATURAL REGION

Scottsburg Lowland Section

Muscatatuck Flats and Canyon Section

Switzerland Hills Section

BLUEGRASS
NATURAL REGION

BLUEGRASS NATURAL REGION

Scottsburg Lowland Section

98. Tangeman Woods

Owned by Sycamore Land Trust

The mostly wooded, thirty-two-acre Tangeman Woods preserve's centerpiece is the Outdoor Lab Nature Trail, which was created in the 1970s by the Bartholomew County Soil and Water Conservation District (SWCD). Located just west of Columbus, this natural area still features a small amphitheater area with wooden bench seats.

The trail traverses the preserve's east end through a mixed hardwood forest, with several bridges crossing intermittent creek ravines. Wolf Creek flows through a small wooded area on the west. The trail runs along State Road 46, where automobile traffic is visible and audible.

Sycamore Land Trust uses the property for its Environmental Education Program. The Bartholomew County SWCD likewise uses it for educational purposes.

The Irwin-Sweeney-Miller Foundation donated the preserve to Sycamore Land Trust in 2007 and named it in memory of Clementine Tangeman, a past owner of the property and sister of local industrialist J. Irwin Miller.

A Bartholomew County Solid Waste Management District rural refuse drop-off site is located near the property's west end.

Activities

Hiking, nature study, photography, wildlife watching.

Directions

GPS coordinates: 39.200794, -86.025347
From State Road 37

- East on State Road 46, through Nashville, to Country Club Road before Columbus, 32.9 miles
- North on Country Club Road to Old Nashville Road, 0.1 mile
- West on Old Nashville Road to preserve, 0.5 mile

(*Facing*) Tangeman Woods, Bartholomew County.

From I-65
- West on State Road 46 at Columbus to Country Club Road, 3.6 miles
- North on Country Club Road to Old Nashville Road, 0.1 mile
- West on Old Nashville Road to preserve, 0.5 mile
- Parking is available at the Harrison Township Volunteer Fire Department on Old Nashville Road.

99. Touch the Earth Natural Area
Owned by Sycamore Land Trust

The ninety-eight-acre Touch the Earth Natural Area west of Columbus has two miles of mowed paths through woods and old farm fields that are reverting to nature and abound in wildflowers such as yellow coneflower (a.k.a. prairie coneflower, gray-headed coneflower), wild bergamot, and others. Sycamore Land Trust planted an area near the parking lot for butterfly habitat with species that are native to Indiana but not to this site.

Touch the Earth is known for hiking, bird watching, and enjoying nature. The trail features several benches, an observation deck, and a tree identification quiz by local Cub Scout Pack 557.

Touch the Earth, purchased by Sycamore in 1995, was expanded in 1998 and is actively managed to protect native species from aggressive invasive species that crowd out native plants to the detriment of the natural ecosystem.

Activities
Hiking, nature study, photography, wildlife watching.

Directions
GPS coordinates: 39.192656, -86.024750
From State Road 37
- East on State Road 46 through Nashville to Country Club Road before Columbus, 32.9 miles
- South on Country Club Road to preserve, 0.3 mile
From I-65
- West on State Road 46 at Columbus to Country Club Road, 3.6 miles
- South on Country Club Road to preserve, 0.3 mile

Selmier State Forest, Jennings County.

A mowed parking area along Country Club Road provides access to the Touch the Earth preserve, with a kiosk by the parking lot on the east side.

Muscatatuck Flats and Canyon Section

100. Selmier State Forest

Owned by Indiana Department of Natural Resources,
Division of Forestry

The 355-acre Selmier State Forest is the smallest state forest in Indiana. Most of the property, originally owned by Jennings County businessman Frank Selmier, was placed in the Indiana Classified Forest Program between 1927 and 1931. The property today is crisscrossed with logging roads and other evidence of timber production such as openings and staging areas that are regenerating.

Located near the Vernon Fork of the Muscatatuck River, Selmier features cliff outcrops and several river overlooks, as well as a pond and an old dam. A one-mile, self-guided "forest management trail" passes the dam and features benches and multiple spurs. The trail does not have signs or other exploratory information.

Selmier's tree species include black locust, black walnut,

sycamore, tulip poplar, American beech, sugar maple, and white oak, many of which were planted by Selmier between 1921 and 1934. Others include flowering dogwood, pawpaw, wild black cherry, northern red oak, eastern redbud, blue beech (a.k.a. hornbeam), American hemlock, sassafras, and box elder.

Wildlife common to the Selmier forest and its environs are turkeys, deer, ducks, skinks, turtles, and songbirds.

The forest floor is covered with ferns and a variety of wildflowers, including orange jewelweed (a.k.a. spotted touch-me-not) and wild ginger.

Three historic buildings are located on the property: a Boy Scout cabin; the Zoar School, which was converted to a church; an old homesite; and a cemetery.

Activities
Hiking Trails: Five short, one self-guided forest management.
Other Activities: Fishing, hunting, nature study, photography, wildlife watching.

Directions
GPS coordinates: 39.036662, -85.599272
From I-65
- East on U.S. 50 at Seymour to State Road 3 in North Vernon, 13.0 miles
- North on State Road 3 to W. County Road 350N, 2.5 miles
- East on W. County Road 350N to forest, 1.8 miles
- The office is located at 905 E. County Road 350N.

From I-74
- South on State Road 3 at Greensburg to W. County Road 350N just north of North Vernon, 27.4 miles
- East on W. County Road 350N to forest, 1.8 miles
- The office is located at 905 E. County Road 350N.

101. Calli Nature Preserve
Owned by Indiana Department of Natural Resources,
Division of Nature Preserves
The 179-acre Calli Nature Preserve is bordered by the Muscatatuck River and features rich biodiversity with karst features,

including high-quality limestone cliffs, spring-fed streams, waterfalls, upland forests, a relic stand of hemlock trees, and successional fields.

A two-mile interpretive trail leads to two loops. The short one leads to an open field with butterfly weed, yellow coneflower (a.k.a. prairie coneflower, gray-headed coneflower), and wild bergamot in summer. The long loop leads to a bluff on the river and features a bench and overlook.

The Calli preserve has been logged and farmed throughout history, and the forest is second growth. In addition to hemlock, tree species include tulip poplar, wild black cherry, white ash, box elder, and a particularly unusual northern red oak with a white oak growing into it.

Forest wildflowers include trout lily, blue phlox, twinleaf, wild ginger, Virginia bluebells, American bellflower (a.k.a. tall bellflower), and Canada violet. The cliff communities feature bulblet bladder fern, ditch stonecrop, bishop's cap, and smooth rockcress.

Nesting bird species on the property include red-shouldered hawk and hooded warbler, both state species of special concern. Other common birds are great blue heron, wood duck, and mallard. White-tailed deer, beaver, and several turtle species are also common.

A Devonian period limestone streambed also has black shale, chert, and brown shale.

Dr. James Calli, Jr., donated the site in honor of his parents, Violet and Dr. Louis J. Calli, Sr.

Activities
Hiking Trail: Two miles, self-guided.
Other Activities: Nature study, photography, wildlife watching.

Directions
GPS coordinates: 39.004047, -85.604198
From I-65
- East on U.S. 50 at Seymour to County Road 40E, east of North Vernon, just past the Muscatatuck River Bridge, 14.4 miles
- South on County Road 40E to parking lot, 0.3 mile

Crosley Fish & Wildlife Area, Jennings County.

From I-74

- South on State Road 3 at Greensburg to U.S. 50 at North Vernon, 30.0 miles
- East on U.S. 50 to County Road 40E, just past the Muscatatuck River Bridge, 1.3 miles
- South on County Road 40E to parking lot, 0.3 mile

102. Crosley Fish & Wildlife Area

Owned by Indiana Department of Natural Resources, Division of Fish & Wildlife

The 4,228-acre Crosley Fish & Wildlife Area is composed of steep to gently rolling hills along a seven-mile stretch of the Muscatatuck River. It is roughly 80 percent forest, with thirteen ponds ranging in size from two to fourteen acres.

The wildlife area is named after Powel Crosley, who originally owned it and was the maker of the Crosley automobile. He purchased the land in 1931 for a private hunting and fishing area.

The hills, ponds, and river attract a variety of wildlife, including songbirds, hawks, waterfowl, turkeys, deer, squirrels, rabbits, quail, and woodcocks.

Activities

Boat ramps (electric motors only), fishing, hunting (for the disabled allowed in designated areas with permit from the property manager), nature study, photography, wildlife watching.

Directions

GPS coordinates: 38.954962, -85.600965

From I-65

- East on U.S. 50 at Seymour to State Road 3 in North Vernon, 13.0 miles
- South on State Road 3 to wildlife area, 3.8 miles

From I-74 to Office in North Vernon

- South on State Road 3 at Greensburg, through North Vernon, to wildlife area, 34.6 miles

103. Muscatatuck National Wildlife Refuge

Owned by U.S. Fish & Wildlife Service

The Muscatatuck National Wildlife Refuge provides resting and feeding areas for waterfowl, other migratory birds, and endangered species on 7,724 acres near Seymour and 78 acres near Bloomington.

Muscatatuck was the first reintroduction site in Indiana for river otters, which, through overtrapping and loss of wetland habitat, had disappeared from the state by 1942 and were added to the state endangered species list in 1994. Since 1995 Muscatatuck has again been home to the once-common creatures.

Since the reintroduction effort began at Muscatatuck, these frisky, furry otters' territories have spread to eighty of Indiana's ninety-two counties. The river otter was removed from the state endangered ranks in 2005. Winter is the best time to see these wary creatures scurrying between ice holes on the marshes, creeks, and ponds on the refuge's auto tour, as well as on Stanfield Lake and Richart Lake. But sightings are increasingly common throughout the year.

Established in 1966 as Indiana's first federal wildlife refuge, Muscatatuck takes its name from the Muscatatuck River, which

Muscatatuck National Wildlife Refuge, Jennings County.

forms the site's southern boundary. The refuge's gently rolling terrain is about 70 percent wetlands, with forests, shrubs/ scrubs, grasslands, and others.

The refuge's wetland forests are of three types: bottomland, floodplain, and beech-maple flats. The bottomland and floodplain forests are mixed with oaks, ashes, maples, sycamores, cottonwoods, birches, and others. The beech-maple flats are upland moist forests with a hardpan clay layer that causes pooling of water. They are not found in the bottomlands.

Muscatatuck has three large lakes: Richart Lake, Stanfield Lake, and Moss Lake; three creeks: Sandy Branch Ditch, Mutton Creek Ditch, and Storm Creek Ditch; and numerous marshes, including the McDonald Marsh, North Endicott Marsh, and South Endicott Marsh.

Other features include a few "moist soil units," which flood in the fall and are drained in the spring; an overlook; a restored cabin and barn; two pioneer cemeteries; the Vernon Fork of the Muscatatuck River; and wildflowers in the spring and fall.

The National Audubon Society has designated Muscatatuck refuge as a Continental Important Bird Area, recording more than 280 species, from ducks to bald eagles. At least 120 species breed there, including a pair of state species of special concern bald eagles in the waterfowl sanctuary, which is closed to the public. Adult and young eagles hunt the wetlands and lakes.

From 2003 to 2008 a remote area of the refuge was used in efforts to reintroduce the federally endangered whooping crane. The stopover routes shifted after 2008 and no longer include Muscatatuck. Between two and nine whooping cranes, however, still winter there.

Among the species Indiana Audubon lists at Muscatatuck with high conservation priority status are American bittern, least bittern, trumpeter swan, yellow-crowned night heron, cerulean warbler, Henslow's sparrow, and sedge wren, all on the state endangered list, and sandhill crane and bald eagle, both state species of special concern. Other noteworthy species that live in or migrate through include wood thrush, grasshopper sparrow, eastern meadowlark, American woodcock, blue-gray gnatcatcher, common moorhen, eastern wood-pewee, great crested flycatcher, Kentucky warbler, prothonotary warbler, yellow-throated warbler, northern flicker, red-headed woodpecker, summer tanager, tufted titmouse, wood duck, yellow-billed cuckoo, double-breasted cormorant, red-winged blackbird, and wild turkey.

Muscatatuck has seen sandhill crane numbers increasing since 2008, when the Fish & Wildlife Service began managing water at lower levels. Their population peaked in 2015 at thirty thousand. They roost in the sanctuary area and frequent the surrounding agricultural fields, where they feed on waste grains and then return to the refuge in the evenings. Several thousand remain on the refuge all day, feeding in Moss Lake and roosting at night. Federally endangered whooping cranes occasionally travel with the sandhills.

Natural springs and creek drainages in the Moss Lake area have created a swamp that is an important sanctuary not just for water birds but for many mammals as well, including mink, muskrat, deer, and raccoon.

The copperbelly water snake is abundant on the Muscatatuck refuge.

The refuge's ninety-seven-acre Acid Seep Spring Research Natural Area is unusual in Indiana. Its boggy environs contain several plant species indigenous to acid seep springs, including marsh bluegrass (a.k.a. bog bluegrass), on the state watch list, winterberry, black chokeberry, and autumn bluegrass.

The Restle Unit of the Muscatatuck National Wildlife Refuge sits due north of the Beanblossom Bottoms Nature Preserve in Monroe County. See no. 51, Beanblossom Bottoms Nature Preserve / Muscatatuck National Wildlife Refuge, Restle Unit, for details.

Activities

Hiking Trails: Four, easy to moderate, 0.2 to 4 miles, one handicapped accessible.

Interpretive Auto Tour: Four-mile loop with twelve stops, open one hour before sunrise to one hour after sunset daily, open to bicyclists.

Other Activities: Boating, nonmotorized on Stanfield Lake, canoes and kayaks on Richart Lake, "belly boats" on all fishing areas; fishing; hunting; interpretive programs; nature study; photography; wildlife watching; visitors' center with exhibits, bookshop, bird observation room, sign-in book.

Directions

GPS coordinates: 38.966664, -85.795951

From I-65

- East on U.S. 50 at Seymour to Muscatatuck National Wildlife Refuge, 2.7 miles

From I-74

- South on State Road 3 at Greensburg to State Road 750 just north of North Vernon, 27.6 miles
- South on State Road 750 to U.S. 50, 4.2 miles
- West on U.S. 50 to Muscatatuck National Wildlife Refuge, 6.5 miles

Tribbett Woods Nature Preserve, Jennings County.

104. Tribbett Woods Nature Preserve
Owned by Oak Heritage Conservancy

The 31.6-acre Tribbett Woods Nature Preserve in southwestern Jennings County is one of the best remaining examples of an old-growth, southeastern flatwoods in Indiana. Situated between the Muscatatuck tributaries Vernon Fork and Graham Creek, this forest type grows on soils referred to locally as "white clay flats," which consist of poorly drained, grayish-white clay that is sticky after rains and brick hard when dry.

These unique growing conditions result in unusual tree associations that are present in Southeastern Indiana's Bluegrass Natural Region but essentially nonexistent elsewhere. Species include American beech, sweet gum, red maple, white oak, big shellbark hickory, black gum, pin oak, and basket oak (a.k.a. swamp chestnut oak). Some beech and oak trees reach 150 feet.

Tribbett's mushy, relatively open understory includes hairy spicebush, pawpaw, and blue beech (a.k.a. hornbeam), with seasonal ponds scattered across the property.

Among the spring wildflower species are bulb bitter cress (a.k.a. spring cress), northern bitter cress (a.k.a. purple cress), spring beauty, yellow adder's tongue (a.k.a. yellow trout lily), and woodland blue violet (a.k.a. LeConte's violet).

On the property's southeast corner, a memorial stone to the Willkom and Tribbett families (1857–1988) commemorates the woodlands' historic owners, who, according to local lore, removed only dead or dying trees.

Tribbett has no trails and can be wet and/or overgrown. Parking is available along the road by the memorial stone.

Activities
Hiking, nature study, photography, wildlife watching.

Directions
GPS coordinates: 38.875044, -85.727805
From I-65
- East on State Road 250 to County Road 700W, 4.3 miles
- North on County Road 700W to West County Road 750S, 2.0 miles
- East on County Road 750S to the preserve, 0.4 mile

From I-74
- South on State Road 3 at Greensburg, through North Vernon, to State Road 250, 43.3 miles
- West on State Road 250 to South County Road 700W, 5.8 miles
- North on County Road 700W to West County Road 750S, 2.0 miles
- East on West County Road 750S to the preserve, 0.4 mile

105. Wells Woods Nature Preserve
Owned by Indiana Department of Natural Resources, Division of Nature Preserves

The twenty-acre Wells Woods Nature Preserve is a mature flat-woods forest situated just south of Main Street in Commiskey. It's located between the Muscatatuck River's two primary tributaries—less than a mile west of Graham Creek and five miles east of the Vernon Fork. That such remnant trees exist on flat land in Indiana is unusual. Most older-growth forests are on steep slopes and in ravines that are difficult to cultivate.

Like nearby Tribbett Woods, Wells sits on what locals call the "white clay flats," level terrain with poorly drained soils that are subject to flooding. Seasonal ponds form during the spring and dry to the point of cracking in the summer.

Also like Tribbett, Wells has developed unusual tree species combinations, including American beech, sweet gum, red maple, black gum, white oak, and basket oak (a.k.a. swamp chestnut oak).

The paved road is lined with private property adjacent to and across from the Wells Woods preserve. Limited parking is available.

Activities

Hiking, nature study, photography, wildlife watching.

Directions

GPS coordinates: 38.856974, -85.647900

From I-65

- East on U.S. 50 at Seymour to State Road 3 in North Vernon, 13.0 miles
- South on State Road 3, through Vernon, to the Commiskey Turnoff (Main Street), 11.2 miles
- West on Main Street, through the stop sign, to Byfield Road, 0.5 mile
- South on Byfield Road to the preserve, park on the curve, 0.3 mile

From I-74

- South on State Road 3 at Greensburg, through North Vernon, to the Commiskey Turnoff (Main Street), 40.9 miles
- West on Main Street, through the stop sign, to Byfield Road, 0.5 mile
- South on Byfield Road to the preserve, park on the curve, 0.3 mile

Guthrie Woods Nature Preserve, Jefferson County.

106. Guthrie Memorial Woods Nature Preserve

Owned by Indiana Department of Natural Resources and Oak Heritage Conservancy

The sixty-three-acre Guthrie Memorial Woods in northwestern Jefferson County—twenty acres of mature forest—is an anomaly among Indiana woods, as it is a mature bluegrass till-plain flatwoods with an elevation change no greater than ten feet. Most remnant forest stands in Indiana are confined to slopes and ravines that are difficult to cultivate.

Like Tribbett Woods and Wells Woods, nearby flatwoods nature preserves, the old-growth Guthrie Woods thrives atop a white clay soil that does not allow water to penetrate and causes spring rains to pool in the woods and the soil to crack in the summer.

The northern section of this beech–sweet gum–white oak forest community contains mature specimens, while the southern two-thirds has medium- and small-sized trees. Basket oak (a.k.a. swamp chestnut oak), white oak, sweet gum, red maple, and tulip poplar are present in large numbers.

The understory supports dwarf ginseng, a state watch list species, partridge berry, and wetland species such as cardinal flower, buttonbush, and ditch stonecrop.

A spring retains water during the spring season but is often dry by late summer and early fall.

The preserve was initially given to the Nature Study Club of Indiana in 1927 by William Guthrie. A stone marker on its southeast corner declares his intent: "This forest land is dedicated to

Sarah Lewis Guthrie for a perpetual sanctuary as a living memorial to one who loved trees, flowers, and birds."

Guthrie has no trails and can be wet and/or overgrown. Parking is along the roadside, which is slightly ditched.

Activities
Hiking, nature study, photography, wildlife watching.

Directions
GPS coordinates: 38.912577, -85.520197
From I-65
- East on U.S. 50 at Seymour to State Road 7 in North Vernon, 13.0 miles
- South on State Road 7, through Vernon, to County Road 500S, 8.1 miles
- East on County Road 500S to the woods, 1.1 miles

From I-74
- South on State Road 3 at Greensburg to State Road 7 at North Vernon, 29 miles
- South on State Road 7, through Vernon, to County Road 500S, 9.1 miles
- East on County Road 500S to the woods, 1.1 miles

107. Big Oaks National Wildlife Refuge
Owned by U.S. Army, managed as an overlay refuge
by U.S. Fish & Wildlife Service

While the fifty-thousand-acre Big Oaks National Wildlife Refuge may be the largest federal refuge and one of the largest contiguous forest blocks and grassland complexes in Indiana, it has visitor restrictions due to its military past. Fencing with double strands of barbed wire on top encircles the sprawling refuge. It's only open for general public use two days a week and two Saturdays a month between April and November. Groups can contact the office and schedule tours of the property throughout the year. These tours can revolve around birding, wildflowers, cultural history, or just a little bit of everything the refuge has to offer.

Big Oaks occupies the northern fifty thousand acres of the

Big Oaks National Wildlife Refuge, Jefferson County.

former Jefferson Proving Ground north of the "historic firing line," where military munitions were tested for a half century. A sign on the gate warns of "unexploded ammunition," illustrated with an image of an exploding bomb beneath what appears to be two dancing teens from the 1960s. Before entering, visitors must attend a safety briefing and sign the "acknowledgement of danger agreement."

This national refuge is named for the mature stands of stately oak trees that represent remnants of the forest that existed around the turn of the twentieth century. With more than fifteen thousand acres of wetlands, grasslands, and shrublands, the refuge also has extensive stands of forest and the 165-acre Old Timbers Lake, all of which provide habitat for more than two hundred bird, forty-six mammal, twenty-five amphibian, and eighteen reptile species.

Federally endangered Indiana bats and federally threatened northern long-eared bats forage, roost, and raise their young in the Big Oaks stream corridors and forested areas. The state-endangered river otter was reintroduced in 1996 and still thrives there. Deer, bobcat, fox, squirrel, coyote, raccoon, and Virginia opossum are common mammals.

The National Audubon Society has designated Big Oaks a Global Important Bird Area in part because of the estimated five hundred–plus pairs of state-endangered Henslow's sparrows that breed in the grasslands, one of the largest populations in the nation. Bald eagles, a state species of special concern, breed on Old Timbers Lake, and golden eagles use the refuge for wintering sites.

State-endangered cerulean warbler and worm-eating warbler, a state species of special concern, have been identified at Big Oaks. Other noteworthy species that live in or migrate through include Acadian flycatcher, blue-winged warbler, Kentucky warbler, prairie warbler, eastern meadowlark, field sparrow, northern flicker, orchard oriole, red-headed woodpecker, and wood thrush.

With a permit, edible mushrooms, berries, and deer antlers may be gathered for personal use. Otherwise disturbing or collecting plants, animals, or their parts is prohibited.

The U.S. Army established Jefferson Proving Ground as an ordnance-testing installation as World War II got under way in 1941. The facility closed in 1995 and became Big Oaks in 2000. During the transition, the U.S. Fish & Wildlife Service managed the wildlife resources. A sign by the gate with boarded-up gatehouse still says "U.S. Army Jefferson Proving Ground, 1941–1995."

Through a twenty-five-year real estate permit, the army retains ownership, and the U.S. Fish & Wildlife Service manages the property. The Indiana Air National Guard still uses the 1,033 acres in the center as an air-to-ground bombing range that is surrounded by, but not designated as part of, the refuge. The south end features a Jefferson County park with fishing lake, trails, and interpretive areas. The remainder of the former cantonment area is mostly private farmland and businesses. World War II–style buildings house businesses and government agencies, such as the Indiana Department of Transportation and Southeastern Indiana Solid Waste District offices.

Activities

Hiking Trails: Big Oaks has two developed hiking trails with an observation platform overlooking a nest of bald eagles, a state species of special concern, and a photo blind, and you may walk the gravel roads or visit the day-use area to observe nature.

Camping: Camping is not allowed in Big Oaks.

Other Activities: Boating (rowboats, kayaks, canoes, paddleboats, and electric trolling motors only), environmental education and interpretation, fishing, hunting, nature study, photography, refuge tours, wildlife watching.

Directions

GPS coordinates: 38.839547, -85.388773

From I-65

- East on U.S. 50 at Seymour, through North Vernon, to U.S. 421 at Versailles, 34.0 miles
- South on U.S. 421 to the refuge entrance, 19.7 miles

From I-74

- South on U.S. 421 at Greensburg, through North Vernon, to the refuge, 41.9 miles

108. Hardy Lake State Recreation Area

Owned by Indiana Department of Natural Resources,
Division of State Parks & Reservoirs

The 2,449-acre Hardy Lake State Recreation Area wraps around Hardy Lake, which, at 741 acres, is the smallest state-operated reservoir in Indiana. The lake water is held in check, however, by the largest state-owned dam.

Aside from the beach area, Hardy Lake is ringed with hardwood forest and rocky limestone bluffs, caves, and fossils. The lake was created in 1970, when Quick's Creek was dammed for water supply and outdoor recreation. Because it's the state's only reservoir that was not created for flood control, Hardy Lake's levels are stable year-round, with positive effects on the shoreline, fishing, and wildlife.

The landscape features climax oak-hickory and beech-maple forests, pine groves, cedar thickets, eighteenth-century gravesites, beaver cuts, scenic lake overlooks, mound-building ants, and hooting owls.

A marsh is maintained below the dam. A raptor rehabilitation center for injured birds of prey educates the public about hawks, owls, falcons, and vultures.

Activities

Hiking Trails: Six, easy to moderate, 0.52 to 2.05 miles.
Camping: 149 electric sites, 18 primitive sites, dumping station.
Other Activities: Archery range, basketball courts, four boat launch ramps, rowboat rental, fishing / ice fishing piers, hunting, interpretive services, nature study, open playfield, picnicking, shelter houses, playgrounds, swimming beach, volleyball courts, waterskiing, wildlife watching.

Directions
GPS coordinates: 38.776638, -85.706205
From I-65
- East on U.S. 256 at Austin to Hardy Lake Road, 6.0 miles
- North on Hardy Lake Road to recreation area, 3.0 miles

From I-74
- South on State Road 3 at Greensburg, through North Vernon, to U.S. 256, 50.0 miles
- West on U.S. 256 to Hardy Lake Road, 3.0 miles
- North on Hardy Lake Road to recreation area, 3.0 miles

109. Pennywort Cliffs Preserve
Owned by The Nature Conservancy
The 210-acre Pennywort Cliffs Preserve features century-old tulip poplar stands, young walnut trees, half-century-old pine plantations, flowing springs, and a thirty-foot waterfall. It was dedicated in 1931 as one of the first classified forests in Indiana.

Pennywort is situated northwest of Madison in a deep canyon along Big Creek. It is named for the state-endangered American pennywort, a wildflower that lives in the base of the preserve's limestone cliffs. Two constantly flowing springs meet and make their way over the waterfall before reaching Big Creek and the preserve's eastern edge.

Pennywort Cliffs Preserve, Jefferson County.

The cathedral-like forest includes tulip poplar, American beech, white oak, northern red oak, shagbark hickory, sugar maple, sweet gum, wild black cherry, sassafras, flowering dogwood, and pawpaw.

Wildflowers at the Pennywort preserve include wood anemone, mayapple, Indian turnip (a.k.a. Jack-in-the-pulpit), Virginia bluebells, and partridgeberry.

In addition to wildflowers, the forest floor features large patches of ground cedar (a.k.a. deep-root clubmoss), rare in the state, and a variety of ferns. Hairy spicebush, whose berries were used by pioneers as a substitute for allspice, is a common shrub.

Wildlife species that frequent the preserve include white-tailed deer, raccoon, Virginia opossum, and wild turkey, as well as a variety of neotropical migrant songbirds.

The preserve's trails are well established and easy to follow.

The Pennywort Cliffs Preserve was donated to The Nature Conservancy in 2002 by Madison resident Mary G. Clashman, a farmer, accountant, restaurant critic, and founding member of the environmental group Save the Valley. A memorial headstone inscribed with her name, 1928–20——, and a Nature

Conservancy logo leaf inscribed on it sits on a knoll by a picnic table overlooking a rugged creek valley.

Activities
Hiking Trails: Easy to moderate terrain, no trail to the waterfall.
Other Activities: Nature study, photography, wildlife watching.

Directions
GPS coordinates: 38.817713, -85.536929
From I-65
- East on U.S. 50 at Seymour to State Road 7 at North Vernon, 13.0 miles
- South on State Road 7 to State Road 250, 16.9 miles
- West on State Road 250 to North County Road 800W, 3.4 miles
- South on North County Road 800W to preserve, 1.4 miles

From I-74
- South on State Road 3 at Greensburg to State Road 7 at North Vernon, 29.0 miles
- South on State Road 7 to State Road 250, 16.9 miles
- West on State Road 250 to North County Road 800W, 3.4 miles
- South on North County Road 800W to preserve, 1.4 miles

110a. Clifty Falls State Park
Owned by Indiana Department of Natural Resources,
Division of State Parks & Reservoirs

The 1,519-acre Clifty Falls State Park just west of Madison on the Ohio River is known for its magnificent waterfalls that plunge over 425-million-year-old bedrock to a canyon floor brimming with fossil-ridden rock. Encompassing some of the state's most precipitous topography, Clifty features an elevation drop of more than three hundred feet between its north and south gates.

Clifty Falls, established in 1920 as one of Indiana's earliest state parks, follows Clifty Creek and its tributaries—Little Clifty Creek, Dean's Branch, and Hoffman Branch—on their way to the Ohio River just outside the park boundaries to the south. A second Ohio feeder, Little Crooked Creek, begins inside the park boundaries on the southeast portion and ends at the Ohio just east of its confluence with Clifty Creek.

Clifty Falls State Park, Jefferson County.

While the broad, picturesque, sixty-foot Big Clifty Falls and Little Clifty Falls are the most recognized, they are the smallest of the park's four in terms of height. Tunnel Falls on Dean's Branch and Hoffman Falls on Hoffman Branch are eighty-three and seventy-eight feet, respectively.

The river, creeks, and canyons trace their origins back some seven hundred thousand years to the Ice Age, when a continental-sized Kansan glacier covered Southeastern Indiana and redirected the region's drainage patterns from north to south, ultimately forming the Ohio River Valley. Through the ages and a subsequent glacial advance that stopped about twenty-five miles to the park's north, melting ice eroded the Ordovician period bedrock, carving Clifty Falls' canyons and gorges.

Clifty Creek's bed is littered with fossils from an ancient marine ecosystem that was abundantly populated with corals, ancestral squids, brachiopods, and more marine life. Searching for fossils is allowed in the park. Collecting them is not.

An observation tower is located on the park's far south end overlooking the Ohio River.

Winter and spring, when the water is flowing and sometimes freezing, are the best times to visit Clifty Falls, though hiking and breathtaking scenery are available year-round.

110b. Clifty Canyon Nature Preserve

The 178-acre Clifty Canyon Nature Preserve lies within the park's northwest section and includes Big Clifty Falls and Little Clifty Falls, with moisture-loving forests on the lower slopes and ravine bottoms and dry oak-hickory forests on the upper slopes and ridgetops. The steep ravines' undisturbed sheet-rock cliff communities support mosses, lichens, and ferns, as well as several rare plants and common wildflowers.

Activities

Hiking Trails: Ten trails, easy to rugged, 0.5 to 4.5 miles.

Camping: 106 electric sites, 63 nonelectric sites, youth tent areas, dumping station.

Other Activities: Meeting and conference facilities, nature center / interpretive naturalist services, nature study, photography, picnicking, restaurant, shelters (reservations), tennis and other games, swimming pool / waterslide.

Directions

GPS coordinates: 38.742143, -85.412633

From I-65

- East on State Road 256 at Austin to State Road 56, 20.4 miles
- East on State Road 56 to Clifty Falls State Park, 2.2 miles

From I-74

- South on U.S. 421 at Greensburg, through Versailles, to State Road 56 at Madison, 49.2 miles
- West on State Road 56 to Clifty Falls State Park, 1.9 miles

111. Chelsea Flatwoods Nature Preserve

Owned by The Nature Conservancy

The 305-acre Chelsea Flatwoods Nature Preserve southwest of Hanover is one of the state's most diverse plots of bluegrass tillplain flatwoods, a forest type that occurs on level ground atop compacted soils that do not drain well and that remain moist or wet year-round. While these conditions resemble those of floodplain forests, flatwoods are not subjected to flooding from nearby waterways.

Situated a few miles west of the Ohio River, the area was glaciated during the Illinoian Glacial some 220,000 to 70,000 years ago, leaving a till plain in its wake. Chelsea's soils are clay that are highly acidic and produce a unique mix of trees, wildflowers, and ferns.

Dominating the woodlands are southern red oak, on the state watch list, swamp white oak, pin oak, basket oak (a.k.a. swamp chestnut oak), white oak, American beech, black gum, sweet gum, and sugar maple.

Chelsea's understory is home to uncommon wildflowers, including the large whorled pogonia, on the state watch list, rare Wolf's spike rush, handsome Harry (a.k.a. common meadow-beauty and Virginia meadow-beauty), and common bur sedge (a.k.a. Gray's sedge). Plentiful fern species include New York fern, sensitive fern, lady fern, marsh shield fern, and Oneida grape fern. Other plant life includes purple chokeberry and strawberry bush.

Chelsea Flatwoods is one of the state's wettest, has no trail, and is easy to get disoriented in, so rubber boots and compasses are recommended. Parking is along the narrow gravel roadside, which can also be wet.

Activities
Hiking (no established trails), nature study, photography, wildlife watching.

Directions
GPS coordinates: 38.664805, -85.524354
From I-65
- East on State Road 56 at Scottsburg to State Road 62, 15.0 miles

Charlestown State Park, Clark County

- South on State Road 62 to West Reardon Road
  (County Road 500S), 3.0 miles
- East on Reardon Road, Chelsea Flatwoods on right

From I-74

- South on State Road 3 at Greensburg, through
  North Vernon, to State Road 56, 52.0 miles
- East on State Road 56 to State Road 62, 6.8 miles
- South on State Road 62 to West Reardon Road
  (County Road 500S), 3.0 miles
- East on Reardon Road, Chelsea Flatwoods on right

112a. Charlestown State Park

Owned by Indiana Department of Natural Resources,
Division of State Parks & Reservoirs

Charlestown State Park's 5,100 acres of 200-foot-plus hill-and-ravine topography sits on the banks of the Ohio River northeast of Louisville. The state's third largest state park features scenic vistas of its two primary natural features: the Ohio River and Fourteenmile Creek.

Before the late 1800s, the Ohio at Fourteenmile Creek was shallow enough to walk across at times in the summer, according to DNR brochures. A series of human-made locks and dams began at that time and transformed the river into its present, navigable state.

The rugged, winding Fourteenmile Creek Valley is one of the oldest unglaciated stream valleys in Indiana. Due to the locks and dams, the creek today in some places looks more like a long, winding "ribbon lake" than a flowing stream.

When the Ohio rises, Fourteenmile Creek appears to flow in reverse, as rising river waters back into the creek valley. This phenomenon is clearly visible from the Portersville Bridge, a 1912 structure that was dismantled at its original site on the East Fork of the White River and reconstructed over Fourteenmile Creek between 2008 and 2011. The bridge connects the park to Fourteenmile Creek Nature Preserve east of the creek.

Charlestown is popular with bird-watchers, with seventy-two species, from bluebirds to vultures to bald eagles, a state species of special concern, living in or migrating through at any given moment. Its natural features include Devonian period fossil outcrops and areas of karst sinkhole topography.

The park property was part of the fifteen-thousand-acre Indiana Armory Ammunition Plant from 1940 to 1995. Before the plant was established, most of the parkland was used for farm or pasture land.

112b. Fourteenmile Creek Nature Preserve

The 1,718-acre Fourteenmile Creek Nature Preserve is bisected by the Fourteenmile Creek, which begins at a peninsula on the Ohio River at an isolated bedrock ridge called the Devil's Backbone. The peninsula is the site of a 1920s-era amusement park called Rose Island, which was accessible only by steamer, bridge, or ferry. The facilities were damaged beyond repair by the 1937 flood and closed.

Though debunked by archaeologists, legend says Devil's Backbone contains the remains of a stone fortress built by twelfth-century Welsh adventurers in the Ohio Valley led by Prince Madoc. Archaeologists say the limestone walls are clearly Native American.

The preserve is composed of deep ravines, sinkholes, caves, high-quality limestone cliffs, and a range of forest types, from dry upland to moist floodplain.

The uplands support eastern red cedar, chinquapin oak, eastern prickly pear cactus, shooting star, hoary puccoon, nodding wild onion, and rare cliff adder's tongue fern (a.k.a. limestone adder's tongue fern). The moist southern end at Devil's Backbone supports sugar maple, tulip poplar, northern red oak, white oak, chinquapin oak, American beech, and a variety of wildflowers, including mayapple, columbine, twinleaf, Jack-in-the-pulpit, and sessile trillium.

A number of rare plants and cave invertebrates have been documented in Fourteenmile Creek Nature Preserve.

Activities
Hiking Trails: Six, moderate to rugged, 1.2 to 2.9 miles.
Camping: 132 electric sites, 60 full hookup sites.
Other Activities: Fishing, interpretive naturalist services, nature study, photography, picnic areas with shelters (reservations), playground equipment, wildlife watching.

Directions
GPS coordinates: 38.449222, -85.646109
From I-65
- East on State Road 160 at Henryville to State Road 3 at Charlestown, 9.0 miles
- South on State Road 3 to State Road 62, 1.1 miles
- East on State Road 62 to park, 1.0 mile

From I-74
- South on State Road 3 at Greensburg, through North Vernon, to State Road 62, 73.4 miles
- East on State Road 62 to park, 1.0 mile

113. Nine Penny Branch Nature Preserve
Owned by Indiana Department of Natural Resources,
Division of Nature Preserves
The 121-acre Nine Penny Branch Nature Preserve features an old-growth upland forest and a moderately deep ravine cut

into limestone bedrock. The forest is dominated by mature oak, beeches, and poplars, with areas of young, second-growth forest.

Nine Penny Run bisects the preserve and features herbaceous plants and a limestone streambed with small waterfalls, pools, and riffles. A two-mile loop trail passes through the preserve. An old stagecoach route runs along the stream. Remnants of early stone fences are still visible.

Activities
Hiking Trail: One, two-mile loop that crosses Nine Penny Branch.
Other Activities: Nature study, photography, wildlife watching.

Directions
GPS coordinates: 38.473859, -85.634470
From I-65
- East on State Road 160 at Henryville to State Road 3 in Charlestown, 9.0 miles
- South on State Road 3 to State Road 62, 1.1 miles
- Northeast on State Road 62 to Monroe Street, 0.4 mile
- Northwest on Monroe Street, 0.3 mile
- Northeast on Tunnel Mill Road to Nine Penny Run trailhead, 2.5 miles

From I-74
- South on State Road 3 at Greensburg, through North Vernon, to State Road 62 at Charlestown, 73.2 miles
- Northeast on State Road 62 to Monroe Street, 0.4 mile
- Northwest on Monroe Street, 0.3 mile
- Northeast on Tunnel Mill Road to Nine Penny Run trailhead, 2.5 miles

Switzerland Hills Section

114. Whitewater Memorial State Park / Hornbeam Nature Preserve
Owned by Indiana Department of Natural Resources, Division of State Parks & Reservoirs
The 1,710-acre Whitewater Memorial State Park is a piece of one of the state's largest outdoor recreation reserves that includes

two lakes, two state recreation areas, and a state-dedicated nature preserve. All together, the Whitewater / Brookville Lake complex totals 12,895 acres that are situated along the historic East Fork Whitewater River Valley north of Brookville and are surrounded by some of Indiana's highest reliefs.

The historic valley is known for traces of prehistoric Native American mounds and is just a few miles east of Whitewater State Historic Site in Metamora, a preserved 1830s canal town that was a stop on the Whitewater Canal. The canal stretched from Cambridge City to Lawrenceburg, with a spur to Cincinnati. It carried boat traffic from 1839 to 1865.

The National Audubon Society has identified Whitewater-Brookville as a State Important Bird Area for supporting "one of the most significant assemblages of migrant and nesting avian species in Eastern Indiana. Congregations of migrant waterfowl, a diversity of neotropical passerines, and nesting endangered raptors are the fundamental characteristics of this Important Bird Area." In early spring, daily counts can exceed two thousand birds, with diving ducks the most prominent. Sizeable concentrations of American black duck frequent Brookville Lake during migration.

The state park surrounds the two-hundred-acre Whitewater Lake and abuts Brookville Lake on the park's west side. Along with the lake and its feeder, Silver Creek, the park features wooded, rolling hills, steep ridges and ravines, and level, open fields. The park naturalist offers programs at the Naturalist Cabin and nearby amphitheater.

Whitewater was initially purchased by Union, Fayette, Franklin, and Wayne Counties after World War II as a veterans memorial. It became the sixteenth park in the Indiana state park system in 1949 and pays homage to its historical roots with a trailside view of Brookville Lake on the two-mile-loop Veterans Vista Trail.

114a. Hornbeam Nature Preserve

The eighty-three-acre Hornbeam Nature Preserve is an example of the mixed hardwood forest that is typically found in this

Hornbeam Nature Preserve, Whitewater State Park, Union County.

part of the state. In successional terms, the preserve's woods is intermediate, between beech-maple and oak-hickory types, trending toward beech-maple, with large numbers of northern red oak and green ash.

Located inside the Whitewater State Park, the preserve is named for the large number of hop hornbeam (a.k.a. blue beech) trees in the understory. Hornbeams are small trees with smooth, blue-gray bark and exceptionally hard wood. They are also called blue beech and ironwood.

The Hornbeam preserve sits atop 450-million-year-old Ordovician shale and dolomite, which is covered by glacial deposits from the Illinoian and Wisconsin glaciers that advanced and retreated in the state between 220,000 and 13,600 years ago. Fossils are exposed where streams have cut through the bedrock.

The preserve also features a small seep spring community. In spring, the forest floor is densely carpeted with wildflowers.

The preserve sits on the Whitewater Lake's southwestern shore and is bisected by the park road. Two trails pass through—the

Redsprings Trail (named after a seep spring whose minerals and iron deposits leave a rust color on the water) and Lakeshore Trail.

Activities
Hiking Trails: Five, all moderate, from 1 to 2.7 miles.
Bridle Trails: Nine miles.
Camping: 236 electric sites, 45 nonelectric sites, 37 primitive horse sites, youth tent areas, camp store, dumping station.
Other Activities: Two boat launch ramps (electric trolling only), canoe, paddleboat, and rowboat rentals; cabins; fishing; interpretive naturalist services; picnicking; shelters (by reservation); swimming.

Directions
GPS coordinates: 39.613920, -84.948336
From I-74
- North on State Road 1 to State Road 101 in Brookville, 12.1 miles
- North on State Road 101, past Brookville Lake, to Whitewater State Park, 14.9 miles

From I-70
- South on U.S. 27 through Richmond to State Road 101 in Liberty, 17.3 miles
- South on State Road 101 to the Whitewater Memorial State Park, 1.7 miles

115. Brookville Lake / Mounds State Recreation Area / Quakertown State Recreation Area

Brookville Lake and its two State Recreation Areas comprise another 11,185 acres of public land south of the Whitewater State Park, including the 5,260-acre reservoir.

Mature forest stands along the lake, especially on its southwestern edge, provide critical breeding habitats for many neotropical migrants, including state-endangered cerulean warbler, wood thrush, Kentucky warbler, Louisiana waterthrush, and prairie warbler. The reservoir and surrounding trees support state-endangered osprey and bald eagle, a state species of special

Brookville Lake, Franklin County.

concern. One eagle nest and two osprey nests are located in the area. Other noteworthy species that live in or migrate through include eastern wood-pewee, lesser scaup, prothonotary warbler, redhead duck, rose-breasted grosbeak, and wood thrush.

The federal government purchased the property and built the lake in 1975 for flood control, wildlife, and recreation. More than eleven thousand acres are managed for a variety of habitats for plants and wildlife.

Nationally known for its recreational sport fishing, Brookville Lake features nine boat launch ramps and four marinas.

Activities
Hiking Trails: Eleven, easy to rugged, 0.7 to 16.5 miles.
Camping: 388 electric sites, 62 full hookup sites, camp store, dumping station.
Other Activities: Archery, boating, horseshoes, hunting, interpretive naturalist services, nature study, picnic tables and shelter house, photography, playground, shooting range, swimming, volleyball, waterskiing.

Directions
GPS coordinates (Brookville Lake): 39.439421, -84.981401
From I-74

- North on State Road 1 to State Road 101 in Brookville, 12.1 miles
- North on State Road 101 to Brookville Lake, 1.9 miles

From I-70

- South on U.S. 27 through Richmond to State Road 101 at Liberty, 17.3 miles
- South on State Road 101 to Brookville Lake, 14.6 miles

116. John Sunman's Woods Nature Preserve

Owned by Central Indiana Land Trust

John Sunman's Woods Nature Preserve is a thirty-three-acre forest that occupies a rolling, ridge-and-gully terrain east of Batesville and features exceptional biological diversity for such a small tract. The forest supports northern red oak, white oak, wild black cherry, American beech, shagbark hickory, sugar maple, tulip poplar, and sassafras trees, with an understory of native shrubs, ferns, and wildflowers.

Sunman's Woods is located at the dead end of a county road adjacent to I-74, is surrounded by private property, and has limited parking. It is named after John Sunman Sr. and is part of a 160-acre plot he homesteaded in 1819.

Activities
Hiking, nature study, photography, wildlife watching.

Directions
GPS coordinates: 39.278923, -85.117873
From I-74

- South on State Road 101 (Sunman exit) east of Batesville to State Road 46, 0.6 mile
- West on State Road 46 to County Road 775E, 1.1 miles
- North on County Road 775E to preserve; preserve begins at northwest intersection

117a. Versailles State Park

Owned by Indiana Department of Natural Resources,
Division of State Parks & Reservoirs

Versailles State Park's 5,998 acres of forested, rolling hills west of Lawrenceburg stretch along and around the scenic Laughery Creek and 230-acre Versailles Lake. The covered 1885 Busching Bridge just before the park gate offers scenic views of the creek.

Laughery Creek's behavior is cloaked in a bit of a natural history mystery. It begins south of Batesville and flows twenty-five miles to the south, through the park, before taking an unpredictable turn to the northeast at Friendship and emptying into the Ohio River south of Aurora. "Complexities in the glacial history of the terrain no doubt explain this perverse behavior," Henry H. Gray notes in Marion T. Jackson's book *The Natural Heritage of Indiana*, "but the exact reasons are unknown" (30).

The state's second largest state park, behind Brown County, is deeply rooted in history. The creek is named after Revolutionary War soldier Col. Archibald Laughery, who in 1781 led his men down the Ohio River to meet with George Rogers Clark at the Falls of the Ohio. Before they arrived, they were killed in a battle with Native Americans where the creek enters the Ohio River, just south of Aurora.

During the Civil War, Morgan's Raiders made their way through the area that is now the park, and the nearby town of Versailles was briefly under Confederate control.

The property became the first federal park in Indiana in 1934, during the Great Depression, when the National Park Service acquired seventeen hundred acres of marginal Ripley County farmland and established the Versailles Recreation Demonstration Area.

The following January, President Franklin D. Roosevelt's Civilian Conservation Corps (CCC), known as the "tree army," began restoring the land by planting trees, implementing watershed and erosion controls, and building roads, paths, and

Versailles State Park, Ripley County.

water construction projects. Artisans constructed buildings and shelters, and most of their original work is still present. A CCC commemorative statue in the park was dedicated in 2010.

In 1943 the National Park Service deeded the property to Indiana, and the Versailles Project became Versailles State Park.

Ancient history abounds beneath the park's surface. Over geologic time, Laughery Creek cut through Silurian reef limestone, creating steep, rocky slopes and exposing fossil-rich, 475-million-year-old Ordovician rock in the process.

Many of the park's creeks contain fossils, including bryozoans, brachiopods, corals, and crinoids. Sinkholes and springs suggest an extensive underground drainage system.

Versailles's hardwood forests provide habitats for songbirds and a variety of wildlife. Herons and other wetland wildlife are commonly spotted near the dam's scenic overlook.

117b. Falling Timber Nature Preserve

While not marked on DNR property maps, the scenic, 109-acre Falling Timber Nature Preserve is located inside the park on the Falling Timber Creek east of the Versailles Lake and is filled with fossil-laden rock. The predominant natural community types are upland and riparian forest.

Activities
Hiking Trails: Three, easy to moderate, 1.5 to 2.75 miles.
Bridle Trails: Day use only.
Camping: 226 electric sites, group camp, youth tent camping area, camp store, dumping station.
Other Activities: Boat launch ramp (electric trolling only); canoeing; paddleboat, rowboat, and kayak rentals; mountain bike trails; fishing; interpretive naturalist services; nature study; photography; picnic areas with shelters (reservations); recreation building (rental); swimming pool / waterslide; wildlife watching.

Directions
GPS coordinates: 39.067656, -85.237282
From I-65
- East on U.S. 50 at Seymour, through North Vernon, to Versailles State Park, 35.6 miles

From I-74
- South on U.S. 421 at Greensburg to U.S. 50, 25.2 miles
- East on U.S. 50 to Versailles State Park, 1.3 miles

118. Oxbow

Owned by Oxbow Inc.

The Oxbow in Lawrenceburg is a three-thousand-acre spread of protected floodplain river bottom on the Ohio River at its confluence with the Great Miami River. Tucked behind a levee, it is named for a small oxbow-shaped lake that was isolated when floodwaters carved a new course for the Great Miami in 1847. In addition to Oxbow Lake, the protected area includes Osprey Lake, Juno Pond, Mercer Pond, Wood Duck Slough, and two overlook areas.

Oxbow, Dearborn County.

Located where Indiana, Ohio, and Kentucky meet, the Oxbow's five-square-mile wetland habitat floods with nutrient-rich waters, whose deposits, plus a high water table, produce prime farmland. Wildlife-friendly agricultural methods practiced on the land provide a winter source of grain that, when combined with small fish left in the shallow waters by receding floodwaters, create rich staging grounds for wading birds and waterfowl migrating between northern breeding grounds and southern wintering grounds in the spring and fall.

As a result, the Oxbow attracts the tristate area's largest concentrations of ducks and herons. Bird-watchers have identified 287 bird species, among them state-endangered black-crowned night heron, as well as bald eagle and great egret, both state species of special concern. Wood duck, prothonotary warbler, Caspian tern, American avocet, and other species of shorebird, wader, duck, songbird, and raptor are also present.

Sixty-six fish species and 472 vascular plant species have also been documented in the Oxbow.

The majority of the refuge—twenty-three hundred acres—is owned by Oxbow Inc., a nonprofit conservation land trust whose mission is to protect, improve, and manage the Oxbow land for wildlife by acquiring land through direct purchase, conservation easements, and donations. Another seven hundred acres are privately owned but managed by Oxbow Inc.

Activities
Hiking, nature study, photography, wildlife watching.

Directions
GPS coordinates: 39.120150, -84.844190
From I-65
- East on U.S. 50 at Seymour to Oxbow Entrance in Lawrenceburg, 62.0 miles
- Turn right on the road between the Shell Station and the Waffle House. Proceed over the levee and drive two blocks to the chain-link fence. Turn right and drive one block to the Oxbow entrance on the left.

From I-74
- South on I-275 to U.S. 50 at Lawrenceburg, 8.9 miles
- South on U.S. 50 to Oxbow Entrance, 0.2 mile
- Turn left on the road between the Shell Station and the Waffle House. Proceed over the levee and drive two blocks to the chain-link fence. Turn right and drive one block to the Oxbow entrance on your left.

119. Splinter Ridge Fish & Wildlife Area
Owned by Indiana Department of Natural Resources,
Division of Fish & Wildlife
The Splinter Ridge Fish & Wildlife Area east of Madison consists of 2,460 acres of contiguous wooded hills and grassy pastures dedicated primarily to hunting. It is named after its major ridge and historic logging road, which the state purchased in 1997.

The steep wooded hills provide excellent habitat for deer, turkeys, and squirrels. Limited hunting opportunities are available for cottontail rabbit, northern bobwhite, and American woodcock.

The rolling hayfields, steep wooded hills, brushy tracts, and small creeks attract a wide variety of songbirds and woodpeckers for wildlife watching and photography.

Activities

Hiking, nature study, photography, wildlife watching.

Directions

GPS coordinates: 38.745861, -85.203905

From I-65

- East on State Road 56 at Scottsburg, through Madison, to Doe Run Road, 32.7 miles
- Northeast on Doe Run Road to Little Doe Run Road, 1.6 miles
- East on Little Doe Run Road to fish and wildlife area, 0.2 mile

From I-74

- South on U.S. 421 at Greensburg, through Versailles, to State Road 56 at Madison, 49.2 miles
- East on State Road 56 to Doe Run Road, 7.7 miles
- Northeast on Doe Run Road to Little Doe Run Road, 1.6 miles
- East on Little Doe Run Road to fish and wildlife area, 0.2 mile

Part 4

SUPPLEMENTARY
MATERIALS

Species List

The following plant and animal species are mentioned in this book. This is not an exhaustive list of the flora and fauna that live in or pass through Southern Indiana. It represents what the areas' land stewards and others, most significantly, various units of the National Audubon Society, prioritized when describing the places.

Rankings for species that are endangered, threatened, or otherwise of conservation concern were drawn from Indiana Department of Natural Resources lists with the following designations.

Animals and Plants

FE (Federally Endangered): Any species that is in danger of extinction throughout all or a significant portion of its range.

FT (Federally Threatened): Any species that is likely to become endangered within the foreseeable future throughout all or a significant portion of its range.

SC (Special Concern): Any animal species requiring monitoring because of known or suspected limited abundance or distribution or because of a recent change in legal status or required habitat. These species do not receive legal protection under the Nongame and Endangered Species Conservation Act.

SE (State Endangered): Any animal species whose prospects for survival or recruitment within the state are in immediate jeopardy and are in danger of disappearing from the state. This includes all species classified as endangered by the federal government that occur in Indiana.

Plants only

SE (State Endangered): Any plant species whose prospects for survival or recruitment within the state are in immediate jeopardy and are in danger of disappearing from the state. This includes all species classified as endangered by the federal government that occur in Indiana. Generally one to five current occurrences in the state.

SR (State Rare): Any plant species that is vulnerable in the state due to restricted range, relatively few populations, recent and widespread declines, or other factors that make it vulnerable in the state. Generally eleven to twenty current occurrences in the state.

ST (State Threatened): Any plant species likely to become endangered within the foreseeable future. Generally six to ten current occurrences in the state.

WL (Watch List): Any plant species about which some problems of limited abundance or distribution in Indiana are known or suspected and should be closely monitored.

Animals

COMMON NAME	SCIENTIFIC NAME	CONSERVATION STATUS
Amphibians and Reptiles		
Banded water snake	*Nerodia fasciata*	
Cave salamander	*Eurycea lucifuga*	
Copperbelly water snake	*Nerodia erythrogaster*	
Eastern box turtle	*Terrapene carolina*	SC
Eastern gray tree frog	*Hyla versicolor*	
Eastern ribbon snake	*Thamnophis sauritus*	
Eastern spadefoot	*Scaphiopus holbrookii*	
Green frog	*Rana clamitans*	
Hellbender	*Cryptobranchus alleganiensis*	SE
Kirtland's snake	*Clonophis kirtlandii*	SE
Leopard frog	*Rana sphenocephala (utricularia)*	
Lesser siren	*Siren intermedia*	
Long-tailed salamander	*Eurycea longicauda*	
Marbled salamander	*Ambystoma opacum*	
Midland painted turtle	*Chrysemys picta*	
Northern copperhead	*Agkistrodon contortrix*	
Northern water snake	*Nerodia sipedon pleuralis*	
Racer	*Coluber constrictor priapus*	
Rat snake	*Elaphe obsoleta*	
Red-eared slider	*Trachemys scripta elegans*	
Red salamander	*Pseudotriton ruber*	SE
Rough green snake	*Opheodrys aestivus*	SC
Scarlet snake	*Cemophora coccinea*	SE
Southeastern crowned snake	*Tantilla coronate*	SE
Spiny softshell turtle	*Apalone spinifera*	
Spring peeper	*Pseudacris crucifer*	
Timber rattlesnake	*Crotalus horridus*	SE
Western chorus frog	*Pseudacris triseriata*	
Birds		
Acadian flycatcher	*Empidonax virescens*	
American avocet	*Recurvirostra americana*	
American bittern	*Botaurus lentiginosus*	SE
American black duck	*Anas rubripes*	
American coot	*Fulica americana*	

American crow	*Corvus brachyrhynchos*	
American golden plover	*Pluvialis dominica*	SC
American kestrel	*Falco sparverius*	
American robin	*Turdus migratorius*	
American tree sparrow	*Spizella arborea*	
American white pelican	*Pelecanus erythrorhynchos*	
American woodcock	*Scolopax minor*	
Baird's sandpiper	*Calidris bairdii*	
Bald eagle	*Haliaeetus leucocephalus*	SC
Bank swallow	*Riparia riparia*	
Barn owl	*Tyto alba*	SE
Barred owl	*Strix varia*	
Bell's vireo	*Vireo bellii*	
Black scoter	*Melanitta americana*	
Black vulture	*Coragyps atratus*	
Black-and-white warbler	*Mniotilta varia*	SC
Black-bellied plover	*Pluvialis squatarola*	
Black-billed cuckoo	*Coccyzus erythropthalmus*	
Black-crowned night heron	*Nycticorax nycticorax*	SE
Black-necked stilt	*Himantopus mexicanus*	
Black-throated green warbler	*Dendroica virens*	
Blue grosbeak	*Passerina caerulea*	
Blue-gray gnatcatcher	*Polioptila caerulea*	
Blue-headed vireo	*Vireo solitarius*	
Blue jay	*Cyanocitta cristata*	
Blue-winged warbler	*Vermivora pinus*	
Brewster's warbler. *See* Golden-winged warbler		
Broad-winged hawk	*Buteo platypterus*	SC
Brown thrasher	*Toxostoma rufum*	
Buff-breasted sandpiper	*Tryngites subruficollis*	
Cackling goose	*Branta hutchinsii*	
Canada warbler	*Wilsonia canadensis*	
Carolina chickadee	*Poecile carolinensis*	
Carolina wren	*Thryothorus ludovicianus*	
Caspian tern	*Sterna caspia*	
Cattle egret	*Bubulcus ibis*	
Cerulean warbler	*Setophaga cerulea*	SE
Chuck-will's-widow	*Caprimulgus carolinensis*	

Common loon	*Gavia immer*	
Common moorhen	*Gallinula chloropus*	
Common yellowthroat	*Geothlypis trichas*	
Connecticut warbler	*Oporornis agilis*	
Dark-eyed junco	*Junco hyemalis*	
Dickcissel	*Spiza americana*	
Double-crested cormorant	*Phalacrocorax auritus*	
Eared grebe	*Podiceps nigricollis*	
Eastern bluebird	*Sialia sialis*	
Eastern kingbird	*Tyrannus tyrannus*	
Eastern meadowlark	*Sturnella magna*	
Eastern screech owl	*Megascops asio*	
Eastern towhee	*Pipilo erythrophthalmus*	
Eastern wood-pewee	*Contopus virens*	
Ferruginous hawk	*Buteo regalis*	
Field sparrow	*Spizella pusilla*	
Forster's tern	*Sterna forsteri*	
Franklin's gull	*Leucophaeus pipixcan*	
Golden eagle	*Aquila chrysaetos*	
Golden-winged warbler	*Vermivora chrysoptera*	SE
Grasshopper sparrow	*Ammodramus savannarum*	
Gray-cheeked thrush	*Catharus minimus*	
Great black-backed gull	*Larus marinus*	
Great blue heron	*Ardea herodias*	
Great crested flycatcher	*Myiarchus crinitus*	
Great egret	*Ardea alba*	SC
Great horned owl	*Bubo virginianus*	
Greater white-fronted goose	*Anser albifrons*	
Green-winged teal	*Anas crecca*	
Hairy woodpecker	*Picoides villosus*	
Henslow's sparrow	*Ammodramus henslowii*	SE
Hooded warbler	*Setophaga citrina*	SC
Horned lark	*Eremophila alpestris*	
Kentucky warbler	*Oporornis formosa*	
King rail	*Rallus elegans*	SE
Laughing gull	*Leucophaeus atricilla*	
Least bittern	*Ixobrychus exilis*	SE
Least flycatcher	*Empidonax minimus*	

Least tern	*Sternula antillarum*	FE
Lesser black-backed gull	*Larus fuscus*	
Lesser scaup	*Aythya affinis*	
Lesser yellowleg	*Tringa flavipes*	
Little blue heron	*Egretta caerulea*	
Long-tailed duck	*Clangula hyemalis*	
Louisiana waterthrush	*Seiurus motacilla*	
Mallard	*Anas platyrhynchos*	
Marbled godwit	*Limosa fedoa*	
Mississippi kite	*Ictinia mississippiensis*	SC
Mourning dove	*Zenaida macroura*	
Northern bobwhite	*Colinus virginianus*	
Northern cardinal	*Cardinalis cardinalis*	
Northern flicker	*Colaptes auratus*	
Northern harrier	*Circus cyaneus*	SE
Northern pintail	*Anas acuta*	
Northern shoveler	*Anas clypeata*	
Northern wheatear	*Oenanthe oenanthe*	
Orchard oriole	*Icterus spurius*	
Osprey	*Pandion haliaetus*	SE
Ovenbird	*Seiurus aurocapilla*	
Pectoral sandpiper	*Calidris melanotos*	
Peregrine falcon	*Falco peregrinus*	SC
Pied-billed grebe	*Podilymbus podiceps*	
Pileated woodpecker	*Dryocopus pileatus*	
Pine warbler	*Dendroica pinus*	
Prairie warbler	*Dendroica discolor*	
Prothonotary warbler	*Protonotaria citrea*	
Red crossbill	*Loxia curvirostra*	
Red-eyed vireo	*Vireo olivaceus*	
Redhead	*Aythya americana*	
Red-headed woodpecker	*Melanerpes erythrocephalus*	
Red-necked grebe	*Podiceps grisegena*	
Red-necked phalarope	*Phalaropus lobatus*	
Red-shouldered hawk	*Buteo lineatus*	SC
Red-tailed hawk	*Buteo jamaicensis*	
Red-throated loon	*Gavia stellata*	
Red-winged blackbird	*Agelaius phoeniceus*	

Ring-billed gull	*Larus delawarensis*	
Ring-necked duck	*Aythya collaris*	
Ring-necked pheasant	*Phasianus colchicus*	
Rose-breasted grosbeak	*Pheucticus ludovicianus*	
Ross's goose	*Chen rossii*	
Rough-legged hawk	*Buteo lagopus*	
Ruddy turnstone	*Arenaria interpres*	SC
Ruffed grouse	*Bonasa umbellus*	
Rusty blackbird	*Euphagus carolinus*	
Sandhill crane	*Grus canadensis*	SC
Scarlet tanager	*Piranga olivacea*	
Sedge wren	*Cistothorus platensis*	SE
Sharp-shinned hawk	*Accipiter striatus*	SC
Sharp-tailed sandpiper	*Calidris acuminata*	
Short-eared owl	*Asio flammeus*	SE
Snowy egret	*Egretta thula*	
Sora	*Porzana carolina*	
Stilt sandpiper	*Calidris himantopus*	
Summer tanager	*Piranga rubra*	
Surf scoter	*Melanitta perspicillata*	
Swainson's hawk	*Buteo swainsoni*	
Tri-colored heron	*Egretta tricolor*	
Trumpeter swan	*Cygnus buccinator*	SE
Tufted titmouse	*Baeolophus bicolor*	
Turkey vulture	*Cathartes aura*	
Virginia rail	*Rallus limicola*	SE
Western grebe	*Aechmophorus occidentalis*	
Whip-poor-will	*Caprimulgus vociferus*	
White-breasted nuthatch	*Sitta carolinensis*	
White ibis	*Eudocimus albus*	
White-winged scoter	*Melanitta fusca*	
Whooping crane	*Grus americana*	FE
Wild turkey	*Meleagris gallopavo*	
Willet	*Catoptrophorus semipalmatus*	
Willow flycatcher	*Empidonax traillii*	
Wilson's phalarope	*Phalaropus tricolor*	SC
Wood duck	*Aix sponsa*	
Wood thrush	*Hylocichla mustelina*	

Worm-eating warbler	*Helmitheros vermivorum*	SC
Yellow-bellied sapsucker	*Sphyrapicus varius*	
Yellow-billed cuckoo	*Coccyzus americanus*	
Yellow-breasted chat	*Icteria virens*	
Yellow-crowned night heron	*Nyctanassa violacea*	SE
Yellow-throated vireo	*Vireo flavifrons*	
Yellow-throated warbler	*Dendroica dominica*	

Fishes

Black crappie	*Pomoxis nigromaculatus*	
Blue sucker	*Cycleptus elongatus*	
Bluegill	*Lepomis macrochirus*	
Channel catfish	*Ictalurus punctatus*	
Freshwater jellyfish	*Craspedacusta sowerbii*	
Goldeye	*Hiodon alosoides*	
Largemouth bass	*Micropterus salmoides*	
Longnose gar	*Lepisosteus osseus*	
Mooneye	*Hiodon tergisus*	
Northern cavefish	*Amblyopsis spelaea*	SE
Paddlefish	*Polyodon spathula*	
Redear sunfish	*Lepomis microlophus*	
Shortnose gar	*Lepisosteus platostomus*	
Shovelnose sturgeon	*Scaphirhynchus platorynchus*	
Skipjack herring	*Alosa chrysochloris*	
Smallmouth buffalo	*Ictiobus bubalus*	
Striped bass	*Micropterus saxatilis*	
Walleye	*Sander vitreus*	
Warmouth	*Lepomis gulosus*	
White crappie	*Pomoxis annularis*	

Mammals

Allegheny woodrat (packrat)	*Neotoma magister*	SE
Bobcat	*Lynx rufus*	
Cottontail rabbit	*Sylvilagus floridanus*	
Coyote	*Canis latrans*	
Fox squirrel	*Sciurus niger*	
Gray fox	*Urocyon cinereoargenteus*	
Gray squirrel	*Sciurus carolinensis*	
Indiana bat	*Myotis sodalis*	FE
Long-tailed weasel	*Mustela frenata*	

Mink	*Mustela vison*	
Muskrat	*Ondatra zibethicus*	
Raccoon	*Procyon lotor*	
Red fox	*Vulpes vulpes*	
River otter	*Lontra canadensis*	
Striped skunk	*Mephitis mephitis*	
Swamp rabbit	*Sylvilagus aquaticus*	SE
Virginia opossum	*Didelphis virginiana*	
White-tailed deer	*Odocoileus virginianus*	
Woodchuck (groundhog)	*Marmota monax*	

Invertebrates

Appalachian brown eye	*Satyrodes appalachia*	
Cave beetle	*Pseudanophthalmus shilohensis*	
Fanshell	*Cyprogenia stegaria*	FE
Fat pocketbook	*Potamilus capax*	FE
Giant swallowtail	*Papilio cresphontes*	
Halloween pennant	*Celithemis eponina*	
Northern cave crayfish	*Orconectes inermis*	
Northern cave isopod	*Caecidotea stygia*	
Painted lady	*Vanessa cardui*	
Question mark	*Polygonia interrogationis*	
Red admiral	*Vanessa atalanta*	
Rough pigtoe	*Pleurobema plenum*	FE
Southern cave cricket	*Ceuthophilus meridionalis*	
Stygian cave cricket	*Ceuthophilus stygius*	
Tiger swallowtail	*Papilio glaucus*	
Zebra swallowtail	*Protographium marcellus*	

Plants

American beech	*Fagus grandifolia*	
American bellflower	*Campanulastrum americanum*	
American elm	*Ulmus americana*	
American lotus	*Nelumbo lutea*	WL
American pennywort	*Hydrocotyle americana*	SE
Angle pod	*Gonolobus obliquus*	SR
Autumn bluegrass	*Poa autumnalis*	
Bald cypress	*Taxodium distichum*	ST
Basket oak	*Quercus michauxii*	

Big bluestem grass	*Andropogon gerardii*	
Big shellbark hickory	*Carya laciniosa*	
Biltmore ash	*Fraxinus americana* var. *biltmoreana*	
Bishop's cap	*Mitella diphylla*	
Bitternut hickory	*Carya cordiformis*	
Black ash	*Fraxinus nigra*	
Black chokeberry	*Photinia melanocarpa*	
Black-eyed Susan	*Rudbeckia hirta* var. *hirta*	
Black gum	*Nyssa sylvatica*	
Blackjack oak	*Quercus marilandica*	
Black locust	*Robinia pseudoacacia*	
Black maple	*Acer saccharum* subsp. *nigrum*	
Black walnut	*Juglans nigra*	
Black willow	*Salix nigra*	
Blazing star	*Liatris scuarosa*	
Bloodroot	*Sanguinaria canadensis*	
Blue beech	*Carpinus caroliniana*	
Blue phlox	*Phlox divaricata*	
Bluets	*Houstonia caerulea*	
Box elder	*Acer negundo*	
Broad-leaved cattail	*Typha latifolia*	
Broad-leaved purple coneflower	*Echinacea purpurea*	
Buffalo clover	*Trifolium reflexum*	SE
Bulb bitter cress	*Cardamine bulbosa*	
Bulblet bladder fern	*Cystopteris bulbifera*	
Bur oak	*Quercus macrocarpa*	
Butterflyweed	*Asclepias tuberosa*	
Buttonbush	*Cephalanthus occidentalis*	
Canada violet	*Viola canadensis*	
Canada wild ginger	*Asarum canadense*	
Canada wood nettle	*Laportea canadensis*	
Cardinal flower	*Lobelia cardinalis*	
Carolina buckthorn	*Frangula caroliniana*	
Celandine poppy	*Stylophorum diphyllum*	
Cherrybark oak	*Quercus pagoda*	WL
Chestnut oak	*Quercus prinus*	
Chinquapin oak	*Quercus muehlenbergii*	
Christmas fern	*Polystichum acrostichoides*	

Cleft phlox	*Phlox bifida*	SE
Cliff adder's tongue fern	*Ophioglossum engelmannii*	SR
Cliff clubmoss	*Huperzia porophila*	WL
Climbing dogbane	*Trachelospermum difforme*	
Columbine	*Aquilegia canadensis*	
Common beggar's tick	*Bidens frondosa*	
Common bur sedge	*Carex grayi*	
Common milkweed	*Asclepias syriaca*	
Common Saint-John's-wort	*Hypericum perforatum*	
Common sunflower	*Helianthus annuus*	
Common water plantain	*Alisma subcordatum*	
Coontail	*Ceratophyllum demersum*	
Creeping bracted sedge	*Carex socialis*	SR
Creeping smartweed	*Persicaria caespitosa*	
Cross vine	*Bignonia capreolata*	
Cucumber magnolia	*Magnolia acuminata*	SE
Cut-leaved coneflower	*Rudbeckia laciniata*	
Cut-leaved toothwort	*Cardamine concatenata*	
Deciduous holly	*Ilex decidua*	WL
Deerberry	*Vaccinium stamineum*	
Devil's paint brush	*Hieracium aurantiacum*	
Ditch stonecrop	*Penthorum sedoides*	
Dutchman's breeches	*Dicentra cucullaria*	
Dwarf ginseng	*Panax trifolius*	WL
Dwarf larkspur	*Delphinium tricorne*	
Early fen sedge	*Carex crawei*	ST
Early low blueberry	*Vaccinium angustifolium*	
Eastern cottonwood	*Populus deltoides*	
Eastern milk-pea	*Galactia volubilis*	WL
Eastern prickly pear	*Opuntia humifusa*	
Eastern red cedar	*Juniperus virginiana*	
Eastern redbud	*Cercis canadensis*	
Ebony spleenwort	*Asplenium platyneuron*	
Evening primrose	*Oenothera triloba*	
False aloe	*Manfreda virginica*	
False gray sedge	*Carex amphibola*	
False sunflower	*Heliopsis helianthoides*	
Featherfoil	*Hottonia inflata*	ST

Fire pink	*Silene virginica*	
Flowering dogwood	*Cornus florida*	
Flowering spurge	*Euphorbia corollata*	
Fox grape	*Vitis labrusca*	
French's shootingstar	*Dodecatheon frenchii*	SR
Giant cane	*Arundinaria gigantea*	
Ginseng	*Panax quinquefolius*	WL
Goat's rue	*Tephrosia virginiana*	
Golden alexanders	*Zizia aurea*	
Golden cassia	*Chamaecrista fasciculata*	
Great chickweed	*Stellaria pubera*	
Green adder's mouth orchid	*Malaxis unifolia*	SE
Green ash	*Fraxinus pennsylvanica*	
Green hawthorn	*Crataegus viridis*	
Green-headed fox sedge	*Carex conjuncta*	
Green milkweed	*Asclepias viridis*	
Grooved yellow flax	*Linum sulcatum*	SR
Ground cedar	*Lycopodium tristachyum*	SR
Hackberry	*Celtis occidentalis*	
Hairy spicebush	*Lindera benzoin*	
Halberd-leaved rose mallow	*Hibiscus laevis*	
Handsome Harry	*Rhexia virginica*	
Harvey's buttercup	*Ranunculus harveyi*	SE
Hay-scented fern	*Dennstaedtia punctilobula*	WL
Hemlock	*Tsuga canadensis*	
Hispid swamp buttercup	*Ranunculus hispidus*	
Hoary puccoon	*Lithospermum canescens*	
Hog peanut	*Amphicarpaea bracteata*	
Hop hornbeam	*Ostrya virginiana*	
Indian grass	*Sorghastrum nutans*	
Indian turnip	*Arisaema triphyllum*	
Jack pine	*Pinus banksiana*	SR
Juneberry	*Amelanchier arborea*	
Lady fern	*Athyrium filix-femina*	
Large whorled pogonia	*Isotria verticillata*	WL
Late low blueberry	*Vaccinium pallidum*	
Little bluestem grass	*Schizachyrium scoparium*	
Lizard's tail	*Saururus cernuus*	

Long-spurred violet	*Viola rostrata*	
Maidenhair fern	*Adiantum pedatum*	
Maple-leaved arrowwood	*Viburnum acerifolium*	
Marginal shield fern	*Dryopteris marginalis*	
Marsh blazing star	*Liatris spicata*	
Marsh bluegrass	*Poa paludigena*	WL
Marsh fleabane	*Erigeron philadelphicus*	
Marsh shield fern	*Thelypteris palustris*	
Mayapple	*Podophyllum peltatum*	
Mistflower	*Conoclinium coelestinum*	
Mockernut hickory	*Carya tomentosa*	
Monkey flower	*Mimulus ringens*	
Moonseed	*Menispermum canadense*	
Mountain laurel	*Kalmia latifolia*	WL
Narrow-leaved bluet	*Stenaria nigricans*	
Netted chainfern	*Woodwardia areolata*	SR
New Jersey tea	*Ceanothus americanus*	
New York fern	*Thelypteris noveboracensis*	
Nodding wild onion	*Allium cernuum*	
Northern bitter cress	*Cardamine douglassii*	
Northern red oak	*Quercus rubra*	
Obedient plant	*Physostegia virginiana*	
Oneida grape fern	*Botrychium oneidense*	
Orange jewelweed	*Impatiens capensis*	
Ostrich fern	*Matteuccia struthiopteris*	SR
Overcup oak	*Quercus lyrata*	WL
Painted sedge	*Carex picta*	
Pale purple coneflower	*Echinacea pallida*	
Partridge berry	*Mitchella repens*	
Pasture rose	*Rosa carolina*	
Pawpaw	*Asimina triloba*	
Pecan	*Carya illinoinensis*	
Pignut hickory	*Carya glabra*	
Pin oak	*Quercus palustris*	
Pinesap	*Monotropa hypopitys*	
Pinnatifid spleenwort	*Asplenium pinnatifidum*	
Plantain-leaved wood sedge	*Carex plantaginea*	
Poison ivy	*Toxicodendron radicans*	

Post oak	*Quercus stellata*	
Prairie dock	*Silphium terebinthinaceum*	
Prairie trillium	*Trillium recurvatum*	
Pumpkin ash	*Fraxinus profunda*	
Purple chokeberry	*Photinia floribunda*	
Purple-flowering raspberry	*Rubus odoratus*	ST
Purple fringeless orchid	*Platanthera peramoena*	WL
Rattlesnake master	*Eryngium yuccifolium*	
Red maple	*Acer rubrum*	
Rigid goldenrod	*Solidago rigida*	
River birch	*Betula nigra*	
Rose gentian	*Sabatia angularis*	
Rosette goldenrod	*Solidago squarrosa*	SE
Rosin weed	*Silphium integrifolium*	
Rue anemone	*Thalictrum thalictroides*	
Sassafras	*Sassafras albidum*	
Scarlet oak	*Quercus coccinea*	
Scotch pine	*Pinus sylvestris*	
Scrub pine	*Pinus virginiana*	WL
Self-heal	*Prunella vulgaris*	
Sensitive fern	*Onoclea sensibilis*	
Sessile trillium	*Trillium sessile*	
Shagbark hickory	*Carya ovata*	
Sharp-lobed hepatica	*Anemone acutiloba*	
Shooting star	*Dodecatheon meadia*	
Shortleaf pine	*Pinus echinata*	
Showy tickseed	*Bidens aristosa*	
Shumard's oak	*Quercus shumardii*	
Silver maple	*Acer saccharinum*	
Slender-stalked gaura	*Oenothera filipes*	
Slippery elm	*Ulmus rubra*	
Smooth rockcress	*Arabis laevigata*	
Southern red oak	*Quercus falcata*	WL
Southern tubercled orchid	*Platanthera flava*	
Spider lily	*Hymenocallis occidentalis*	WL
Spotted wintergreen	*Chimaphila maculata*	
Spring beauty	*Claytonia virginica*	
Stout blue-eyed grass	*Sisyrinchium angustifolium*	

Strawberry bush	*Euonymus americana*	
Sugarberry	*Celtis laevigata*	
Sugar maple	*Acer saccharum*	
Swamp cottonwood	*Populus heterophylla*	
Swamp milkweed	*Asclepias incarnata*	
Swamp white oak	*Quercus bicolor*	
Sweet gum	*Liquidambar styraciflua*	
Sycamore	*Platanus occidentalis*	
Tall ironweed	*Vernonia gigantea*	
Tall scouring rush	*Equisetum hyemale*	
Trumpet creeper	*Campsis radicans*	
Tulip poplar	*Liriodendron tulipifera*	
Twinleaf	*Jeffersonia diphylla*	
Virginia bluebells	*Mertensia virginica*	
Virginia creeper	*Parthenocissus quinquefolia*	
Virginia dayflower	*Commelina virginica*	
Virginia willow	*Itea virginica*	SE
Walking fern	*Asplenium rhizophyllum*	
White ash	*Fraxinus americana*	
White basswood	*Tilia americana*	
White oak	*Quercus alba*	
White pine	*Pinus strobus*	SR
Wild bergamot	*Monarda fistulosa*	
Wild black cherry	*Prunus serotina*	
Wild geranium	*Geranium maculatum*	
Winterberry	*Ilex verticillata*	
Wolf's spike rush	*Eleocharis wolfii*	SR
Wood anemone	*Anemone quinquefolia*	
Woodland blue violet	*Viola affinis*	
Yellow adder's tongue	*Erythronium americanum*	
Yellow buckeye	*Aesculus flava*	
Yellow coneflower	*Ratibida pinnata*	
Yellow crownbeard	*Verbesina helianthoides*	
Yellow ladies' tresses	*Spiranthes ochroleuca*	ST
Yellowwood	*Cladrastis lutea*	ST

Glossary

Barrens—A landform that has very few plants, that is generally not suitable for plants.

Biodiversity—The variety of life in the world or in a particular habitat or ecosystem.

Bog—Wet, muddy, spongy ground too soft to support a heavy body; a body of water—lake or pond—with a floating mat of vegetation; a poorly drained area, usually acid, rich in accumulated plant material, frequently surrounding a body of open water.

Driftless region—A tract of land that was surrounded by but never covered by a continental glacier.

Dune—A mound or ridge of sand or other loose sediment formed by blowing wind.

Ephemeral—Lasting for a brief period of time; specifically, plants that grow, flower, and die in a few days or ponds or streams that dry up in summer.

Escarpment—A long cliff or steep slope separating two comparatively level or more gently sloping surfaces that results from erosion or faulting.

Exotic—A nonnative species originating in or characteristic of a location distant from where it is found.

Extinct—No longer in existence; having no living members anywhere.

Extirpated—The condition of a species that ceases to exist in a geographic area but still exists elsewhere.

Fen—A low and marshy or frequently flooded area of land; a wetland community where water flows to the surface in a diffused manner, commonly through an organic substrate, such as peat, muck, or marl.

Flatwoods—Woodlands that occupy low-lying regions and have little drainage.

Forb—An herbaceous (nonwoody) flowering plant other than a grass or fern / fern ally; generally, a flowering plant.

Glade—An open area in a forest vegetated primarily by herbaceous plants, usually having thin soil over a rocky substrate such as siltstone or limestone.

Hay press barn—A structure where hay is formed into bales for shipping.

Herbaceous—Flowering plants whose stems do not produce woody tissue and generally die back at the end of the growing season.

Indigenous—Originating or occurring naturally in a particular place; native to a particular place.

Karst—Landscape underlain by limestone that has been eroded by dissolution, producing ridges, swallow holes, fissures, sinkholes, caves, and other characteristic landforms.

Marl—Unconsolidated sedimentary rock or soil consisting of clay and lime.

Marsh—An area of low-lying land that is flooded in wet seasons and typically remains waterlogged at all times; shallow wetlands with emergent herbaceous plants.

Mesic—An environment or habitat that contains a moderate amount of moisture; not excessively wet or dry.

Mesophytic—A land plant that grows in an environment having a moderate amount of moisture.

Pasture—Land covered with grass and other low plants on which animals graze.

Prairie—A large open area of grassland; an extensive flat or rolling area dominated by grasses, especially the species that once covered much of central North America.

Riffle—A rocky or shallow part of a stream or river with rough water.

Savanna—A grassy plain in tropical and subtropical regions,

usually with sandy soil, with scattered trees and drought-resistant undergrowth.

Sink—A habitat where the plants do not produce enough young to increase the population. Also another term for *sinkhole*.

Sinkhole—A cavity in the ground, especially in limestone bedrock, caused by water erosion that provides a route for surface water to disappear underground; sometimes referred to as a *sink*.

Succession—The process by which the composition of a biological community evolves over time.

Swale—A low or hollow place, especially a marshy depression between ridges, that carries water during rainstorms and snowmelts.

Swallow hole—An opening or depression where water from a surface stream disappears underground.

Swamp—An area of low-lying, uncultivated ground where water collects; a bog or marsh with emergent woody vegetation.

Terrace—A raised, level space that was once the bottom of a glacial river.

Till—Unsorted material that was deposited directly by glacial ice and shows no stratification (rock layers). Composed of clay, boulders of intermediate sizes, or a mixture of the two, till is sometimes called "boulder clay."

Wildflower—A flower of uncultivated varieties or a flower that grows freely without human intervention.

Resources

Print

Allison, Harold. 2006. "Bluffs of Beaver Bend." *The Nature Conservancy's Guide to Indiana Preserves*.

Audubon, Maria R. 1897. *Audubon and His Journals*, vol. 2. London: John C. Nimmo.

Corydon Democrat. 2005. "TNC Dedicates Latest Acquisition on Saturday; Sally Reahard's Gift Allows Purchase of 294 Acres at Mosquito Creek." October 12.

Cox, E. T. 1874. *Fifth Annual Report of the Geological Survey, Made during the Year 1873*. Indianapolis: Sentinel Company, Printers.

Deam, Charles C. 1919. *Trees of Indiana*. Indianapolis: Wm. B. Burford, Contractor for State Printing and Binding.

——. 1924. *Shrubs of Indiana*. Indianapolis: Wm. B. Burford, Contractor for State Printing and Binding.

——. 1929. *Grasses of Indiana*. Indianapolis: Wm. B. Burford, Contractor for State Printing and Binding.

——. 1940. *Flora of Indiana*. Indianapolis: Department of Conservation, Division of Forestry.

Fennel, David. 2008. *Ecotourism*. 3rd ed. Abington, UK: Routledge.

Frushour, Samuel S. 2012. *A Guide to Caves and Karst of Indiana*. Bloomington: Indiana University Press.

Homoya, Michael A. 1997. "Land of the Cliff Dwellers: The Shawnee Hills Natural Region." *The Natural Heritage of Indiana*. Bloomington: Indiana University Press.

——. 2012. *Wildflowers and Ferns of Indiana Forests*. Bloomington: Indiana University Press.

Homoya, Michael A., D. Brian Abrell, James R. Aldrich, and Thomas W. Post. 1985. "The Natural Regions of Indiana." *Proceedings of the Indiana Academy of Science*.

Homoya, Michael A., and Hank Huffman. 1997. "Sinks, Slopes, and a Stony Disposition: The Highland Rim Natural Region." *The Natural Heritage of Indiana*. Bloomington: Indiana University Press.

Jackson, Marion T., ed. 1997. *The Natural Heritage of Indiana*. Bloomington: Indiana University Press.

——. 2003. *101 Trees of Indiana*. Bloomington: Indiana University Press.

Jordan, Christopher, and Ron Leonetti. 2006. *The Nature Conservancy's Guide to Indiana Preserves*. Bloomington: Indiana University Press.

Lindsey, Alton A., Damian Vincent Schmelz, and Stanley A. Nichol. 1969. *Natural Areas in Indiana and Their Preservation*. Lafayette: Department of Biological Sciences, Purdue University.

Logan, W. N., et al. 1922. *Handbook of Indiana Geology*. Indiana Department of Conservation, Publication 21.

Mallott, Clyde. 1922. "The Physiography of Indiana." *Handbook of Indiana Geology*. Indiana Department of Conservation, Publication 21, pt. 2: 59–256.

Minton, Sherman A. 1972. *Amphibians and Reptiles of Indiana*. Indianapolis: Indiana Academy of Science.

School of Public and Environmental Affairs, Indiana University. 1996. *Lake Monroe Watershed Pilot Study*. September 21.

Seng, Phil T., and David J. Case. 1992. *Indiana Wildlife Viewing Guide*. Falcon.

Simons, Richard S. 1985. *The Rivers of Indiana*. Bloomington: Indiana University Press.

USA Today. 2011. "Great Places to See Wildlife." July 28.

Whitaker, John O., Jr. 2012. *Habitats and Ecological Communities of Indiana: Presettlement to Present*. Bloomington: Indiana University Press.

Yatskievych, Kay. 2000. *Field Guide to Indiana Wildflowers*. Bloomington: Indiana University Press.

Online

CENTRAL INDIANA LAND TRUST
http://www.conservingindiana.org/

CIVILIAN CONSERVATION CORPS
http://www.ccclegacy.org/

HARRISON COUNTY PARKS
http://www.harrisoncountyparks.com/parks/

INDIANA DEPARTMENT OF NATURAL RESOURCES
http://www.in.gov/dnr/

Division of Fish & Wildlife
http://www.in.gov/dnr/fishwild/

Division of Forestry
http://www.in.gov/dnr/forestry/

Division of Nature Preserves
http://www.in.gov/dnr/naturepreserve/

Division of Parks & Reservoirs
http://www.in.gov/dnr/parklake/

INDIANA GEOLOGICAL SURVEY
http://igs.indiana.edu/Surficial/

INDIANA KARST CONSERVANCY
http://ikc.caves.org/

NATIONAL AUDUBON SOCIETY—IMPORTANT BIRD AREAS
http://netapp.audubon.org/iba/

OAK HERITAGE CONSERVANCY
http://www.oakheritageconservancy.org/

OXBOW INC.
http://www.oxbowinc.org/

SYCAMORE LAND TRUST
http://sycamorelandtrust.org/

THE NATURE CONSERVANCY
http://www.nature.org/

U.S. FISH & WILDLIFE
http://www.fws.gov/

Big Oaks National Wildlife Refuge
http://www.fws.gov/refuge/Big_Oaks/

Muscatatuck National Wildlife Refuge
http://www.fws.gov/refuge/muscatatuck/

Patoka National Wildlife Refuge
http://www.fws.gov/refuge/patoka_river/

U.S. FOREST SERVICE
http://www.fs.fed.us/

Hoosier National Forest
http://www.fs.usda.gov/hoosier/

WESSELMAN NATURE SOCIETY
http://www.wesselmannaturesociety.org/

Index

Salt Creek SRA, 256
salt licks, Northern Kentucky, 42, 288
saltpeter, 152
Saltpeter Cave, 152
sand deposits, windblown, 55, 69
sand dunes, 19; windblown, 55
sand-dwelling species, 55
Sand Island, 288
sandstone: bedrock, 61; bluffs, 47, 141, 146, 164, 167, 169, 170; canyons, 61; cliff alcove, 143; cliffs, 57, 60, 61, 146; detached blocks, 61; glades, 60, 61; honeycombed, 152; Lower Mississippian, 279; Mansfield, 151; Mississippian, 169; outcrops, 144, 165, 167, 171; rockhouses, 61; rock shelter, 149; shale, 62; sheer faces, 61; soils, 61; Tar Springs Formations, 156; Wickliffe, 151
Sarah Lincoln Woods Nature Preserve, 75, 98
Saunders Woods Nature Preserve, 23, 75, 102, 103
savanna, 79, 106, 349
Save the Valley, 312
sawmills, 189, 203
Scarlet Oaks Woods, 185, 228, 229
Schlamm Lake, 278
Schmelz, Damian Vincent, 190, 351
School of Public and Environmental Affairs, Indiana University, 232, 254, 352
Schulz, Adolph, 242, 244
Scott County, 46, 50, 51, 279
Scottsburg, IN, 277
Scottsburg Lowland, 45, 46, 50–51, 70
Scottsburg Lowland Section, 50, 69, 70, 273, 291, 293
Scout Ridge Nature Preserve, 185, 221
Section Six Flatwoods Nature Preserve, 75, 115, 116
sedge meadows, 194
sedimentary deposits, windblown, 56
seeps, 169, 322, 323; acid springs, 57, 61, 65, 70, 302
Selma Steele State Nature Preserve, 186, 242

Selmier, Frank, 295, 296
Selmier State Forest, 22, 46, 291, 295–296; forest management trail, 295
Seymour, IN, 16, 45, 299
Shades State Park, 16, 78, 219
Shakamak Lake, 81
Shakamak Prairie Nature Preserve, 75, 81, 82
Shakamak State Park, 18, 81
shale: bedrock, 51; black, 297; brown, 297; Devonian, 51, 69, 297; Lower Mississippian, 279; Mississippian, 51, 52, 69, 221, 270; nonresistant, 69; Ordovician, 49, 71, 322
Shaw Lake, 278
Shawnee Hills Natural Region, xii, 60, 62, 135, 138, 176
Shawnee Indians, 60
Shelby County, 50, 69
Shirley Spring, 197
Shirley Spring Cave, 197
Shoals, IN, 45, 47, 141, 146, 147
shrublands, 86, 106, 308
Shrubs of Indiana (1924), 281, 351
silt: acid loams, 56, 57, 65, 69; loams, 64; neutral, 56, 57, 69
siltation, 126
siltstone, 349; glades, 65, 68, 283; Mississippian, 51; nonresistant, 52; Pennsylvanian, 52
Silurian period, 34, 35, 70, 327
Silver Creek, 69, 321
Simons, Richard, 42, 43, 44, 352
sinkhole, 349, 350; plain, 204, 212; ponds, 62, 63, 64; swamps, 63, 64; topography, 318
sinking stream, 207
sinks, 64, 208, 350
Skyline Drive, 273
Slim Pond, 116
Slim Pond Road, 116
sloughs, 48, 57, 104, 121, 124, 125, 126, 194
Smith bridges, 139
Smith trusses, 139
soils: acidic, 55, 56; acid silt loam, 57, 65, 69; clay, 91, 306; dry, 64;

Teal Marsh, 224
Teays River, 37
Tecumseh, Shawnee Indian
    Chief, 239
Tecumseh Trail, 220, 238
Teeple Glade, 215, 216
Tell City, IN, 14, 259
Tennessee, 62, 173
Terre Haute, IN, 30, 38, 44, 77, 286;
    West, 77
Terrill Ridge, 265
Thousand Acre Woods Nature Pre-
    serve, 75, 98, 100
timber famine, 14
Tipsaw Lake, 161
Tipsaw Lake Recreation Area, 135,
    161, 268
Tipton Till Plain, 47
Titanic, 201
T Lake, 88
Toledo, Ohio, 109, 139
Totem Rock, 151, 152
Touch the Earth Natural Area,
    291, 294
Treaty of Vincennes, 124
tree army, 326
Tree Identification Trail, 221
Trees of Indiana, 281, 351
Trevlac Bluffs Nature Preserve,
    186, 236
Tribbett Woods Nature Preserve, 66,
    291, 303
trilobites, 287
tropical sea. *See* Devonian Sea
Troy, IN, 43
Tucker Lake, 155
Tunnel Falls, 314
Turtle Creek, 42
Twain, Mark, 288
Twin Bridges. *See* Arches: Twin
    Bridges
Twin Cave, 204
Twin Creek, 210
Twin Creek Valley Nature Preserve
    and Henderson Park, 185, 209, 210
Twin Swamps Nature Preserve, 75,
    117, 118, 120
Two Lakes Loop Hiking Trail, 159

unexploded ammunition, 308
Union County, 19, 49, 54, 321, 322
United Nations, 4
Upper Cataract Falls, 138
U.S. Army, 223, 309
U.S. Army Corps of Engineers, 18,
    20, 39, 42, 65, 138, 148, 253, 255,
    256, 288
U.S. Army Reserve, 224
USA Today, 149, 352
U.S. Bureau of Fisheries, 15
U.S. Congress, 14, 15, 263
U.S. Department of Agriculture, 13;
    Office of Economic Ornithology,
    15; Office of Special Agent, 14
U.S. Department of the Interior,
    14, 15
U.S. Fish & Wildlife Service, 3,
    14–15, 104, 110, 193, 194, 299, 301,
    307, 309; Ecological Services Field
    Offices, 15
U.S. Fish Commission, 15
U.S. Forest Service (USFS), 3, 13–14,
    155, 156, 158, 159, 161, 163, 164,
    166, 167, 173, 174, 208, 209, 251,
    252, 258, 259, 260, 263, 264, 265,
    267, 353
U.S. Geological Survey, 207
utopian communities, 44
utopian settlement, 93

Vallonia Nursery, 273
Vanderburgh County, 52, 129
Velpen, IN, 113
Versailles, IN, 326
Versailles Lake, 326, 328
Versailles Project, 327
Versailles Recreation Demonstra-
    tion Area, 326
Versailles State Park, 20, 35, 291,
    326, 327
Veterans Vista Trail, 321
Vigo County, 52, 77, 78
Vigo County Courthouse, 77
Vincennes, IN, 42, 44, 155, 262
Virginia Pine-Chestnut Oak Nature
    Preserve, 187, 279

Works Progress Administration, 20, 278
World War II, 224, 309, 321
Worthington, IN, 47
Wyandotte Cave, 61
Wyandotte Woods State Recreation Area. *See* O'Bannon Woods State Park

Yellowwood Lake, 237, 239
Yellowwood State Forest, 186, 219–220, 236, 237, 238, 254

Zoar School, 296

Steven Higgs is one of Indiana's senior environmental writers and photographers. He is the author of *Eternal Vigilance: Nine Tales of Environmental Heroism in Indiana* (IUP, 1996), and his experience includes eleven years as an environmental reporter at the *Herald-Times* in Bloomington and four as a senior environmental writer/editor at the Indiana Department of Environmental Management. He is an adjunct lecturer at the Indiana University Media School, where he teaches introductory classes in reporting, writing, and editing and advanced classes in online journalism. On the side he leads nature tours through his business Natural Bloomington Ecotours and More and through the Sierra Club Hoosier Chapter. He lives in Bloomington, Indiana.

James Alexander Thom was formerly a US Marine, a newspaper and magazine editor, and a member of the faculty at the Indiana University School of Journalism. He is the acclaimed author of *Follow the River; Long Knife; From Sea to Shining Sea; Panther in the Sky,* for which he won the prestigious Western Writers of America Spur Award for best historic novel; *The Children of First Man; The Red Heart; Sign-Talker;* and *Warrior Woman,* which he cowrote with his wife, Dark Rain Thom. The Thoms live in Indiana hill country near Bloomington.